PEN
S
EXPERIMENTS WIT

Dionne Bunsha is a Special Correspondent with *Frontline*, one of India's most respected newsmagazines. She has won two journalism awards for her reportage on the Gujarat violence—the Sanskriti Award and the People's Union for Civil Liberties Human Rights Award. Dionne Bunsha studied for a Master's degree in Development Studies at the London School of Economics in 1999-2000, and completed a diploma in Social Communications Media at the Sophia Polytechnic, Mumbai, in 1995.

Scarred: EXPERIMENTS WITH VIOLENCE IN GUJARAT

DIONNE BUNSHA

PENGUIN BOOKS

PENGUIN BOOKS

Published by the Penguin Group

Penguin Books India Pvt Ltd, 11 Community Centre, Panchsheel Park, New Delhi 110 017, India

Penguin Group (USA) Inc., 375 Hudson Street, New York, New York 10014, USA

Penguin Group (Canada), 90 Eglinton Avenue East, Suite 700, Toronto, M4P 2Y3 (a division of Pearson Penguin Canada Inc.)

Penguin Books Ltd, 80 Strand, London WC2R 0RL, England

Penguin Ireland, 25 St Stephen's Green, Dublin 2, Ireland (a division of Penguin Books Ltd)

Penguin Group (Australia), 250 Camberwell Road, Camberwell, Victoria 3124, Australia (a division of Pearson Australia Group Pty Ltd)

Penguin Group (NZ), cnr Airborne and Rosedale Roads, Albany, Auckland 1310, New Zealand (a division of Pearson New Zealand Ltd)

Penguin Group (South Africa) (Pty) Ltd, 24 Sturdee Avenue, Rosebank, Johannesburg 2196, South Africa

Penguin Books Ltd, Registered Offices: 80 Strand, London WC2R 0RL, England

First published by Penguin Books India 2006

Copyright © Dionne Bunsha 2006

ISBN-13: 978-0-14400-076-0 ISBN-10: 0-14400-076-8

The views and opinions expressed in this book are the author's own and the facts are as reported by her which have been verified to the extent possible, and the publishers are not in any way liable for the same.

Typeset in Sabon by Mantra Virtual Services, New Delhi
Printed at Chaman Offset Printers, New Delhi

For the people who died in vain, the people who survived and fought the fear, the people of Gujarat who will overcome the barriers that divide them.

My family: Victy, Russi, Rhea and Nana Ratty.

Contents

27 February 2002:

A compartment of the Sabarmati Express from Varanasi to Ahmedabad was set on fire at 8.05 a.m. after a fight at the Godhra station platform between Hindutva activists travelling on the train and a Muslim tea vendor. Fifty-nine people were killed in the clash. Several activists of the fundamentalist groups, the Vishwa Hindu Parishad (VHP) and the Bajrang Dal, were in the train on their way back from a ceremony to build a temple at the disputed site of the demolished Babri Masjid in Ayodhya.

28 February 2002:

During the VHP bandh the next day, mobs targeted Muslims in Ahmedabad, Vadodara and villages in 20 of Gujarat's 26 districts,* mainly in north and central Gujarat. More than 1000 people were killed.

The violence continued for three months in some places. Refugees were stuck in relief camps for many months afterwards.

Three years later:

Many refugees cannot return home.
The culprits remain unpunished.
Muslims and Christians in Gujarat still live in fear.

---

* According to the Election Commission of India order no. 464/GJ-LA/2002 of 16 August 2002 on the holding of General Elections to the Gujarat Legislative Assembly.

'The golden rule of conduct is mutual tolerance, seeing that we will never all think alike and we shall always see truth in fragment and from different angles of vision.'

—Mahatma Gandhi

Foreword

28 February 2002—a day which I will never forget. I pray for all those who were killed—children, young girls; so many who lost their lives even before they could figure out what had happened to them. Young boys and girls who left their homes to play in the neighbourhood would never see their parents and relatives again. Mothers searched for their children in the commotion, and many still don't know whether their children are alive or dead. They are still waiting. There was not enough time to react. Indifferent government statistics can never account for those lakhs of people who died silent deaths, and are still suffering today.

When I go back in my mind to that awful day, my thoughts circle the same path and always come back to where they started. What happened, and why? I, and indeed many others like me, are still unable to come to terms with what happened.

During the 1969 riots in Ahmedabad, we—my children, relatives and neighbours—spent months in a relief camp set up by the government after our houses were burned in Chamanpura, next to Gulbarg Society. We were not afraid to go back and establish Gulbarg Society which was under construction, as people still had faith in their neighbours and family friends. We could distinguish our friends and foes in the establishment and organizations. But today when we narrate our story, we come across a different environment.

There are many whose arguments are aimed at justifying the death and destruction which took place.

Whenever I remember the attack on us, I wonder why Jafrisaab didn't climb up on the roof. Why didn't he take shelter in another house or flat? Why didn't he hide? The whys don't end. I just don't have an answer for these questions. What made him confront the killers? He knew death was waiting for him, and he opted for it. I have tried to comprehend and make sense of the events of that day, and how it changed our lives forever.

This book is a great tribute to those who have undergone unimaginable suffering, and is an excellent attempt to provide a place in history to those known and unknown victims who lost their life in Gujarat's communal riots in 2002. How many of those who died in Ahmedabad's horrific riots of 1969 do we remember? The events narrated and the views of those who were responsible for protection and administration gives an accurate account of the feelings of the sufferers, rioters and their abettors.

No amount of patience can bring what we have lost back to us. The very least we expect by way of consolation is justice, however delayed. I pray that all those who read this book will take a vow to wipe out hate and jealousy from their hearts to prevent such ghastly events from happening again.

September 2005   Zakia A. Jafri

Zakia A. Jafri is the widow of the late Ahsan Jafri, an ex-member of parliament (Congress) who was lynched by a mob outside his house in Gulbarg Society in Ahmedabad during the riots. Gulbarg Society saw one of the worst communal attacks in Gujarat, in which more than fifty-nine people were killed and many others attacked and injured. None of Gulbarg Society's residents have managed to return home. Mrs Jafri now lives in Surat with her son, Tanvir.

Author's Note

'Jai Shri Ram!'
'Hello, can I please speak to Mr Jaideep Patel?'
'Jai Shri Ram!'
'Hello?'
'Say Jai Shri Ram!'
'Namaste, I am a journalist and I would like to speak to Mr Patel.'
'Jai Shri Ram! You have to say Jai Shri Ram or I will not talk to you any further. Which country are you from? Aren't you living in Bharat?'
'But I did say Namaste to you, sir . . .'
'Jai Shri Ram!' (hangs up the phone.)

This telephone conversation was my first taste of the Vishwa Hindu Parishad. On my first visit to Gujarat to cover the communal violence, I had called up their office hoping to speak to their leaders.

I didn't want to go back. One trip to Gujarat to report on the communal violence in March 2002 had been enough. Hearing stories of inhumanity repeated in relief camp after relief camp, making people relive their torture while telling me their stories. Sure, they were eager that I hear them out and record their testimonies—it had to be done—but it made me feel sick in the stomach. And it still hurts. The first time I left Gujarat, I hoped it would disappear.

But Gujarat would not let me be. What I saw and heard was too shocking to forget. The story didn't seem to end; it just kept unfolding with more and more grisly twists and turns. For the refugees, the nightmare was just beginning. There was no way out of the camps. New victims poured in as more violence followed. Then, the police actually attacked two relief camps, claiming they sheltered 'terrorists'. Here were people with little to eat, still trying to find work, rebuild their homes. The attitude of the police alone could have easily driven them to violence. But it didn't. They just wanted to get on with their lives.

The government's disregard made the refugees' dilemma even more tragic, and at times, bizarre. Speaking to people from the administration or the middle classes made me wonder—were we talking about the same thing?

Any mention of the massacres was brushed aside, as if they had never happened. Gujarat had to get on with business. Nothing should be said to damage Gujarat's name. The thousands who suffered didn't matter. Many felt 'they (Muslims) deserved it.'

Could people really think like that? Did children deserve to be thrown into fires? Did women deserve to be gang raped and later burned to death? Did innocent men, indeed anyone, have to be cut into pieces? Even after hearing these stories often, I couldn't fully come to grips with them. I wanted to understand the minds of the people who could inflict such barbarism on others.

I sought out both the big and the small fish. Funnily enough, some of them are now familiar faces to me, friendly when we meet. And they are important characters in this book. (To be honest, it's hard to always see them as murderers, although I know they are.) In some strange way, these are people who have been programmed. They are whole-heartedly proud of what they did, and can't see it any other way. The violence is something that they have been trained and conditioned for, prepared and psyched for all these years at countless meetings, fed by local street gossip. The same doesn't hold true for bigger leaders. Their motives were cynical in the extreme, and they made no bones about it.

I still remember a senior Bharatiya Janata Party (BJP) leader telling me, with a glint in his eye, that yes, he too had gone out on the streets to lead the trouble in his constituency. But then, '*Bus, ek do din ke baad bahut ho gaya. Itna nahin karna chahiye.*' (After one or two days, enough. It shouldn't go too far.) But it did. Chief minister Narendra Modi allowed it to move to a dangerous extreme. (Over a span of more than two years I tried to get an interview with him, but he kept refusing to grant me one.)

My conversations with people like Mangubhai Maharaj, one of the main accused in the Naroda Patiya massacre, made me aware of how confident the perpetrators were of getting away with murder, rape and kidnapping. Mangubhai recounted with relish how he and his volunteers thrashed Muslim boys who married Hindu girls. Or happily described how he told the media waiting outside the riot commission, 'Muslims are like diabetes and the Bajrang Dal is the medicine.' He proudly displayed press clippings as proof. Mangubhai could get away with it because he knew he was pleasing the most powerful and had their support.

Curious about what makes people like Mangubhai, I visited a VHP camp where they train their fighters in rifle shooting, karate and lathi practice. The recruits also attend a daily lecture where 'knowledge' is imparted, which mainly spews hate against the minorities and glorifies Hindutva. I have tried to place the violence in the larger context of the social and political processes that have contributed to the closed climate that prevails today. Communal education, ghettoization, the saffron take-over of the administration and the absence of any other organized political force have all led to the dominance of saffron groups. They keep the fear of 'the other' brewing on both sides, and foster a climate that is ripe for any small incident to spark an outbreak of violence. Long after the killings were over, not only the victims, but Gujarat's people and its social fabric remain scarred by intolerance.

There are less obvious victims of the riots too—top police officers who happened to be Muslim—they were forced to watch helplessly while the city burned. Their high-ranking positions meant little in that period. They were not even posted on official duty, and as thousands called begging to be saved, they couldn't do much to help. Their own safety was fragile and the buildings they lived in were attacked. It drove them crazy. To de-stress, one officer practiced golf at the Police Stadium. It disturbed him that he was playing golf while the city was burning. Months after the violence abated, a senior police officer was still scared to venture out for his morning walk. Two years down the line, they are more reluctant to discuss their marginalization than they were at the time that it was happening.

As time passed, I saw outspoken people lose their nerve. With the BJP winning the state assembly elections less than a year after the violence, the dissenters ran out of steam. Too many people were lapping up the BJP's version of events, however twisted. That's when I realized the need to document what I had seen. To share with others the encounters I had had with different kinds of people—on either side of the fence, some even sitting on the fence.

Prominent businessmen publicly lionized Narendra Modi. One of them, a Parsi, told me that top industrialists like Jamshed Godrej and Anu Aga (also Parsis) were a bunch of idiots—because they publicly criticized Modi. 'Nothing happened. Leave Gujarat alone,' was the refrain. As one newspaper editor joked, 'In a year, the BJP may succeed in convincing people that the riots didn't happen. It was a mere fabrication of the "pseudo-secular" English press.' He was not far off the mark. That was indeed the BJP's line.

After the election, Gujarat virtually disappeared from the news pages. There was no violence. But that didn't mean things were normal. Many refugees hadn't left relief camps, especially in rural areas. Even Salim Sindhi, the sarpanch of Kidiad village, was living in a tent at the Modasa relief camp in Sabarkantha until April 2004. None of the Muslims in his village could return home. They sold all their agricultural land there. Here was an entire community camping miles away from home, with no idea of how to find work and survive—landowners reduced to casual labourers, roaming the streets every day in search of work. In cities and towns too, an economic boycott was enforced. Shops were warned not to hire Muslims, and many employers were scared to take back their Muslim staff.

Witnesses weren't fighting battles only against the accused, but also against the police and prosecutors, who did their best to botch up cases or close them down. They were also wrestling against their own fears. Around half the cases were closed as 'true but undetected'. Literally, there were thousands of people waiting outside police stations every day as if to say—'Listen! This is what happened to us! This is how my mother was killed! My wife gang raped! My son burned!' But the police were deaf to their cries, and also heartless.

Refugees were fighting not only to rebuild their lives, but to get justice. It would have been easier to give up and move on. What a brave front they put up. It isn't easy, fighting with everything possible ranged against you. Being the target of lewd remarks in court while you narrate how your daughter was raped, or describing how your husband and children were brutally killed to an intimidating courtroom. Few would have the stamina or the courage to go through even one of those court hearings, but many did. Their stories had to be told. I wanted to take the story of Gujarat beyond the violence, to give faces and names to the numbers. I also wanted people to see the 'other side'. To understand Mangubhai and his fellow activists in the VHP. Who were the 'mobs' in saffron bands and khaki pants?

Children are always the most eloquent. I remember a small girl at the Godhra civil hospital, standing beside her father, Razak Ghachi, who was slashed with sword wounds. As her father narrated the story of the attack in Pandharvada, the seven-year-old daughter kept looking up at me with big eyes. She waited for her father to pause for a second so that she could pipe in, 'You know, they grabbed small children from their homes and threw them into the fire.' She was anxious to tell me this, to let me know that she could have been one of those in the fire. Many months later, I met a young thirteen-year-old Bajrang Dal recruit at a procession in Rajkot. I asked him why he joined the Bajrang Dal. His answer was straight: '*Miyaon ko marna*' (to kill Muslims). I couldn't ask another question. This book is for those children, and countless others like them.

Hindus, too, suffered. Like the fifty-nine who were burned to death in the Sabarmati Express. In the riots that followed, some of those who lived within Muslim colonies had to flee when their homes were burned. A few Hindu bastis were attacked in Muslim-dominated areas of Ahmedabad and Vadodara. Their trauma, too, matters. However, those killed were overwhelmingly Muslims (713 of 975, according to government statistics.) They were the targets of the pogrom. It was common in Gujarat to accuse the English-language press of being 'pro-Muslim'; the truth is, you didn't have to go looking for Muslim victims, the relief camps overflowed with them.

Gujarat's violence wasn't a spontaneous Hindu versus Muslim conflict. It was politically engineered violence with a communal excuse. A planned, deliberate attempt to wipe out as many Muslims as possible. The targeting of Muslims had shades of the persecution of Jews by the Nazis in pre-Second World War Germany. The marginalization of the Muslims in Gujarat continues till today. I have tried to describe the daily forms of bias that this minority encounters— ghettoization, school segregation, job discrimination. Going beyond the stories of the victims, I have tried to understand how saffron politics affects people's lives. Looking further back in time, I've tried to analyze what made Gujarat the BJP's 'Hindutva Laboratory', a prototype for the Hindu right-wing party. What happened to Gandhi's Gujarat, where intolerance reached such an extreme that VHP activists even attacked his Sabarmati Ashram?

After the pogrom, Muslim refugees faced a hostile administration and social boycotts. With every riot, they are pushed further into ghettos. In spite of having their families hacked to death, their homes burned, their wives gang raped, they are the ones branded as 'terrorists'. Such labels are often used to justify the killings.

'What about Godhra? Didn't the Muslims burn the train?' Actually, there is no clear evidence to show that the burning of the Sabarmati Express was a pre-meditated terrorist act. In fact, it might have been the result of a fight on the railway platform that escalated into gruesome violence. There is no clear-cut conclusion either way. It is unlikely that we will ever know the truth about Godhra because of the political implications. But even if it was a terrorist attack, does it justify the killing of 1000 other people who had nothing to do with the crime? Because of the actions of a handful of criminals, can we punish all those who follow the same religion? By that logic, do the actions of the Gujarat rioters damn all those of the Hindu faith? Hardly. In fact, most Hindus had nothing to do with it, and many rescued their neighbours and friends.

People always expect that as a reporter who covers such violence, I would have many interesting stories to tell about how I saw someone killed, was attacked by a mob, or had my camera snatched from me. 'So tell us what happened in Gujarat.' I dodge the question. For one, I don't think violence makes for great conversation. Besides, I have no such 'I was in deadly danger' stories; the only time I was anywhere close to being mobbed is—believe it or not—at a relief camp in Godhra.

As soon as we entered, hundreds of people descended on us. Everyone wanted their story recorded. I was whisked away into a room. People were brought in individually to speak to us. Those outside banged on the windows, desperate for their turn. When there's no hope, you cling on to anything. I tried to temper their expectations. People have more faith in journalists than we deserve. These are the times when you feel like a skunk journalist. There is nothing you can do for so many, except interview a handful. And then what?

Yet people always went out of their way to help us. I remember driving down a dark road towards Halol, calling the relief camp organizer, Mehboobbhai, to ask him how to get to his house. There were trees on both sides, but nothing else for miles around. Mehboobbhai told me, '*Bump pe milenge.*' (We'll meet at the bump.) What? 'At the speed bump on the Halol Road. It's a famous landmark.' He didn't want me to get lost trying to find his house. But how did he ever expect me to find him in the darkness at the appropriate speed bump? Finally, I found my way through the narrow lanes of the town and reached his home.

Writing this book has been somewhat like looking for that elusive speed bump. I never really planned it. My editor, N.Ram (always incredibly encouraging and supportive), suggested the idea. I've been going down a road that has pulled me along. I only hope it gets somewhere. You be the judge. And watch out for those bumps.

(Some of the names in this book have been changed to protect identities.)

'An eye for an eye only ends up making the whole world blind.'

—Mahatma Gandhi

Introduction

In search of anonymity

Sometimes you get the feeling you know someone just because you've seen their picture so often. A stranger may seem so familiar that you're curious to meet him. That's how a room packed with journalists and photographers felt as they jostled for space, anxiously awaiting the arrival of Qutubuddin Ansari.

He wasn't a film star, politician, or sports star, but we had grown accustomed to his face. Qutubuddin Ansari had become the symbol of the Gujarat pogrom. The photograph of his hands folded, pleading for mercy with the hungry mob, his eyes brimming over with tears, looked out at millions from newspaper pages around the world.

Finally, we would get a chance to meet him. Hopefully he would have a smile on his face this time. When he walked into the room, it was almost like he was walking out of the photograph into real life. But there was no smile. He seemed nervous. Being recognized made life difficult. 'Someone asked my seven-year-old daughter, "Why do we always see your father crying?"' he said.[1]

Qutubuddin's face captured Gujarat's agony as no other. His photograph portrayed the utter helplessness of ordinary people, targeted only because of their religion. Even a year and a half after the violence, he couldn't shrug off the stigma.

Now, in August 2003, he was on his way to Kolkata, at the other end of the country, 1500 km away.

'I can't go anywhere in Ahmedabad. Wherever I go, people recognize me. The media has made me the face of Gujarat. I can't carry the burden,' said Qutubuddin. 'It's very difficult for me to lead an ordinary life. Everything is back to normal in Gujarat, but it's not normal for me. When it is, I'll go back.'

Qutubuddin's family has lived in Ahmedabad for decades. Their basti was looted and burned during the riots. No one in his family was killed.

He was haunted by his own face. 'If I stand at a street corner, at a bus stop—anywhere—people recognize me. Even at the cinema, my photograph was on the screen for a peace campaign. "We are all Indians", it said.' Qutubuddin wasn't allowed to feel that way.

'Why can't I roam freely? I can't even go to a park without being recognized. When I went with my family, a crowd gathered. I got scared, so we immediately got into a rickshaw and left,' he said.

Recognition came at a price. His earnings reduced by half. 'I'm afraid to go into the market. I have to work only in my mohalla. The wages are lower there,' said Qutubuddin, who is a tailor. This is not the first time he has run away from his city. After the riots he fled to Malegaon, an industrial town in Maharashtra, to look for work. 'Two months after the riots, we were still stuck in the relief camp. There was curfew in the city. We couldn't work. My sister lives in Malegaon, so I went there to earn something to survive,' he told us.

But Qutubuddin's photograph followed him to Malegaon. 'Everything went well for fifteen days,' he said. 'Then, the local newspaper published my picture. One of my colleagues brought it to the workshop. At the end of the day, my boss asked me to leave. He said the police or press could come and ask questions. He didn't want his business to be in danger.'

His picture still hounds him. It pops up in several national publications. 'The photographer did his job. But why does the media keep printing my picture? They didn't come back after that to ask me about my problems or to help,' he said.

'I don't know how people look at me when they recognize me. Maybe they are sympathetic. But after all that I have been through, I can't help being scared.' Despite all that he had been through, the young, amiable Qutubuddin remained remarkably composed even when he had to face a barrage of cameramen once again at the press conference.

After reading about Qutubuddin's dilemma in *Communalism Combat* magazine, the West Bengal government offered to help him start a new life in Kolkata. They paid his rent for one year and set up a tailoring workshop for him with two or three sewing machines.

'I am leaving for a better future for my children. I don't want them to grow up like this.'

But he still hoped to return to Ahmedabad. 'Gujarat is my desh (homeland). My entire family lives there. I have grown up there. I will go back to celebrate Id. Many of our Hindu friends also come to celebrate Id with us. I hope I can settle back in Ahmedabad after a few years.'

In August 2004 Qutubuddin returned home to look after his mother, who has a heart problem. Then too, he was upset when the media announced his return. He just wanted to be left alone. Even in Kolkata, Ansari couldn't escape recognition as 'the riot victim'.[2]

The face that defined the violence also symbolizes the situation in Gujarat today. 'Law and order' may be back to normal, but the riot victims aren't.

There are many other Qutubuddins holed up far away from their homes, hoping to return one day.

The burning train

It was sparked off by the burning of a train.

Yet the human tragedy of Godhra began for some as an all-expenses-paid holiday. Gayatri Panchal, seventeen, was one of the kar sevaks who went to Ayodhya to pray for the construction of a Ram temple there. Her mother, Nitaben, was a local activist of the Durga Vahini, the women's wing of the VHP. Nitaben gathered around twenty kar sevaks from their neighbourhood, Ramol in Ahmedabad, for a trip to Ayodhya sponsored by the VHP. They were returning home on the Sabarmati Express on 27 February 2002 when the train stopped at Godhra, a town in central Gujarat, at 7.43 a.m.

What began as a fight between kar sevaks and some Muslim hawkers on the Godhra station platform exploded into a horrific massacre. 'First, there was stone throwing at the station,' recalls Gayatri. 'Then the train started. A little ahead, it stopped again, and burning rags and bottles were flung at us.'

'I managed to escape through a broken window. But my family was stuck inside. There was too much smoke. I could not find them.'[3]

Gayatri boarded the train with her family intact. She got off it an orphan. Two of her sisters and both her parents died on the Sabarmati Express that day. Today, she lives with her three surviving sisters in Ahmedabad. Fifty-nine people were scorched to death inside the S6 compartment.

'I don't like them (Muslims). They are dirty. Eat dirty food. Only bathe every Friday,' she says. 'Of course I am going to hate them. If they come near us I feel, *'Salon ko kaat do'* (Kill the bastards). We had Muslim neighbours. After my parents were killed, I don't talk to them.' Try and reason with Gayatri that her Muslim neighbours had nothing to do with the attack on the train. But she is too emotionally overwrought. 'Did any of the people who attacked the train know my mother? Why did they kill her? What was her fault?'

When I met these teenaged sisters at their home in Ramol, an industrial area on the outskirts of Ahmedabad, they appeared to be fairly independent while dealing with the real world, but it seemed as if they felt very empty inside. Photographs of their dead parents and sisters looked down from the frames on the walls.

'We live off the interest from the compensation money. The VHP has given us this house. We converted our old home into a temple,' she explained. 'We asked the Gujarat VHP general secretary, Jaideep Patel, for a job. But he told us, "Job? Why do you need a job? We are there to get you married."'

But there was a trade-off for the VHP's help. The BJP milked public sympathy for the Panchal orphans, using them as the poster girls of the Godhra tragedy. The VHP took them to inaugurate Narendra Modi's election campaign in Maninagar and Ahmedabad, and even put them up on the pedestal at one of the chief minister's election rallies. Why did the young girls go along with them? Well, these aren't people you can refuse easily. Besides, like most victims, perhaps they hoped that by cooperating, they could squeeze more out of them too.

No one knows whether the attack on the train in Godhra was pre-planned or not, but nothing can justify the planned attacks that followed. The burning of the train was used by Hindutva forces in Gujarat to carry out a systematic pogrom against Muslims. The government and the police gave them full control of the streets.

Chief minister Narendra Modi had an election to win, and he planned to polarize people by making the Godhra tragedy the main issue in his campaign.

His ticket to victory was a burning train.

The burning state

Was the burning train the only reason why an inferno spread across Gujarat the next day?

<u>Don't come in the way of the 'Hindu backlash'.[4] That's what Gujarat's top cops were told by the chief minister Narendra Modi, no less.</u>

The VHP announced a bandh on 28 February 2002, which the government supported. The mob hit the streets armed with gas cylinders, petrol bombs, trishuls, swords and electoral lists. Muslim houses, shops and masjids were systematically burned and destroyed. At places like Naroda and Chamanpura in Ahmedabad, Sardarpura village in Mehsana, and the Best Bakery in Vadodara, people were burned alive. They gang raped women and hacked little children to death. In Naroda Patiya, which saw one of the worst massacres in Ahmedabad, they made a human bonfire.

After three months of mayhem, more than 1000[5] people were slaughtered and around 1,50,000 were left homeless.[6]

The police did little to stop the carnage. In some cases, they guided mobs towards Muslim homes. Modi, a police sub-inspector in Salatnagar, Ahmedabad, was seen giving petrol from his jeep to the mob. When I spoke to the residents of Patel ni Chali in Gomtipur, Ahmedabad, I was told that the police fired on those being attacked, rather than on the mob. To show that they were taking action, they arrested Muslim victims, not their Hindu attackers, and when the victims begged to be rescued, the police said they were helpless.

Not only the police, even the President of India felt 'helpless'. After his term ended in August 2002, President K.R. Narayanan said that he felt 'helpless, sad, agonized and ashamed' when he couldn't help those who came to him after the communal violence[7]. He said there was 'a conspiracy' between the BJP government at the centre and in Gujarat, in an interview to *Manava Samskriti*, a Malayalam monthly magazine.[8] 'There has been government participation in the Gujarat riots. I had sent several letters to the then PM Vajpayee and also talked to him. But he didn't do anything effective,' the ex-President said. He felt the violence could have been controlled if the army had been allowed to work freely. 'How many instances of the serial killings could have been avoided if the army had resorted to shooting against the rioters? . . . But neither the Central nor state government gave the permission. It shows there was a Central–State conspiracy behind the riots,' Narayanan said.

Even a prominent political leader like Ahsan Jafri, a former Congress MP, was ambushed in his home at Gulbarg Society in Chamanpura, Ahmedabad. His house had been burned even in the 1969 riots. After that, he and some others built Gulbarg Society. During this attack, he was on the phone for six hours calling for help, but no one came even though the police were posted in his locality from 7 a.m. The police commissioner, P.C. Pandey, visited his house and assured him protection. At 3.30 p.m. the mob stripped the seventy-two-year-old ex-MP, paraded him naked, cut off his hands and feet and threw him into a fire, say eyewitnesses.[9] Around seventy-three[10] others were also burnt alive.

Ahmedabad and Vadodara were the worst affected. Saurashtra, Kutch and southern Gujarat remained relatively peaceful. Mainly villages in north and central Gujarat (Congress strongholds) experienced communal violence. In parts of central Gujarat, the Sangh Parivar mobilized adivasi mobs, reportedly giving liquor, cash and the opportunity to loot without fear. Those who escaped the attacks ran into the neighbouring jungles, or were saved by Dalit or adivasi neighbours.

The survivors fled this nightmare to relief camps—the second nightmare. Crammed together in dargahs, open fields or even graveyards for months, they endured the blazing sun and were drenched in the rain. Shah Alam camp in Ahmedabad had 13,000 people sharing thirty-eight toilets.[11] Pregnant women delivered their babies in the camps because it was too dangerous to even venture out. Going home was out of the question. Some who tried to return home—only to collect their belongings—were killed, even though they were escorted by the police.

Camps were set up mainly by Muslim charities and later supported by the state government. The administration didn't supply some sites with rations, and pressurized relief organizers to close down, even though refugees couldn't return home because their houses had been reduced to rubble and they had nowhere to go. The government wanted to show that things were back to normal. They were in a hurry to hold elections, to win the majority vote while the fear and hate was still fresh.

'Don't let the Muslims come back'—the graffiti on the broken walls said it all. 'Muslim-free village', declared a board in Khed Brahma, Sabarkantha district. In some villages like Kadiadra in Sabarkantha, the VHP threatened to fine anyone who patronized Muslim shops or even talked to them. Muslim farm labourers were not given employment. In Ahmedabad, businesses were threatened not to take back their Muslim staff. The aim was to make it impossible for refugees to return to normal life. For those living in relief camps, even a year after the carnage, it was difficult to find work in the new towns where the camps were located. Many landed farmers were reduced to roaming the streets, looking for odd jobs or selling vegetables.

Six months later, just when many refugees were leaving relief camps and returning home, terror struck again. On 24 September 2002, two terrorists stormed the Akshardham temple in Gandhinagar, killing thirty-seven devotees. National Security Guard (NSG) commandos flown in from Delhi gunned them down after a night-long siege operation. After that, no serious attempt was made to trace their identities. But the fear of the 'terrorist threat' gave the BJP's election campaign new impetus.

'This time, we had to show them. We couldn't let them get away with this (Godhra). Otherwise, more Hindus would have died than Muslims,' said Pramodbhai, the owner of a taxi service in Vadodara. Pramodbhai drove me around central Gujarat two weeks before Gujarat's election day.[12] 'Whatever happens, Narendra Modi will win the election. For three days after Godhra, he let us react. He said, "do what you want, you won't be caught." The police didn't do anything. That's why so many Muslims were killed. Godhra was pre-planned. Later, it was a Hindu reaction,' he explained.

Those outside Gujarat find it difficult to understand how a party that is widely believed to have abetted a pogrom of more than 1000 people has come to power. But within Gujarat, few were surprised by Modi's landslide victory in the December 2002 state elections. By playing on people's fears, and with the help of fierce anti-Muslim propaganda, the BJP gained support.

The party's entire campaign was based on the Godhra tragedy and the 'terrorist threat', even though it is still not clear how the train caught fire, or who the culprits are. The facts about the Akshardham attack are even foggier. But the BJP's campaign ignored reality and fed on underlying communal prejudices built up over decades. Ahmedabad and Vadodara have seen many communal riots in the past, and the 9/11 attacks in New York made it even easier to build up a fear of 'Islamic terrorists'.

It was a cynical political manipulation of a human tragedy. 'Pay your homage to the Godhra martyrs. Cast your vote,' read a huge BJP advertisement in the Gujarati media on election day. In his last campaign speech, Narendra Modi told his audience, 'You decide whether there should be Diwali in Gujarat or whether firecrackers should burst in Pakistan.'[13] He added, 'Friends, when you all go to vote this time, if you press your finger on the hand symbol you will hear the screams of Godhra! The pain of Godhra! I took a vow on the Godhra platform that I would not spare the sinners of Godhra. I'll teach a lesson to the merchants of death . . . if your son can't return home safe in the evening, what's the use of money or development?'[14]

For ten months, the BJP ensured that its sustained propaganda seeped deep into the public psyche. It wanted to consolidate the 'Hindu vote', gathering different caste and class strata under the communal umbrella.

There was virtually no escape from the burning train. Godhra merchandise flooded the state. The BJP distributed T-shirts with the slogan 'I Will Not Make My Village Another Godhra'. Posters of the burning Sabarmati Express portraying Narendra Modi as the saviour were sprawled across Gujarat. Matching Modi's anti-Pakistan rhetoric were posters with Modi and Musharraf's pictures, depicting them as adversaries. It prompted a Congress leader from Madhya Pradesh who was campaigning in Gujarat to comment, 'I didn't know Musharraf was contesting elections in Gujarat!'

Modi had pulled off a brilliant Goebbelsian trick. He was not the instigator of violence, but the protector of Hindus. 'There's no security. We could walk out of the house and terrorists could shoot us. See what happened at Akshardham. It could happen anywhere,' said a middle-class housewife from Maninagar, Modi's constituency in Ahmedabad.[15] 'Modi will do something to protect us. During the riots, he helped Hindus.'

Modi won the BJP an election. It was considered a victory for Hindutva's hardliners. The VHP's international president, Praveen Togadia, hailed it as the start of the 'Hindu Rashtra'.[16] From now on, his mobs knew they could get away with murder, and even win elections with it. The polls weren't the end, they were just the beginning.

Criminal justice

Medina Sheikh drew up all her courage as she stepped into the witness box. Talking about the massacre of your family is difficult enough; testifying in the presence of those who killed them is sheer torture.

As Medina described how her daughter and niece were gang raped, the crowd in the courtroom, wearing saffron bands, smirked. She broke down while describing how seven of her family were murdered. They laughed and hooted.

'My daughter Shabana was only seventeen, we were to get her married next year. Those men—all our neighbours and "friends"—caught hold of her and flung her around. I heard my daughter's screams, begging them to get off her. But instead, they continued raping her one after the other. They cut off her breasts. My niece Suhana and sister-in-law Rukaiyya were also raped. They hacked my old in-laws. They killed seven members of my family. Taufiq was only eighteen months old. They sliced off his thumb. They gathered all the bodies—piled wood and dry leaves on them and set them on fire. Then they left. Suddenly there was silence. It was all over. Right before my eyes, I lost the very people who I lived for. Life will never be the same again.'[17]

Many of the accused weren't arrested.[18] The police said they were 'absconding'. Medina sees them roaming around her village Eral, in Panchmahal. But she can't live there; she lives 18–20 km away, in Kalol town. The 'absconders' do not attempt to hide. In fact, they have been pressuring her and other witnesses. Both threats and temptation came Medina's way—offers of money not to testify, warnings of what would happen if she did.

Medina's difficulties had only just begun. The magistrate

insisted that all thirty-two witnesses show up for every hearing. The court is 60–70 km away from the village. Under threat, the witnesses travel together in a bus. Most of them are men. Their wives are afraid to stay alone in the village, so they are dropped to the nearest camp and wait there till their husbands return to take them home.

Yet, in some sense, Medina considers herself lucky. At least she got her police First Information Report (FIR) filed. Many like Firdos Sheikh, a young tailor from Delol village, had to wait twenty-two months and endure endless abuses from policemen before they acknowledged the death of his parents and five relatives while fleeing an attack on the village.

Another strategy to sabotage cases is the group FIR. Violent incidents were not registered separately; even crimes that occurred in different places were registered in one FIR. In Kalol police station, four separate crimes within a 20 km radius were clubbed together[19]—the burning of Rabbani Masjid and police firing in Kalol town, the torching of ten persons in a tempo at Ambica Society, the killing of an injured victim who went to Kalol Referral Hospital for treatment, and the burning of Boru village six km away. It's a legal nightmare, virtually impossible to fight in court.

Witnesses had to fight a system intent on subverting justice. The police did their best to conceal evidence, botch up testimonies and protect the accused. In fact, 2120 of the 4252 cases[20] (see table on riot cases) were closed as 'true but undetected'. The police could confirm that the crime had occurred (the complaint was 'true'), but it could not gather enough evidence to file a charge-sheet (it remains 'undetected'). In several cases, the police deliberately destroyed evidence and didn't record statements properly so that cases could be shut. Bilkis Yakub's[21] case was closed until the Central Bureau of Intelligence (CBI) took over. Then the skeletons came tumbling out of the closet. Six policemen were later arrested for falsifying proof, failing to conduct a proper investigation and conspiring with the accused.

When charge-sheets were filed, victims became the accused. The police charged them with provoking the mob or even, in some cases, being part of it. Police officer Rahul Sharma protested the blatant bias in the charge-sheets of the horrific massacre in Naroda Patiya, Ahmedabad. He was soon transferred.

Government lawyers who were supposed to defend the witnesses worked against their interests. Many public prosecutors were VHP members, and didn't bother to fight the cases. The only time witnesses met them was during the trial. But the VHP looked after 'their boys'. They even had a fund-raising drive to send food to the accused in jail. BJP MP Bhupendra Solanki, a lawyer by profession, defended another local BJP leader Kalubhai Malivad, who was accused of burning seventy-three people in a tempo at Limbadia Chowkdi near Kalol. Malivad was acquitted by the district court and was later elected as an MLA.

There was no hope for justice in Gujarat. That's why Zaheera Sheikh, the young witness in the Best Bakery killings in Vadodara (in which her sister and uncle were burned alive), asked for the case to be transferred outside the state. Under pressure and threats from local politicians, Zaheera lost her nerve and turned hostile in the sessions court. After the court freed the accused, she emerged from hiding in Mumbai and pleaded for a retrial outside the state. Zaheera won in the Supreme Court, but during the retrial in Mumbai her family turned hostile once again. At a press conference in Vadodara in December 2004, just before her deposition in the retrial, Zaheera accused activist Teesta Setalvad of forcing her to falsely blame the accused, claiming she said had not seen anything that night. The press meet was held at a hotel owned by BJP supporters. The lawyer accompanying Zaheera had once defended the accused in the sessions court. Setalvad had kept Zaheera secure in Mumbai for more than a year. But for witnesses keen to return home, a compromise sometimes seems a safer option to fighting the powerful.

In Bilkis's case, the Supreme Court has asked the CBI to take over investigations, and all the twelve accused, including six policemen, were arrested. Her case will also have a retrial in Mumbai. In August 2004 the Supreme Court also ordered an inquiry into the 2000 plus cases that were closed as 'true but undetected' and asked the Gujarat police to review all bail applications and acquittals.

But even if justice is delivered, the witnesses are walking targets. Like Zaheera and Medina, they have to live in hiding. Is the hope of justice worth such a high price?

The Saffron web

From high-rise homes in Ahmedabad to huts in remote villages, the Sangh Parivar's network is well laid out.

It uses different ways to spread its message. It gets housewives to arrange Ram Dhun poojas, satsangs and religious discourses. It gives young boys a place to hang out, at the RSS and Bajrang Dal shakhas. Here they are taught drills, exercises, fighting techniques and are brainwashed with 'patriotic' lectures, and are also trained to 'defend the Hindu religion'. It has ashram shalas (residential schools) for adivasi children—their only access to education—where it teaches them warped versions of history and science.

The Sangh's reach also spreads overseas. It uses several channels, from the internet to business and community networks, as well as temple contributions to collect funds for its activities. Sometimes it's the Ram temple, at other times, it's disguised as 'earthquake relief'. But the money is used to further its ideological agenda—Hindutva.

To 'unite Hindus', there has to be a common enemy. Several methods are used to spread propaganda against minorities—religious lectures, schools, songs, rumours. Across class and caste barriers, biases against Muslims are similar. They are labelled 'traitors', 'jehadis', 'antisocial'. Muslim areas are called 'mini-Pakistans', 'breeding grounds for criminals'.

Rajat, a chartered accountant, told me, 'The minorities have been overprotected. People were frustrated. This feeling was so strong that thousands came out on the streets. The police couldn't do anything. Hindus have always been soft. This is the first time we stood up and fought.'[22]

The Ahmedabad elite, people like Rajat, looted shops on the upmarket C.G. Road after mobs had broken into them. They excitedly rushed into stores, grabbing whatever they could, filling their cars with stolen goods. They even sent messages on mobile phones informing their friends of the booty. It was just another wild but free shopping spree.[23] Yet, Rajat says, 'They (Muslims) are all antisocials, but we are described as dangerous.'

In Ahmedabad's ghettos, it's no different. 'Borders' divide Muslim bastis from Hindu ones. These 'borders' are considered the most sensitive areas to live in. Poor Dalits and lower castes live next to Muslims, but they harbour the same prejudices. 'All of them (Muslims) do illegal business,' said Hiren (name changed), a slight, lively Dalit youth who is a bootlegger and local BJP leader.[24] He boasted, 'I haven't worked a day in my life. I earn my living through cheating. I take haftas.' He also led a mob during the riots. Hiren explained to me the economic benefits of communalism. 'After the BJP government came, the Hindu bootleggers have more power than the Muslim ones.'

The BJP gives youth like Hiren an opportunity to flex muscle locally, but it has done little else for them. Hiren is from Ahmedabad's old textile mill area, Gomtipur. His father was one of the 1,00,000 workers who lost their jobs when the mills closed down here. But the BJP has no new jobs to offer, only Hindutva.

Because it was the first state to have a BJP government
with a clear majority, Gujarat is called the 'Hindutva
laboratory'. The foundations for its support are nurtured not
only by the BJP, but also other Sangh Parivar organizations.
They are building a model for the 'Hindu Rashtra' here.
Narendra Modi's election victory re-enforced their bases. 'The
experiment of the Hindutva lab will be repeated in Delhi,'
said Praveen Togadia, VHP international president.[25] 'When
madrasas in various parts of the country can train jehadis,
why can't the VHP set up its Hindutva lab? A Hindu Rashtra
can be expected in the next two years . . . we will change
India's history and Pakistan's geography by then.'

The Sangh Parivar's Ram Janmabhoomi movement has
led to the mass spread of Hindutva since the late 1980s. It
reached out to lower castes and adivasis, who do not normally
support the Sangh, which is seen as a 'bania' party. The Ram
Mandir campaign culminated in the demolition of the Babri
Masjid on 6 December 1992. The VHP had assured the central
government and the Supreme Court that only kar seva,
singing of bhajans and a religious ceremony would take place
at the disputed structure on 6 December. But twelve 'Balidan
Senas' (suicide squads) had been trained to bring down the
Babri Masjid. Construction equipment had been brought to
the site in late November 1992. Ayodhya's residents feared
trouble as their town was swamped by VHP volunteers, many
of whom were being trained for combat.[26] A day before the
kar seva, Atal Bihari Vajpayee, who later went on to become
India's 'statesmanlike' prime minister, gave a speech in
Lucknow hinting at the obliteration of the Masjid. 'I don't
know what will happen there tomorrow, but everything will
be decided by the kar sevaks,' he said.[27] Top BJP leaders like
L.K. Advani, Murli Manohar Joshi and Uma Bharati were at
the site, overseeing the demolition. In July 2005, Advani and
seven other Sangh leaders were charged by a special court in

Rae Bareli with rioting and provoking riots during the kar seva.[28] Which 'religious ceremony' has ever involved the destruction of a sacred historic monument, looting of its idols[29] and the subsequent killing of thousands of innocents?

The destruction of the Babri Masjid led to large-scale violence across India, in which more than 2000[30] were killed. More importantly, it changed the course of Indian politics. The polarization it brought about struck at India's secular fabric. From then on, communal forces like the BJP gained ground. The party's mass growth was also aided by the fact that all these processes came to a head at a time when people were fed up with fifty years of Congress rule, and were looking for change. By 1998,[31] the BJP came to power for the first time by forming a coalition government.

In the last fifteen years, the Sangh, through its Vanvasi Kalyan Kendras, has been trying to gain ground in adivasi areas of central and south Gujarat, where the Congress has a very old support base. Until now, it didn't yield any electoral gains, and the Congress retained a large majority of seats in these regions. These were precisely the areas targeted during the communal violence. In the state elections after the 2002 violence, the BJP swept the polls in the riot-hit areas of Panchmahal, Dahod and Vadodara, winning every seat in this Congress bastion.

The Sangh Parivar has been working hard to make inroads here. 'After Godhra and Modi's Gujarat Gaurav Yatra, adivasis have also become kattar (hardline) Hindutva. After Godhra, they looted Muslims. They are against the Congress because it supports Muslims,' said Rajubhai Rathwa, a BJP panchayat leader in Joz village, Chotta Udaipur.[32] The RSS has also been mobilizing support. 'We do a lot of work within villages. We want to awaken Hindus,' said Madhusudan Pancholi, an RSS leader in Tejgadh.[33]

In the Dangs district in south Gujarat, the Bajrang Dal and its affiliate, the Vanvasi Kalyan Parishad has been holding 're-conversion ceremonies' for adivasis. The 'reconverted' are given a picture of Hanuman and a trishul. In Jhabua, a district in Madhya Pradesh bordering Panchmahal in Gujarat (where some of the worst massacres occurred), the VHP has been consistently trying to gain a foothold. In March 2005, the Vanvasi Kalyan Parishad launched Project Shivganga, a seemingly innocuous scheme to build ponds, check dams and stop dams in villages.[34] But there was a catch—only those villages that set up a Shivling would be given aid. Several Christian adivasis in the area would have been left out. It is a part of the Sangh's ongoing campaign against Christian missionaries in this tribal area, who they feel are taking adivasis away from 'Hinduism'.

The Sangh's cadres have been systematic and organized. The Congress has been complacent and virtually non-functional. In fact, the Congress defeat in its strongholds is also, in some way, an anti-incumbency vote against long-time MLAs who have done nothing for their constituencies.

The VHP had been laying the ground for years to establish a network that is now so well organized that when its leaders called for a bandh, several parts of Gujarat were in flames. Gujarat's violence shocked the nation because it wasn't a mere riot, it was engineered mayhem with a political motive.

This pogrom signified the culmination of the politics that followed after the demolition of the Babri Masjid. This is how the 'Hindu Rashtra' would work—with the most unashamed disregard for human rights. The Sangh wanted to replicate the Gujarat 'experiment' all over India (and Pakistan). The plan was to divide people at any cost and deflect political discourse away from the real problems of social and economic deprivation. Their propaganda made people temporarily believe that a burning train was more important than an empty belly.

An uncanny coincidence

27 February 1933: The burning of the Reichstag.

Germany was shocked when a huge fire engulfed the Reichstag, the German government's headquarters. Hitler immediately declared it a 'Communist conspiracy'. The next day, he got the president to sign a decree suspending civil liberties, then arrested all his political opponents from the Communist, Social Democratic and Liberal parties. Publication of documents which proved a Communist conspiracy was promised, but never done.[35]

The Reichstag fire proved to be a turning point in Hitler's rise to power. In the election on 5 May 1933, Hitler got only 44 per cent of the vote, but managed to scrape together a majority in the Reichstag with his allies.

Uncannily, the burning of the Sabarmati Express in Godhra and the burning of the Reichstag in Berlin—a key element in Hitler's rise to power—occurred on the same day—27 February.

Unlike the Reichstag fire, the burning of the Sabarmati Express might simply have been an accident. Yet, the fallout of both bears some resemblance. Both tragedies were used as an excuse for 'retaliatory' violence. Political leaders immediately built up the fear of the 'terrorists'/communists. Soon after both events, the hysteria which was generated helped to win an election.

Hindutva's ideologues like M.S. Golwalkar were admirers of Nazi Germany, and the Sangh's organizations draw inspiration from European fascism. While it projects itself as a 'nationalist' group, the Sangh Parivar is really a chauvinistic Hindu organization. Its parent body, the RSS, was inspired by European nationalism, which is exclusionary.[36] 'It tried to create a uniform citizenry on tried and tested European nationalist principles—a shared language, an authorized history, a single religion and a common enemy . . . none has any interest in plurality,' says Mukul Kesavan.

One of the RSS's founders, B.S. Moonje, even visited Italy under Mussolini in 1931 and tried to adapt fascist models to Indian society and to organize militarily according to fascist patterns.[37]

The 'nationalist' RSS did not participate in the freedom struggle. Its idea of nationalism is very different from that of the Congress, which is open and not based on any identifying traits such as race, culture or language. The nationalism of the Congress produced Gandhi, while the nationalism of the RSS produced Nathuram Godse, his assassin, who was an RSS member. The guiding principle is not equality and secularism, but majority rule.

Hindutva views Muslims and Christians as 'the other'. The goal is a 'Hindu Rashtra', where the minorities have to live according to the will of the majority.

In the Sangh's view, Muslims are 'outsiders' who should be treated like second-class citizens. 'Pseudo-secularist' parties have 'pampered' them to create vote banks.

'It is characteristic of majoritarian politics (whether in Malaysia, Indonesia, Bangladesh, Sri Lanka or Nazi Germany) that the demonized minority in every case is resented for being socially or economically more powerful than the 'indigenous' majority,' says Mukul Kesavan. 'So the Jews are rootless financiers responsible for the subversion of the German economy, the Tamils are guilty of monopolizing Sri Lanka's professional and bureaucratic institutions, the Chinese in Southeast Asia stand accused of shutting local populations out of business through racial conspiracy (besides being guilty of being different) and Bangladeshi Hindus are stigmatized for the centuries of oppression their educated and (relatively) prosperous co-religionists (Hindu landlords) unleashed upon Bengal's plebeian Muslims.'[38]

However, unlike in other countries, a large chunk of India's Muslims are poor, and cannot be called 'privileged'. Muslims are one of India's impoverished communities, but they have been the most regular targets of communal violence. It's an effort to create divisions amongst the poor. That's why the BJP's opponents sometimes refer to it as the 'Bharat Jalao Party' (Burn India Party). Political parties like the Congress have often used communal violence to further their clout, but for the BJP it is not only about opportunity, it's an article of faith.

In some ways the Gujarat violence was similar to past communal incidents in India like the 1984 anti-Sikh riots or the 1992 anti-Muslim violence after the demolition of the Babri Masjid by VHP activists. Then too, the violence was politically instigated. Most 'riots' in modern India aren't spontaneous chaos, but are sometimes planned by vested interests. Often, there is some element of state and police collusion with the instigators; only the degree of state involvement varies.

So what was different about the Gujarat carnage? For one, the level of state complicity was unprecedented. Never before has a chief minister instructed top police officials to let the mobs have their way.[39] Never have ministers sat in the police control room and overseen whole-scale slaughter without doing anything to stop it. Never have MLAs defended the accused in court. Never has the top police chief of a city visited an MP's house while it was under attack and then allowed it to burn. During the 1992 violence in Mumbai and the 1984 attacks in Delhi, there were delays in sending out troops. The governments were ineffective. The police was biased. But persecution was not state policy.

In the 1984 Delhi and the 1993 Mumbai pogroms, mobs were as organized. The VHP president Keka Shastri admitted that they made lists of targets on the morning of the attack.[40] They used electoral rolls and tax records to identify Muslim property. Their corporators and party workers had easy access to them. Leaders coordinated the mobs using cellphones. They were well stocked with gas cylinders, swords and knives. The VHP network made sure that the call to arms reached far-off villages. Some sections of the local media helped them in provoking violence and stirring hate.

What shocked most was the sheer scale and viciousness of the attacks. There were gory attacks on women and children, and more than 1000 people in 20 of Gujarat's 26 districts[41] were killed.

Months of violence, institutionalized terror and subordination. Muslims were now second-class citizens. After 2002, political parties don't need another riot in Gujarat—the marginalization of the minorities is complete.

Notes

1. Press conference in Mumbai on 7 August 2003.
2. 'Face of riots returns home', *Hindustan Times*, 30 August 2004.
3. Interview on 30 January 2004.
4. Manu Joseph, 'From the Devil's lair', *Outlook*, 3 June 2002.
5. Official police estimates place the number of dead as 975, human rights activists estimate that 2000 died. The number killed is surely over 1000, because a lot of bodies were never found and were classified by the police as 'missing' rather than 'dead'.
6. Estimates by Citizen's Initiative, an organisztion involved in relief after the violence.
7. Press Trust of India, 'I felt helpless during riots: Narayanan', *The Hindu*, 14 August 2002.
8. United News of India (UNI), 'Gujarat riots a BJP conspiracy: K.R. Narayanan', *The Hindu*, 2 March 2005.
9. Eyewitnesses quoted in Human Rights Watch report titled 'We Have No Orders to Save You': State Participation and Complicity in Communal Violence in Gujarat, pp. 18–20.
10. Police records say that thirty-nine were killed and thirty-five were missing (their dead bodies were never found).
11. At the end of April 2002, after the PM had visited the camp, there were 38 toilets. Before the PM's visit, it had just four toilets.

According to interviews with camp organizers in March and April 2002.

12. Interview on 25 November 2002. Gujarat state elections were held on 15 December 2002.

13. 'Modi's final pitch: Cong win Pak win', Express News Service, 10 December 2002.

14. Sujan Dutta, *The Telegraph*, *'Beti or Behn*, Modi sells a one-point message', 11 December 2002.
    'What use development if your son can't return home safe?', Sheela Bhatt, 11 December 2002, http://www. rediff.com/election/2002/dec/11spec1.htm

15. Interview on 24 November 2002.

16. Press Trust of India, '"Hindu Rashtra" in two years: Togadia', 15 December 2002, http://www.rediff.com/election/2002/dec/15guj13.htm

17. Navaz Kotwal, 'Untold Tragedies', *Frontline*, 16-29 August 2003, http://www.flonnet.com/fl2017/stories/20030829007601300.htm

18. They were arrested later. In April 2003, thirty-eight of the forty-one accused were out on bail. Three were in custody.

19. FIR no. 36/02 in Kalol police station, Panchmahal.

20. According to Gujarat police records, violence from 27 February 2002 to 1 January 2003. A year later, when the matter was taken to the Supreme Court, the Gujarat police website said there were 2022 cases closed.

21. Bilkis Yakub's case became one of the landmark cases of the Gujarat communal violence when the Supreme Court ordered the CBI to investigate the case after the Gujarat police closed it. The CBI investigation found the police guilty of doctoring evidence and sheltering the accused.

22. Interview in Ahmedabad on 11 December 2002.

23. Sourav Mukherjee and Amit Mukherjee, 'High-society looters roam scot free', *The Times of India*, 16 September 2002.

24. Interview on 3 September 2002 and 24 September 2002.

25. Press Trust of India, '"Hindu Rashtra" in two years: Togadia', 15 December 2002.

26. Venkitesh Ramakrishnan, 'Flashpoint Ayodhya and tension in the air', *Frontline*, 5-18 December 1992. In fact, *Frontline* magazine's correspondent Venkitesh Ramakrishnan had

forewarned that all signs indicated that VHP squads planned to demolish the Babri Masjid.

27. Venkitesh Ramakrishnan, 'This Vajpayee speech campaigns against the NDA & Atal Speak', *The Hindu*, 25 April 2005. This article talks about the contents of Vajpayee's speech of which the journalist obtained a video-taped copy. The Babri Masjid Action Committee was planning to move court to include Vajpayee as an accused in the Ayodhya case. 'Video weapon against liberal Atal', *The Telegraph*, 21 February 2005.

28 *The Hindu*, charges framed against Advani, seven others, 29 July 2005.

29. Venkitesh Ramakrishnan, 'Looting the "mandir"', *Frontline*, 15 January 1993.

30. Estimates by the press and the BBC.

31. In the 1996 Lok Sabha elections, the BJP was the party with the single largest majority, but not enough for a clear majority. It was invited to form an alliance government. But the coalition it formed broke within thirteen days. In 1998, it was able to form a stronger coalition.

32. Interview on 25 November 2002.

33. Ibid.

34. Rohit Bhan, 'For Jhabua tribals, Sangh dams come with a check: Shivlings first', *The Indian Express*, 9 February 2005.

35. William L. Shirer, *The Rise and Fall of the Third Reich*, Secker and Warburg, London 1962, p. 192.

36. Mukul Kesavan, *Secular Common Sense*, Penguin Books India, p. 32.

37. Marzia Casolari, 'Hindutva's foreign tie-up in the 1930s: Archival evidence', *Economic and Political Weekly*, 22 January 2000.

38. Mukul Kesavan, *Secular Common Sense*, Penguin Books India, p. 46.

39 Manu Joseph, 'From the Devil's lair', *Outlook*, 3 June 2002.

40. Sheela Bhatt, 'It had to be done, VHP leader says of riots', 12 March 2002, http://in.rediff.com/news/2002/mar/12train.htm

41. According to the Election Commission of India order no. 464/GJ-LA/2002 of 16 August 2002 on the holding of general elections to the Gujarat legislative assembly.

'I know that no religion teaches madness.'

—Mahatma Gandhi

2

Our Children Still Wake Up
Screaming: The Violence

'It was decided there should be a model for reprisals. The Hindu community in Gujarat would teach a lesson that Hindus can emulate elsewhere in case they are attacked again.'
—Kaushik Mehta, General Secretary, Gujarat VHP.[1]

'What happened in Gujarat after the Godhra carnage had the blessing of Lord Ram.'
—Ashok Singhal, Working President, VHP.[2]

A prisoner in her own home, Rehanabibi still lives with the ghosts of the dead.

She prefers not to venture out, though she has lived here for twenty years. If she does step out, it's only within her own basti in Naroda Patiya. She dare not cross the line into the Hindu areas. She is even scared to be seen on the road or highway just outside her home. 'Nowhere is safe. Those who attacked us live just behind. They are powerful people here. They haven't been arrested and can do anything,' Rehanabibi told me,[3] while other women sat with us in her small, dark, newly rebuilt home.

Her fears are etched on her weary, anxious face. Her dark eyes turn away, and she clutches her faded green sari as she braces herself to try and narrate what she saw. Rehanabibi has lived through one of India's worst communal nightmares. It is here that attackers slit a pregnant woman's belly and executed other equally heinous acts of terror that brought this slum on the outskirts of Ahmedabad into the national spotlight. Naroda Patiya—India's capital of communal carnage.

After eighteen months of being refugees, the elderly Rehanabibi and her family are back. They couldn't afford to rent a place anywhere. This is their neighbourhood where they have lived for more than twenty years, since they migrated from Rajasthan. Now they are exiles at home, fighting back fears of the massacre they survived.

Meet Salim Sindhi. He is sarpanch of a village he cannot live in. When I met the tall, well-built, affable Salim, he had been staying in a tent at a relief camp ground in Modasa for more than two years.[4] No Muslim from Kidiad village has been able to return home since the violence, not even the sarpanch. Most have sold off their land to the Patels, a powerful middle caste.

Salim and his family were fleeing the attack on the village when death caught up with them. Their vehicles were stopped on the road. Minutes later, seventy-three people lay dead, Salim's wife amongst them. Because Salim and other survivors are witnesses to the case, their lives are in danger. While the killers roam free, Salim and the other victims are refugees.

Firoze has 24-hour police protection but he doesn't feel safe—only imprisoned. The police were nowhere when he needed them most—to save his family when their home in Gulbarg Society, Ahmedabad, was attacked. The gaunt young Firoze lost his parents, two brothers and a sister. He watched helplessly from a roof as the mob hacked his mother with swords.

Today, he is trailed by police guards because he is a key witness to the butchery in his colony. 'I can't go out anywhere alone. What if someone attacks me? The police haven't arrested some of the accused whom we named,' says Firoze,[5] who now stays in Sarkhej in the outskirts of the city. 'With the police guards trailing me, I avoid going to people's houses. It's embarrassing, yet I need security. My life is still in danger.'

Spontaneous combustion

'The Hindu community today is not what it was in 1984. In the years since then, the VHP has given it a spine and the courage to react. There are a whole range of feelings that have come into play, chiefly the perception that we are meek—we send our army to the border but dare not wage war; our people get driven out of the inner-city, but dare not return. After 28 February 2002, those perceptions stand corrected.'

—Hareshbhai Bhatt, vice-president, Bajrang Dal.[6]

The Bajrang Dal, 'Hanuman's Army', is what they call themselves. A cadre of young boys trained to 'defend their religion'. The bandh called by the VHP a day after the Sabarmati Express massacre gave these young men a chance to put their training into practice.

'It was a spontaneous reaction of people against the terrible events of Godhra.'[7] That's how chief minister Narendra Modi described the precise attacks on Muslim homes and shops. There was nothing spontaneous, though, about the VHP's decision to engineer a pogrom the next day.

While supervising the removal of bodies from the train compartment at Godhra, VHP and BJP leaders discussed their strategy for the killings that were to follow. VHP leader Jaideep Patel wanted to call a bandh for '*jawabi karvai*' (revenge), to give a 'fitting reply' to the attack on the kar sevaks. Later, when Modi arrived, they consulted him and state home minister Gordhan Zadaphia, a former secretary of the VHP for six years before he joined electoral politics. They wanted the BJP to support the bandh.[8]

Narendra Modi told them that he would take no hasty decisions, but within a matter of hours he had made up his mind. At 8 p.m. the ruling party released a press note announcing its support of the bandh.[9] High-level warnings didn't seem to affect his decision. State police intelligence chief, additional director-general of police (DGP) G.C. Raigar, had alerted him that the bandh could have violent consequences. Modi insisted on letting the VHP bring the bodies of the Godhra victims to Ahmedabad, despite fears that it could spark more trouble.[10] Former additional chief secretary (home) Ashok Narayan, told the Nanavati–Shah commission of inquiry that the CM took the controversial decision of bringing all the fifty-eight bodies of the Godhra carnage victims to Ahmedabad. This decision, seen as a major provocation for the communal violence in the city, was despite the fact that only twenty-six of them were from Ahmedabad. The rest were from Mehsana, Sabarkantha and Anand. The bodies were brought to the Sola civil hospital where the atmosphere got tense by the night of 27 February 2002.

In fact, there were already signs of trouble. When the Sabarmati Express, carrying the survivors of the Godhra carnage stopped at Vadodara, mobs were waiting. They took over the station, waving sticks, broken bottles, trishuls and daggers—raising slogans, swearing revenge. Soon after, a thirty-five-year-old man was knifed in Vadodara. The violence had begun. In Ahmedabad, a fifty-year-old rickshaw driver was stabbed and seven buses were burnt.[11] Four persons were killed in Godhra—three succumbed to knife injuries, and one died in police firing.[12]

The mobs were out. The government handed over the streets to them. The chief minister instructed police chiefs to 'let the Hindus vent their frustration' over the Sabarmati Express burning.[13] At a meeting in the CM's bungalow on the night of 27 February, Modi instructed top police and home ministry officials like DGP K. Chakravarthi, the Ahmedabad police commissioner P.C. Pandey, and the DGP (Intelligence Bureau), G.C. Raigar, that 'the police should not come in the way of the Hindu backlash.' Some officers foresaw serious trouble and discussed whether or not the army should be requisitioned.[14]

Perhaps the CM felt he would be able to control the violence within a day or two, since it was his people triggering it. As Modi's own ministerial colleague told a tribunal of retired judges, his only motive was to use religious polarization to win the elections.[15] Godhra provided the opportunity. There were plans to use other triggers—he had toyed with the idea of making an issue of a cow slaughter video that the BJP had in its possession, but Godhra made it unnecessary.[16]

The VHP worked overnight, gathering their troops. They held meetings, distributed weapons, drew up lists of Muslim targets[17] and were ready to hit the streets the next day.

The floodgates burst open on the morning of 28 February, unleashing unimagined carnage across the state.

As chaotic as it looked on television screens—houses on fire, people running through the streets—there was a method to the madness. There were clear targets, and gangs moved around with cellphones, lists, trishuls and swords—hi-tech planning for primitive hatred. This was no riot, it was a pogrom.

Dhamaal: Organized chaos

Ahmedabad
No one was spared.

Not even high court judges. Status or wealth didn't matter, only the tag of religion did.

The VHP made sure that its bandh went off with a bang in Ahmedabad, its strongest base. The 'outburst of Hindu sentiment' was premeditated, well designed.

From Paldi, a posh locality, to the slums in Gomtipur, Ahmedabad's industrial area, saffron-clad mobs surging on to the streets had only one target—Muslims.

Judges, businessmen, hoteliers, doctors, hawkers, policemen, tailors, workers—all had to run for their lives. A nervous Justice M.H. Kadri, a sitting judge of the Gujarat High Court, called the chief justice to ask him to ensure his family's security, but all his boss could advise him to do was to hide at a fellow judge's house. Kadri had to leave his official home in Law Gardens, in the heart of the city.[18] Even the chief justice could not ensure his protection. Retired judge Akbar Divecha's house in Paldi was set on fire. Divecha hasn't returned there, and still lives in government quarters.[19]

As mobs closed in, people had nowhere to run. 'We were surrounded from all sides. They were like an army on a rampage for two days continuously,' said Farukh Azam, a resident of Sundaram Nagar,[20] a huge Muslim settlement in Gomtipur. 'Jeeps would come in, adding new batches of people to the mob. The looters had stocked water and biscuits in their pockets. After completely destroying us, they handed us over to the army.'

Minority businesses were targeted with precision. The mobs had lists of Muslim shops and hotels. Even Muslim-owned hotels with Hindu names were burned, but Hindu businesses or homes adjacent to Muslim establishments were left untouched. In Naroda's fruit market, which has 200 shops, the seventeen Muslim stores were the only ones looted and destroyed.[21] At the upmarket C.G. Road, only Muslim shops were raided. Ahmedabad's elite sent text messages on mobile phones informing each other where the booty was. They picked up the loot, even tried on clothes for size and drove off in their cars.[22]

Besides shops, masjids were a priority target. Within Ahmedabad alone, fifty-five[23] masjids were destroyed. The shrine of the Urdu poet Wali Gujarati, located just a few minutes walk from the police commissioner's office, was demolished in a matter of hours, and a makeshift Hindu temple took its place. The temple was removed a few days later, and the Ahmedabad Municipal Corporation quickly built a road over it. The Babanshah mosque at Swami Narayan chawl in Naroda was destroyed. A framed photo of a Hindu idol was placed where the Imam stands to lead the namaaz. They performed a puja and wrote '*Jai Shri Ram*' in red on the walls. The 100-year-old dargah opposite the Jagannath Mandir[24] in Ahmedabad's walled city was also broken.

The only areas of Ahmedabad that remained relatively untouched were the 'purged' areas. Middle-class Hindu areas—Navrangpura, Naranpura, Satellite—where Muslims would never have been sold a home in the first place. This is the new Ahmedabad that has emerged over the last twenty years on the other side of the Sabarmati river,[25] far away from the narrow lanes of the violence-scarred old city.

Ahmedabad's old walled city, which is supposed to be its most 'communally sensitive' area, was relatively trouble free. 'The old city has large Muslim and Hindu pockets. They are so used to violence that now they are careful and know how to respond by taking precautions. Local leaders keep in touch with the police,' explained a police officer. 'Moreover, since trouble was anticipated, there was heavy police security in the walled city. The VHP couldn't target areas with a large Muslim population. In areas where Muslims were secluded, like Naroda, the worst violence occurred.'

Poorer, industrial parts of Ahmedabad, like Gomtipur and Shah Alam, stayed under curfew for several months. The city was under siege, and people were stuck in their homes or in relief camps for several months. There were an estimated 1,00,000 refugees[26] in Ahmedabad's camps alone. Later the curfew was lifted, but the tension didn't ease. Muslims and

Hindus on either side of the 'border' armed themselves—an edgy stand-off waiting to explode.

In Ahmedabad, a few Hindu areas were also burned. Small Hindu colonies in the old city, which has a large Muslim population, faced retaliatory attacks. Few were killed, but houses were totally destroyed.

It took several months for the tension in Ahmedabad to die down. In some parts of the city, curfew remained in force for upto two months. Today, an underlying unease still exists. Every festival brings the threat of violence, with thousands of Muslims temporarily vacating their homes.

Naroda Patiya, Ahmedabad

Rehanabibi was still rubbing the sleep from her eyes, when people came running through the lanes saying that the Noorani masjid across the highway was being destroyed. Still, she never imagined that her home would be attacked—it had never happened before. 'When our boys went to see what was happening, the police started firing on us instead of stopping the mob,' said Rehanabibi.[27] Four persons were killed and two injured in police firing.[28] Among them was Mushtaq Razzak Kaladia, running across the road for safety with his little son.

Naroda is VHP head honcho Dr Jaideep Patel's home turf. Dr Maya Kodnani, the local BJP MLA, has a big following amongst the Sindhi community. The good doctors didn't heal. Rather, as witnesses at Naroda Gaam say, they directed the attack.

Rehanabibi watched as the masjid went up in flames. Then the mob descended on the colony. 'We tried to escape into the State Reserve Police (SRP) colony next to our basti. There was a police point there and they wouldn't let us go in. We waited near the wall till 4 p.m., begging them to save us,' said Rehanabibi.[29] When Asifbhai asked the police to let them go, they took him inside, pushed him on the ground and started hitting him with the rifle butt, she remembered. 'They showed us a newspaper with a headline of the burning train and said, "We have no orders to save you. We will burn you and kill you the same way today. Call your Allah to save you." There was no one to help us.'

Inspector K.K. Mysorewala, who was in-charge of Naroda police station, said that field officers like him had instructions not to send any messages to the police control room over their wireless sets. While more than 100 were killed in Naroda on 28 February 2002, Mysorewala could not inform the police control room of the massacres in his jurisdiction.[30]

By the evening the mob had taken over the entire colony. 'When people started running out of their homes, the mob surrounded them from all sides and set them on fire,' said Rehanabibi. At least eighty people were burnt alive. Their corpses were recovered from Teesra Kuan, a well behind the State Transport workshop. Many employees at the workshop joined the mob and even supplied them with petrol and diesel.

'When we ran into Gangotri Society behind, they had pipes and sticks and didn't let us enter. They were tearing off women's clothes, raping and burning them. I saw them rape at least five women,' Rehanabibi told me, reliving the horror as she spoke.

Rehanabibi also witnessed the infamous belly-slitting murder. 'I was hiding on a roof when they caught Kauser Bano. Bhavani Singh and Suresh were hitting her with swords. Kauser begged them not to. She told them she was pregnant,' said Rehanabibi. But they didn't hesitate for a second. 'Still, Bhavani put his sword into her stomach, took out the unborn child with his sword, held it up in the air and said, '*Dekho tere bacche ko duniya mein aane ke pehle upar pahuncha diya.*' (Look! We have sent your child to heaven before he even arrived in this world.) Then they threw it into the fire and burned her as well.'

By night, all that was left in Naroda Patiya were charred,

mutilated bodies. Ninety-seven were slaughtered[31] here and in the nearby Naroda Gaam, eleven[32] were killed.

Now it's not hard to see why Rehanabibi won't leave her home.

Gulbarg Society, Ahmedabad

Gulbarg Society is a small, innocuous middle-class colony in the heart of Ahmedabad, tucked away in a lane behind shops in the market. One of its residents was a well-known former Congress MP, Ahsan Jafri.

As the mob swooped in, people sought refuge in 'Jafri Uncle's house. Little did they know that it was the most dangerous place to hide—he was the main target. Some weeks before the attack, Jafri had been to Rajkot to campaign for the Congress against Narendra Modi, who was seeking election to the state assembly. Those close to him suspect that it might have been the main reason why he was targeted. Ahsan Jafri was a respected public figure, not only as an MP, but also as a lawyer and a poet (he was a member of the Progressive Writer's Association).

None of his influential friends came to his rescue. He desperately tried to contact everyone he knew—the mayor, the police commissioner, his friends in the Gujarat Congress.

The attack started at 7 a.m., when the VHP started closing down shops. The police knew what was happening. Constables posted outside watched as the mob killed the owner of Ankur cycle shop just outside the society. A frightened Mr Jafri immediately called the police commissioner. Joint commissioner of police M.K. Tandon came for ten minutes at 11 a.m., while the crowds were swelling and shouting 'Jai Shri Ram'.[33] He left, assuring that he would send SRP troops. Soon after, a bakery and autorickshaw were burned right outside. The owners of the bakery were the first to be savaged by the mob.[34]

'Then they started throwing stones, bottles, petrol bombs.

We ran to Jafri's house,' said Salimaben,[35] a frail, gentle old lady who was brave enough to venture back to the remains of her old home to meet me. Still aghast at the carnage, she was keen to tell her story. 'On the way, I saw them gang rape many young girls. Two sisters and their mother were raped and burned. Firoze's sister was raped and killed. They didn't spare any woman they came across—young or old.'

Around twenty-seven families were left to face an armed attack. 'They had instruments to break open windows. They threw cylinders and burning rags inside. There was a lot of smoke and many people fell unconscious,' Salimaben remembered, her slender frame shaking as she told me of the horrors. Her husband stood behind her for moral support.

At around 2.30 p.m. the mob entered Jafri's house. 'They caught my hands, put me on a table and said, "strip her". I pleaded with them. One boy took pity. He said, "You are my friend's mother." Then he fought with the rest to let me go. While getting off the table, they pulled out my necklace and earrings. He made sure they left me and my daughter-in-law on the road,' said Salima.[36] While she was outside they killed her son and four other relatives.

Inside the house, Jafri pleaded with the mob to spare the women. They dragged him out on to the street. Outside, the former MP was stripped, paraded naked and asked to say 'Jai Shri Ram'. He refused. His fingers were chopped off. Half dead, he was paraded around the neighbourhood. Then they hacked off his hands and feet. His body was dragged down the road and thrown into the fire.[37] Later, the chief minister said that Ahsan Jafri was the first to fire at the mob.[38] Witnesses deny this, and police officers say that there is no proof of this except a gun found in the remains.

Inspector K.G. Erda, in charge of Meghaninagar police station, was stationed outside Gulbarg Society but did not think it necessary to enter, claiming that if he went inside the crowd would follow him and the situation would go out of control. Although he was stationed at Gulbarg Society throughout the day, he did not try meeting Jafri even after Tandon sent a message at 2 p.m. saying that Jafri needed help.[39]

'We desperately called top police officials and politicians, but the police arrived only towards evening. When all that was left were a few survivors and mounds of dismembered bodies,' said Rupa Modi, a Parsi resident of the society.[40]

Gulbarg Society was allowed to burn for a week after the massacre.[41] According to police records,[42] 39 were killed and another 23 bodies were not found and are considered 'missing'. Rupa lost her thirteen-year-old son Azhar while they were hiding in Jafri's house. Still hoping that he was alive, she travelled all over Gujarat searching for him. A year after the massacre, some of Gulbarg Society's residents returned to the abandoned graveyard that was once their home. In Jafri's backyard, they buried the charred remains of the dead—hacked, dismembered bodies.[43]

Gulbarg Society remains deserted—no one dares to go back home.

Vadodara

This time, Professor J. Bandukwala was prepared. He had been targeted during two earlier riots because he had gone on peace satyagrahas. When the VHP announced its bandh, the police sent him security guards. But that didn't stop the mob.

'My house was the first place in Vadodara to be attacked on 28th morning. There were two armed policemen posted at my door for protection. They told the mob that they had fifteen minutes to do whatever they wanted. There was nothing we could do. If this could happen to me, just imagine the plight of a poor Muslim,' said the mild-mannered Bandukwala.[44] A popular physics professor at the M.S. University, and a peace activist, Bandukwala is a well-known personality in Vadodara who has been constantly critical of both Hindu and Muslim fundamentalists. The next day, a bigger mob returned with gas cylinders and weapons to burn down his house. 'BJP corporator Pradeep Joshi and BJP leader Ajay Dave led the attack. Later, they boasted about it in public, hoping it would boost their political careers,' he said.

The Bandukwalas' Hindu neighbours helped them escape the first attack, but then they too had to leave their home for a few days, under threat for saving the Bandukwala family. Later, they were asked why they helped Muslims. Rumours were spread that this dedicated teacher was an ISI agent and stored guns, just because his name was 'Bandukwala'. His friends asked him to leave the city, fearing he would be killed. Bandukwala and his family could return only in July, after the violence had died down. His daughter was to marry her Hindu boyfriend, but it was too dangerous for them to marry in Gujarat; couples who intermarried were also being targeted. They had to migrate to the US so that they could marry and be together. Professor J. Bandukwala had to start again from scratch; abandon the burned remains of his old home. Yet, what strikes you is his lack of bitterness, or a desire for revenge.

Gujarat's cultural capital, a gentle city with beautiful old architecture, a centre of art and learning, Vadodara has a reputation to live up to. But culture was thrown to the winds, its glory was in a shambles, when almost the entire city became the VHP's stomping ground. Men with saffron scarves and swords took over. Police atrocities and the abuse of women were a marked feature of these attacks.

Local cable channels helped broadcast the call to arms. As early as January 2002, a VHP meeting at ITI grounds was broadcast by the local channel. Here, Praveen Togadia asked Hindus to cut all relations with Muslims—to stop buying from Muslim shops, not even offer them water if they visited their homes.[45] During the mayhem, the cable channels kept interviewing VHP leaders, who said, 'Muslims will have to live the way we want, otherwise we will pull them out of their houses and kill them.'[46] The mass broadcasts led to mass murder.

At Dabhoi Road, an industrial area on the outskirts of the city, a mob attacked the Best Bakery and roasted fourteen people alive, including three Hindu workers.

In some parts of the city, Hindu neighbours saved their Muslim friends. In Kisanwadi, a poor neighbourhood of eastern Vadodara, residents of both communities were at a Muslim family's wedding when a mob started climbing the masjid on the evening of 28 February 2002. Ramdas Pillai, one of their neighbours, tried to stop them. They managed to fight them, but the mob returned the next day to tear it down. Ramdas and his brother sheltered 500 Muslims in their homes.[47]

During the second phase of the violence, Sangh Parivar activists targeted areas that had so far remained peaceful. This time the trigger was the VHP's call for a shila daan in Ayodhya on 15 March 2002. The VHP took out a huge procession through the city, violating curfew orders. Participants shouted insults at Muslims and burned shops en route. The police watched, but did nothing.

Then the procession entered the Muslim area of Macchipith in the old city, which had been untouched by the carnage until then. People left the procession and rushed into residential lanes with weapons, shouting slogans like 'Bandiao (circumcised), go away to Pakistan.' Some took off their pants and danced inside the colony. Local residents who threw stones in defence were arrested in police raids, but the assailants went free.[48]

For months, Sangh activists kept tensions brewing. They had dealt a body blow to the state's cultural capital, but they couldn't break its spirit. Dr Bandukwala's children are now abroad, but he refused to follow them, preferring to live alone in Vadodara. 'Why should I leave?' he asked. 'I won't feel at home anywhere else.'

Panchmahal
They hid in the fields, fleeing an attack on their village, Delol, but the mob caught up with the refugees. Eight dead bodies were piled up and set on fire. Hameed, nine, and Ijaz, eleven, were made to go around the pyre and shout *'Jai Shri Ram'*. Then they were thrown in and nailed there with sharp weapons as they struggled.[49]

In Godhra civil hospital, there's a calm that chills. The corridors are empty, but the wards are full, crammed with patients, all of them badly injured, heads and limbs bandaged from knife and rod wounds. As I walked into the burns ward, I had to look away. Women so badly charred, you could barely imagine what they must have looked like. From faraway villages, these were the few survivors, some not thankful to be alive.

I met Maksooda Rahim from Anjanwa village. She was one of the few patients who could speak (many others were so badly burned, they were wrapped up in bandages like mummies.) 'The attackers came beating drums and yelling *"Maaro, Kaapo, Baalo"* (Kill, Cut, Burn). I was with my two little ones. They threw us into a well. I managed to cling on to the wall. But my two infants drowned. Eight people were thrown into the well, including four children. Outside, they cut and burned an elderly couple,' said Maksooda, straining in her hospital bed, but fighting the pain so as to be able to tell her story.

Panchmahal, a parched, poor district of central Gujarat, was still in shock. Villages here had never known communal violence. After the burning of the Sabarmati Express in Godhra, the district capital, VHP volunteers made sure that violence spread to distant villages. They distributed newspapers with provocative photographs and headlines about Godhra. Muslims were driven out of more than twenty towns and villages. Camps were mainly in the towns, and people lived in the wilderness for days before they were rescued. Many were never found.

According to Police FIRs filed in Kalol police station on 17 December 2002, as well as eyewitness accounts, the attacks began on the day of the VHP bandh itself. In Delol village, sixty Muslim families took shelter in Hindu homes. The attackers chased them out on to the fields. That night they surrounded those hiding in the farms and told them they could leave. Then they attacked from behind, hacking and burning twenty-four people.

In several villages, electricity and phone lines were snapped the day before the attack—clear evidence of pre-planning. For ten days no bus service, newspapers or police reached Anjanwa.[50]

Sangh activists patrolled the highways. The police were nowhere to be seen. Mobs blockaded the roads and nabbed refugees fleeing their villages. When Salim Sindhi's village, Sabarkantha in Kidiad, was attacked, he bundled in as many people as possible into two tempos and fled. 'On the road, there was a lot of stone-throwing. All the windows were broken. One rock hit my four-month-old nephew. He died instantly,' said Salim.[51]

'Two men on a motorbike kept trailing us. Then, near Limbadia Chowkdi, they barricaded the road and made us stop,' he said. While trying to avoid the blockade, the tempo turned, skidded and overturned. As people tried to run out, the mob hacked six of them in one tempo. They set the other tempo on fire, killing sixty-seven, of whom thirty-four were children. A total of seventy-three people were killed, of which thirty-two were children.[52] Only eleven bodies were found. The rest are 'missing' according to police records.

In several villages in Panchmahal there were similar horror stories. The VHP was intent on avenging the Godhra massacre, particularly in the district where it occurred. Here and in nineteen other districts, Hindutva's soldiers unleashed mass violence on a scale never experienced before in rural Gujarat.

Pandharvada
The writing was on the wall. But they didn't see it.

Two weeks before the Godhra tragedy, the VHP held a meeting in their village. Over the loudspeaker, local leader Dr A.B. Pandya threatened to remove Muslims from the village and 'break their necks'. Police and district officials posted at the village sat there laughing, sipping tea.[53]

Suddenly, a day after the Godhra massacre, telephone wires were snapped. The next day, electricity was also cut off.[54] Then local leaders went in for the kill.

'A local lawyer and also a VHP activist called around 200 people and offered them protection in his house. Then, he bolted the door from outside. They brought Bhil tribals with them. They had given them money and liquor,' said Mariambibi Sayyed. 'They threw stones, acid and set the house on fire. Small kids were roasted alive.'[55]

Another village leader also offered Muslims protection on his farm. There, the waiting mob threw acid on them, hit them with swords on their head and burned them. 'My two sons were in the field. They were hacked to pieces in front of my eyes,' the elderly Nathubhai Sheikh told me,[56] still shaking with fear. He was also locked inside the lawyer's house, but managed to escape.

Thirty-three people were killed. Many ran to the hills. They were rescued after three days. 'We ran out of our homes without even chappals. Our feet were full of thorns. For three days, we ate bitter neem leaves. It was like some action film. The men in the mob even told us, 'Have you seen the film *Gadar*?[57] Watch! Now it's happening live in front of you.' We still have nightmares about that day,' Saira Sayyed, one of the survivors, told me.[58]

Mumtaz Fakir Sheikh's husband, Fakir, was running with their two-year-old son in his arms when the mob accosted him and cut his head off with a sword. 'I gave the police the names of those who murdered him, but there was no investigation,' she says.[59] Mumtaz hasn't been able to go back home, and lives in a nearby town.

Akeela's daughter saw them slice off her father's neck and drown people in the water tank. Children are scared at the very mention of their village. Their immediate response is— 'The Bhils will kill us.'[60]

Dahod

They were only safe across the border, in Rajasthan.

Fleeing from the attack on their village, Muslims from Fatehpura sought protection at the police station. 'But the police said that they couldn't help us. "Go wherever you want," they told us, said Iqbal Sisoli, a young refugee from Fatehpura, who owned a paan shop there. He took his wife and two young children and ran. 'But where could we go? For two nights we camped outside the police station without even water to drink.' The police shoved them into tempos and took them across the border to Rajasthan. On the way, five-year-old Shabnam Quereshi died of suffocation. 'No one realized she was dead until we got out of the tempo,' said Ismail. It was only in Rajasthan that they were given food and shelter.

Dahod, adjacent to Panchmahal district, is a dry, rocky terrain with villages spread far apart from each other. Here too, the attacks to drive away Muslims seemed well planned. 'Around two weeks earlier, they had put saffron flags on all Hindu houses,' said Abdul Karim, a carpenter from Jhalod. His twenty-two-year-old son went for namaaz and came back with bullet wounds in his neck. In Sanjeli, Fatehpura and Sukhsar villages, Hindu houses were marked with a cross or with saffron flags.[61] Sanjeli had seen VHP hate campaigns in the past as well, against adivasi women who had eloped with Muslims from the village.

A day before the attack on 1 March 2002, BJP MP

Babubhai Katara's cars traversed Jhalod all day, possibly preparing for the attack. The next day, his son Bhavesh roamed the streets with an armed mob. 'His son shot my brother Anees,' said Hafiz Patel, an owner of a garage on the highway near Jhalod.[62] The operation was so well planned that in the mob there was one group only loading weapons[63] and passing them on to the foot-soldiers.

The violence lasted for three continuous days. On 3 March 2002 the Muslims of Jhalod pleaded with the collector and the police to hold a peace meeting. Political leaders including BJP MP Babubhai Katara and RSS leaders put down a list of conditions. These included:

- No mikes should be used during the azaan in the mosque.
- Muslim children should not enter Hindu areas after 10 p.m.
- All butcher shops should be closed down.
- Muslims would not be allowed to sell meat in the vegetable market.
- The Muslim orphanage that was burned in the riots should not be restarted.
- No intermarriages.[64]

The Muslims agreed. But outside, the carnage continued.

'We couldn't even bury my son,' said Abdul Karim.[65] 'The mobs were everywhere—at the hospital, at the graveyard. After my son was shot in the neck, we couldn't get an ambulance. When he died, we couldn't even take him to the graveyard. Finally, we buried him in the jamaatkhana (eating hall).'

Inside the mosque at Sanjeli they wrote, 'Hindustan is for Hindus and Muslims should go back to Pakistan.' They didn't want to go to Pakistan. Rajasthan was safe enough.

North Gujarat
Till the very end, Yusuf Khan Pathan never believed his neighbours would harm him. But his faith proved fatal. Yusuf

lost eleven family members when his home in Deepda
Darwaza, a small cluster of Muslim houses in a predominantly
Hindu area, was attacked on 28 February 2002. 'They cut
my family into pieces and burned them. They took the remains
and threw them into the Malab Talao so that there would be
no evidence,' said Yusuf, a resident of Visnagar in Mehsana.[66]

During the violence, the VHP also instigated trouble in
the northern districts of Sabarkantha, Banaskantha and
Mehsana. These are parched regions, partly adivasi areas,
partly controlled by rich tubewell farmers. A Congress
stronghold, north Gujarat was one of the last bastions left
for the BJP to capture.

They took over highways. Five people returning to
Ahmedabad via Himmatnagar were stopped at Pratinj,
Sabarkantha. Only one was left alive. Two of those killed
were British nationals of Gujarati origin, who were visiting
Jaipur with their relatives.[67] At Madhopur Kampa, five truck
drivers were burned alive and twenty trucks were set ablaze.[68]

In Sardarpura, Mehsana district, the Patel community led
attacks on the Muslim bastis. The violence started on the
night of 28 February 2002 when several small shops were
burned. The police was alerted, but did nothing to stop the
violence. The next day, frightened Muslims and Dalits made
several attempts to call a village meeting to prevent further
violence. But the Patels did not attend. A street-light that
had not been working for months was suddenly repaired.
Then they put up halogen lights and swooped in for the
kill.[69]

In the Sheikh (a community of poor landless labourers)
basti, around thirty-one[70] people huddled together in one
house. The mob surrounded the house, locked them in and
started throwing stones and acid. They threw in live wires
through a steel door and electrocuted twenty-nine[71] people.
In all, thirty-three people were murdered. As usual, the police
remained spectators. Dalits, who sheltered some refugees, were

later harassed by the Patels. Long after the attack, the Patels imposed a boycott on Muslims in the village and took over their shops. In 2004, Sardarpura was still a 'Muslim-free' village.

'*Hindu Nagari*', read the sign at the Khed Brahma bus stand. This town in Sabarkantha remains hostile to the minorities. The first to go were the homes and shops of the Muslims, then their owners were chased out. To this day, the local dadas won't let them return. For some refugees from this town, a trip back home could be their final journey.

Anand

'They burned everything. They even looted goats,' Rashida Vora, a survivor from Odh village in Anand, told me.[72] Anand, the home of Amul, India's most successful dairy co-operative, is considered one of the more prosperous areas in Gujarat. A large proportion of its residents are NRIs. In this land of plenty, the VHP made sure that Muslims were reduced to paupers. In several villages like Padoli, there were reports of rich NRIs instigating mobs with the temptation of money and liquor, and funding the operation by providing cash, weapons and gas cylinders.

In Odh, thirty people hiding in their homes were locked in and burned alive. 'After the Godhra incident, the Bajrang Dal had a meeting at midnight in the Jalaram temple. That's when they planned to attack us. They put Hanuman statues in our masjid. They used our gas cylinders to destroy our homes,' said Aslam Vora, a refugee from Odh.[73]

'We used to work in their fields. We never imagined this would happen.' Around 200 houses, shops and mosques were razed to the ground.[74] Bulldozers were used to flatten the land. No one was allowed to return to Odh.

Graffiti on the walls said it all—'Don't let the Muslims come back.'[75]

Rashidabibi now knows what the writing on the wall means. Even when you're back, you're not.

Firoze too understands. Even with police protection, you're not safe.

Salim Sindhi won't go back even though he is the sarpanch of his village.

Whether they returned home or didn't, they are still exiles. Whether they had police protection or not, they are not safe. From now on, they know they are marked for life.

The Police: We have no orders to save you

'That's the whole problem. The police are equally influenced by the overall general sentiment.'
—P.C. Pandey, Ahmedabad Police Commissioner, on
Star News, 28 February 2002

When they burst into her home and shot her in the head, eighteen-year-old Naziabibi was studying for her 12th standard exams. Her father, Mehmud, took a bullet in the nape of his neck. The three young girls studying with her for the exams, also trapped in the shooting, were terrified. No, it wasn't one of Gomtipur's mobs out on the rampage—it was the police 'combing the area' for criminals.

Her uncle Wali rushed them to the hospital in an autorickshaw. 'At the Saranpur bridge, the police tried to stop our rickshaw, but we just went on. Then they fired on us,' remembers Wali.[76] They made it to the hospital, but daughter and father didn't make it to see another day. They died the same night from gunshot wounds.

Whether those who died in police firing in Patel ni chali on the afternoon of 21 April 2002 were guilty or innocent was irrelevant. They were criminals by definition—they were Muslims.

On the morning of 28 February 2002, former MP Ahsan

Jafri frantically called the police commissioner asking for protection. The commissioner visited his home and assured him security, but no police reinforcements were sent. There was no one to stop the mob that dragged him on the street and slashed him to bits.[77]

In Naroda Patiya, the police stopped people from escaping through the SRP colony gate. They told them that it was their day to die.[78] Just outside the Naroda police station, the mob blocked the road with burning tyres and drums. When they parked a tanker to provide water to their foot-soldiers at the gate of the police station, no one stopped them. Men in saffron bandanas roamed freely, while refugees who ran for help were scared to enter the station.[79]

The police response was remarkably similar in most places—they sat back and watched as Gujarat burned. They were merely following orders. The night before, chief minister Narendra Modi had called a top-level meeting, telling the director-general of the Gujarat police and the Ahmedabad police commissioner to let the 'Hindu mobs vent their frustration'.[80] They obeyed.

The invisible hand: Government complicity

On the day of the VHP bandh, BJP ministers took over the police control rooms.[81] Urban development minister I.K. Jadeja, considered Modi's right-hand man, sat at the state police room, updating the chief minister on the latest developments. In the Ahmedabad police control room, health minister Ashok Bhatt oversaw operations. Ironically, Bhatt is accused of the murder of a constable during the 1985 communal riots.[82]

Both ministers were present when desperate calls for help flooded the control rooms, but they did nothing to respond. The only person Bhatt instructed the police to save was his son Bhushan, a BJP councillor, who was mobbed at Gaekwad

Haveli.[83] As a rule, no one can interfere with the working of the police control room; not even senior police officers enter without permission. But rules mattered little in a state that discarded the rule of law.

The chief minister boasted that his government brought the situation under control within seventy-two hours. In fact, violence continued until July. The union government admitted that 216 died, 790 were injured and property worth Rs 417.07 crore[84] was lost in communal violence between April and June.[85]

As proof of action, Modi said that police firing was more than in previous riots; what he didn't mention is that most of the people killed by the police were victims, not aggressors. Of the 184 people who died in police firing since the violence began, 104 were Muslims.[86] On 28 February the police shot dead forty men near the Bapunagar police station in Ahmedabad. All were Muslims, most of them shot in the head and chest while trying to defend themselves against a mob attack.[87] Normally, the police are supposed to shoot below the waist to immobilize the mob, not kill them.

Even though trouble was brewing, the police didn't take precautions that are standard procedure, such as preventive arrests, deployment of extra forces, intelligence gathering, and firing at violent sections of the mob. Violence had already broken out in Vadodara and parts of Ahmedabad on the night of the Godhra massacre. Though the VHP called a bandh the next day, the Ahmedabad police made only two preventive arrests in response.[88]

The pattern of police complicity has been remarkably similar in communal massacres across India. During the Mumbai violence of 1992–93, Delhi's anti-Sikh pogrom in 1984 and numerous other massacres, the police stood back and let mobs attack. They often refused to file cases and deliberately jeopardized investigations, sometimes naming the victims as the accused. It is similar to the stereotyping of the African-Americans in the US, who are more vulnerable to police atrocities and arbitrary arrests.

Many including Ahmedabad's police commissioner P.C. Pandey have an explanation for this inherent bias. 'After all, policemen are part of society and have the same biases as ordinary people.' But experience has shown that in places where there are strong police officers directing operations to quell violence, police personnel have shown remarkable skill and courage in restoring peace. Surat, which was aflame in 1992 after the Babri Masjid demolition, was peaceful after the Godhra incident thanks to an effective police commissioner, V.K. Gupta. He prevented violence by merely doing his duty—with the help of standard precautions like making preventive arrests and mobilizing forces. After the demolition of the Babri Masjid, the West Bengal government issued strict orders to prevent violence, and so Kolkata remained peaceful. But because the then Maharashtra chief minister Sudhakarrao Naik was ineffective, Mumbai burned and more than 900[89] lives were lost.

It's the will of the rulers that matters most. Actually, it is easier for the police to prevent a riot than to allow it to happen. Sometimes senior officers respond according to the mood of their political masters, and that is why they hesitate to act—because politicians are often more interested in manipulating the violence for their own gain rather than stopping it.

Refugees

Injured and barefoot, fifteen Muslim families in Kisangadh village, Sabarkantha, limped to the Bhiloda police station. When they finally reached their destination they were turned away—the police told them that they should leave quickly or they would be attacked. When they pleaded with police officers to escort them to Idar, a nearby town, they said they couldn't because they had orders from above.[90]

In Fatehpura, the police did nothing as the mob gang raped women in full public view, just a kilometre away from the police station. Three men who tried to rescue them were killed. Several people, some of them naked and battered women, poured into the police station seeking help, but none was given.[91]

At the police station, brimming over with refugees, there wasn't even room to sit. Most of them just stood there for one and a half days. The police didn't give them any food or drink. Just once, they gave the children some water. On the morning of 4 March 2002, the police bundled them into vehicles so tightly packed that a five-year-old child died. They were taken to the Rajasthan border and handed over to the local police. It was there that the refugees got their first meal. The dead child was buried in Rajasthan.

The police even targeted refugee camps. Bharat Barot, the food and civil supplies minister, wanted to get rid of the refugees in his constituency. He wrote to the home minister asking him to shut down the Dariya Khan Ghummat camp in his area because 'his Hindu voters didn't feel safe'.[92] Later, he got the police to attack, claiming that the camp was sheltering criminals and terrorists. When they stormed in, an old lady died of shock. The police threw tear gas shells, injuring several people.[93]

Transfers
Police officers were punished for doing their duty and saving lives.

While the state was still tense, the government transferred twenty-seven IPS officers without consulting the top brass of the force. Several of those shifted were officers who had done an impressive job preventing violence. They were either sent to remote districts or to assignments that were not as challenging; non-executive posts that did not involve fieldwork.

Special inspector-general (Vadodara range) Deepak Swaroop, was transferred from Godhra hours after he was posted there on 27 February 2002. Swaroop had reportedly warned political leaders against visiting Godhra that day, keeping in mind the fragile communal situation there.[94]

Rahul Sharma, the police superintendent in Bhavnagar, came down hard on troublemakers. When he arrested twenty-one VHP and BJP activists, he got a call from the home minister, Gordhan Zadaphia, asking him to book them under 'safe clauses' of the law. Sharma saved 400 children in a madrasa, which was attacked from all sides by a huge mob. His alertness ended trouble in Bhavnagar in a matter of two days. But for Sharma, the trouble began after he brought peace to the city. He was soon shunted out to the Ahmedabad city control room.

Sharma also wrote to the state director-general of police asking for action to be taken against *Sandesh*, a Gujarati newspaper, for publishing an article that incited trouble during the violence. The article claimed that while so much violence had occurred in the rest of the state during the VHP bandh, the leaders of Bhavnagar were sitting like cowards. This sparked off violence in the city. Sharma's letter got no response.

While he was supervising the Ahmedabad crime branch investigations, he disagreed with the manner in which the charge-sheets for the two worst massacres—Gulbarg Society, Chamanpura and Naroda Patiya—were filed. They blamed Muslims for provoking the attack and ignored crucial evidence that showed the involvement of local politicians like Dr Maya Kodnani and Dr Jaideep Patel. When Sharma insisted that the truth be told, he was reassigned once again, this time to the SRP in Vav, a small town in south Gujarat.

Kutch was one of the few areas that remained trouble-free during the violence. Much of the credit goes to the superintendent of police, Vivek Srivastav, who immediately arrested VHP leaders who attempted to attack Muslim areas, including Vasant Patel and Akshay Thakkar, also a home guard commandant. Zadaphia badgered him with several phone calls asking for their release, but he did not relent.

When shops and a dargah were burned by a mob, Srivastav tracked down the culprits and made them pay for the reconstruction costs. When VHP activists attacked a dargah in Bhimsar village, he stopped them. Thanks to Srivastav, Kutch remained peaceful. But he was too independent for the government's liking; soon he was transferred too. A week after his departure, violence hit Kutch for the first time, when rioting broke out in Anjar.

Praveen Gondia, DCP Zone IV, Ahmedabad, was punished because he registered FIRs that named Dr Jaideep Patel and Dr Maya Kodnani for their involvement in the Naroda Patiya massacre. He was transferred to civil defence. Once Gondia left, the FIRs he filed vanished into thin air—they simply ceased to exist in police records. The investigating officers produced alibis for Kodnani and Patel in court, claiming that they were at Sola civil hospital at the time of the attack.

Himanshu Bhatt, superintendent of police in Banaskantha, suspended a sub-inspector who let a mob plunder Muslim homes. Soon he too received calls from the chief minister's office asking him to revoke the suspension. The sub-inspector had friends in high places within the VHP and BJP. Bhatt was shunted to a desk job in the state Intelligence Bureau.

In official lingo these were 'routine transfers', but the motive behind them was all too obvious. DGP K. Chakravarthi was so incensed that he wrote a letter to the home ministry in protest, saying 'the transfers will demoralize officers who stood their ground and effectively checked communal violence.'[95] But that was the whole idea.

Pandora's box

They couldn't contain the silence for too long. Even though the cops, the politicians and the accused were partners in crime, all it took was one person to blow the lid on them.

The first to speak out was an insider—R.B. Sreekumar, Gujarat's additional director-general of police (Intelligence Bureau). Two months after the violence, his warnings about police complicity with the accused fell on deaf ears. The chief minister's office asked him to tap the phones of Haren Pandya, Shankarsinh Vaghela, a Muslim corporator and the chief police inspector of Ellis Bridge police station in Ahmedabad. He refused, and when he recommended police action against Modi for his anti-minority speech at Becharji on 9 September 2002, no one dared to act. Predictably, he was transferred out of his post.

It was in his testimony before the Nanavati–Shah commission that someone finally listened. The government did not heed his warnings about police collusion with the riot accused, he stated. Sreekumar gave the court a letter he had written to Ashok Narayan, additional chief secretary (home) in late April 2002. In the letter, Sreekumar had warned that the police's complicity in shielding the accused and its failure to properly record and investigate cases had made Muslims feel both insecure and belligerent. The police bias against Muslims was one of the reasons why Ahmedabad was not fully back to normal even two months after the violence began, he said. Inspectors in police stations were taking orders directly from politicians, rather than their senior officers, weakening the effectiveness and morale of the police force. Based on Sreekumar's report on the law and order situation to the election commission, the chief election commissioner, J.M. Lyngdoh, felt that elections in Gujarat had to be delayed, angering Modi and foiling his plans of an early election victory. Sreekumar's candid warnings of the deterioration of law and order in the state and the persistent persecution of minorities were the first on official record that were made public.

Two months after the pogrom, Sreekumar warned that the police were conspiring with the accused. 'A major complaint of the Muslims is that the investigating officers are avoiding the arrest of Hindu leaders, even though their names are figuring in the FIRs of major offences . . . the accused persons from the Hindu community arrested for non-bailable cases are also immediately released because of the partisan stand taken by the government public prosecutors.' In fact, several government prosecutors in Gujarat are VHP members. After the release of the accused, 'local leaders of the ruling party made arrangements for giving them a hero's felicitation,' he informed the government. But the police let it slide for more than a year until Zaheera Sheikh's case in the Supreme Court pressured the state to make amends.

'The police were not fair in recording the complaints (FIRs) of the minority community,' he said, 'and often pressure and strong persuasive tactics are adopted to dissuade complainants from giving complaints.' They were intentionally not recording the names of the accused in the FIRs. Policemen deliberately clubbed together many crimes that took place in different places in a single FIR. This 'provided loopholes to the accused persons during prosecution'.

The 'abnormally' high rate of Muslim casualties and losses, disproportionate to their population, had fostered a sense of revenge amongst some sections, the Intelligence Bureau official said. He had warned that Islamic militants from within and outside the country were sending weapons to Ahmedabad. A high degree of 'self-destructive' communalism by extremist elements in both communities was keeping hate alive, Sreekumar cautioned. No one cared to listen. It suited the BJP in building up public hysteria for the elections.

While the then Gujarat police chief K.Chakravarthi and former Ahmedabad police commissioner P.C. Pandey nervously approached the commission, trying to save their skins, Sreekumar and his colleague Rahul Sharma boldly produced new evidence of police complicity. Fearing what he would say in his testimony before the Nanavati–Shah commission, lawyers for the Gujarat government called Sreekumar for a meeting and warned him of the consequences if he testified against the state. But the professional spy was one up on them—he taped the entire conversation and gave it to the newspaper *Tehelka* to publish.

Rahul Sharma's biggest revelation was records of mobile phone conversations between top politicians and police officers in the first three days of the violence, which reveal that key riot accused were in regular touch with the police, politicians and VHP leaders during the time of the massacres. They also establish that Kodnani and Patel were at Naroda when the killings occurred, putting to an end speculation about the whereabouts of accused, police, and politicians, establishing at what place, when, and who was in touch with whom. Even after this damning proof was made public, police investigators have not included this evidence in the case papers and not taken action accordingly.

Not only did Sharma have to cross swords with the attackers on the streets, he had to also fight with his bosses. He told the commission how he argued with Gujarat's top cop, K. Chakravarthi, for forty-five minutes when he called and asked Sharma to free those arrested for rioting in Bhavnagar.[96] He said he was pressured from 'all levels'—by the collector, the range IG, the DGP, and local BJP leaders—to free on bail twenty-one rioters arrested for attacking a local madrasa on 23 March 2002. When he refused to do so, he was transferred within twenty-four hours. This was the first time that deliberate police negligence was spoken about publicly by people within the force.

Home minister Gordhan Zadaphia called up Sharma and told him that the community-wise ratio of those killed in the police firing was 'not proper' because more Hindus were killed than Muslims in Bhavnagar.[97] Overall, as per state records, until 30 April 2001, eighty Hindus and 103 Muslims were killed in police firing. In Bhavnagar, five Hindus and one Muslim were killed in police firing.[98]

The conflicts continued when Sharma was asked to oversee investigations of the Ahmedabad crime branch. Here, he told the court that he disagreed with police commissioner P.C. Pandey and ACP D.G. Vanjara, who were in charge of the investigations. They were reluctant to get the mobile phone records of prominent politicians, policemen and the accused and to probe any further, while Sharma was convinced that these records would yield valuable evidence.

FIRs

It took Firdos Ghanchi 657 days to get his statement registered with the Kalol police. He had witnessed the murders of ten members of his family on 1 March 2002, but the police only recorded his statement on 17 December 2003.

The police asked Firdos to remove the names of the accused and produce the remains of the dead before agreeing to register his testimony. Since the bodies were not found, they were considered 'missing persons'. The police even asked this young, penniless tailor to produce Rs 4,50,000 in collateral for each dead person, just in case they turned up alive in the future.[99] They were acting on a government order which laid out this procedure. Later, that order was revoked.

Firdos, who had seen ten of his kin killed, was intent on justice. When the mob attacked Muslims in his village, Delol, he and his neighbours fled and ran away into the fields. He watched as they hacked his father, mother, brother, sister, niece and nephew to death.

While hiding in the shrubs with Firdos, eleven-year-old Ijaz saw the mob slash his mother's neck. He screamed with fright. The mob caught hold of him, stacked the dead bodies into a pile, set them ablaze, made Ijaz walk around the pyre and finally threw him and a friend into the fire as well.

For almost two years there was no record of this gory massacre. Finally, when officials in Kalol police station were transferred, Firdos was able to get his complaint registered. Now round two had begun—the struggle for justice in the courts.

When the police agreed to take down statements, they deliberately missed out names and important facts. Before the commencement of the trial, witnesses of the Chamanpura massacre went to court asking that their statements be recorded accurately and proper investigations be conducted, fearing that the outcome of the trial could have been manipulated if this was not done.

Going one step further to shield the accused, the police also destroyed evidence. In Bilkis Yakub's FIR in Randhikpur, the police closed the case as 'true but undetected', even though the main witness was willing to testify. When the Supreme Court ordered a CBI probe, skeletons came tumbling out—literally. The CBI team found that the police had asked panch witnesses to bury the bodies with sixty kg of salt so that they would disintegrate faster, and there would be no trace of evidence. The police made no effort to investigate her complaint, closing it as soon as possible. The CBI later arrested six policemen for negligence and conspiring with the accused; they are part of the small handful of policemen punished for their complicity in the violence. Inspector Patil, who clubbed Firdos's FIR with three others' was arrested in August 2004.

The Gujarat police shielded culprits brazenly. In Delol village, Jaggubhai sits opposite the police station and sells vegetables to police constable Patil every day. Jaggubhai is accused of burning to death thirteen people who were escaping the attack on their basti in a tempo. He shares a joke with the good inspector every day, and can afford to. In public view, he is present; in police records, he's absconding.

Khaki is not uniform

He trained them at the police gym and watched them grow up. But Inspector Rashid Khan's 22-year dedication to the police force dissolved in just one day. The boys he had nurtured were the men who burned his house.

'The boys who I have trained and looked after were part of the mob that looted and destroyed my home,' Rashid told me. 'They were sons of fellow policemen. They were like my children. I couldn't believe it.'[100]

Rashid is still reeling from the hurt of being betrayed by his own people, his own brothers in the police.

Rashid smelt something fishy when his neighbour, a local Bajrang Dal leader, held a late night meeting on the day of the Godhra carnage. Once the VHP bandh was announced, Rashid took precautions. He shifted as much as he could from his home in Pratap Nagar, Dhanteshwar in Vadodara, locked it all up and fled.

'I put all my stuff in a flat in the police lines near my home,' says Rashid. 'Two days later, a mob led by constable Deepak Badgujar (who lives there) broke the lock, looted it, poured kerosene and set it on fire. I watched it all from a distance, but I couldn't do anything.'

They didn't spare other Muslim homes in Rashid's housing society either. The flats of two other Muslim policemen, Salim and Iqbal Sheikh, were attacked.

Their families had to run for cover on the night of 1 March 2002. 'I called for a police van, but it would just pass by without doing anything. One of my brothers had to crawl at night from house to house begging for help. Another hid in a toilet all night. They even stole our baby's cradle,' said Salim.[101]

None of them have returned to their homes, but have shifted to Tandalja, considered a Muslim area of the city. Rashid was able to sell his home—for less than half the price he had paid for it, but Salim and Iqbal haven't managed even that. 'The society people stand at the gate and scare off anyone who comes to see the house. They want to buy the flats cheap,' says Rashid.

Rashid has been working in the Pratap Nagar police headquarters for more than twenty years, but his colleagues didn't help him. The first time round they gave him a police van to shift his belongings. 'But after everything was burned, I literally had to beg them for a van to shift whatever remained. They didn't feel anything when I was attacked. It was as if we were complete strangers. They didn't even help me pick up my stuff,' he says.

The atmosphere at work has also chilled. 'The feeling of brotherhood has gone. They don't trust us. And I don't have faith that the police will help me if my life is in danger,' says Rashid.

A fitness freak and gym instructor, Rashid has won the 'Mr Vadodara' title twice. But his enthusiasm has waned. 'I'm still training boys at the police gym. But it's not from my heart. Why should I do this after being betrayed?'

Several Muslim policemen were attacked during the violence. Their uniform offered them no security. Suddenly there was a huge inflow of application forms for police housing—they were applications by Muslim personnel who had lost their homes, sometimes within police quarters itself.

It doesn't get much better as you go higher up. Even senior Muslim officers, the cream of the force, experienced similar problems. On 28 February 2002, a mob gathered outside their building in Ahmedabad, ready to attack. They were surrounded from all sides. One of the officers called a friend in the control room, who sent a police squad to fight back the mob.

Considering that trouble was expected and it was the only Muslim building in Navrangpura, there should have been more police security arranged for the building. But not a single police constable was posted outside until after the attack.

'We feel neglected. There was no sympathy for us,' said an officer.

Even after the attack, small groups would gather outside the building, throwing stones or blinking car lights and honking. For three months after the attack, one officer wouldn't go out of his house for a walk, for fear of being attacked.

Even at work, Muslim officers were sidelined. While the state was burning, they were not assigned any field duties. Though there was a dire shortage of staff, they were never deployed. There was a desperate feeling of powerlessness. Outside, there was mayhem on the streets. People kept calling them for help—this was a time when a policeman is most needed. But there was little they could do except make a few phone calls. Some were even reluctant to ask their colleagues to save people; they were not sure what reaction it would elicit.

'We couldn't do anything to help. We were scared to even visit the camps for fear of being sidelined within the force,' said one officer. 'They didn't want people to know what was going on. That's why they didn't put Muslim officers on the streets.'

Since 1995 no Muslim officer in Gujarat has been given a field posting involving law and order or investigation. They are only given assignments like police housing, logistics, etc. Constables under them were waiting in the wings. Although there was a shortage of manpower, even they had to stay put while the city was in flames.

Muslim policemen were afraid to even wear their name tags on their uniform, some even asked for special permission not to wear them. Many were attacked while on duty. A.I. Saiyed, special inspector-general, went to help some people on the way to Karai, Gandhinagar. But when the mob saw his name, they pounced on him.[102]

Today, Muslim officers are afraid to talk about their

marginalization. Many would prefer to be transferred outside Gujarat. After Modi was re-elected, they were more fearful of being harassed, so they choose silence—the path of least resistance. Not everyone is as brave as Mr Vadodara, Rashid Khan.

Women and children: Easy prey

'My younger brother Siraj, who is seven, still wakes up screaming at night: '*Mat maaro meri ammi ko*' (Don't kill my mother). He was in her lap last. She made him run,' said Mustafa Khan, all of ten, from Limkheda, Panchmahal.[103] Both brothers saw their mother being raped and killed, along with nine other family members.

They were on their way to meet their two older sisters, who are married and live in Pandu. Their mother was taking them to a mela there along with a group of twenty from their village. On the 28th, the group took a train to Derol and reached the next morning. While walking towards Pandu, they were accosted by a mob.

'They were carrying sharp weapons and wearing brown shorts and half-sleeve shirts,' says Mustafa. 'We all started to run . . . we hid behind a bush . . . from there we saw that the attackers had grabbed my mother Khatunabibi, my cousin Akbar Khan, his pregnant wife Rehanabibi, and seven other young cousins.'

'The mob caught hold of them, stripped every man, woman and child, and started beating them mercilessly. They raped the women. They forced them all to say "*Jai Sia Ram*",' he said. 'When they tried to rape my mother, one of my brothers tried to save her. He was instantly killed with a sword. Siraj shouted in fear and I shut his mouth . . . Then one by one they killed all ten of our family, cut them and burnt them near the canal after noon. We were like dead bodies hiding in the shamshan (graveyard).'

The mass rapes and carnage had women terrified. Many were still trying to come to terms with the torture they had lived through, or seen others suffer. Some still get palpitations and hypertension. Children have seen their mothers, sisters or friends gang raped and mauled in public view. The nightmares still haunt them.

Terror even spilled over into playtime. At the Rang Avadoot camp in Juhapura, children played war games. 'They would shoot, fight, kill, throw bombs at each other and team up saying, "You're Hindu, we're Muslims, you're the Bajrang Dal/VHP, we are Muslims. You wear saffron, I'll wear green" . . . they refer to Hindus as the Bajrang Dal or the VHP. Now we have got them out of those games,' said a volunteer.[104]

Many women walked into the camps stark naked. Men took off their shirts to cover them. Some women could barely walk. Their genitals were torn in gang rapes. One woman from Naroda Patiya was brought unconscious, her body covered with bites and nail marks. Pieces of wood had been shoved up her vagina. Women at the camp pulled them out and dressed the wounds.[105] After raping a thirteen-year-old, they shoved a rod into her stomach and burned her.

'The mob started chasing us with burning tyres after we were forced to leave Gangotri Society. It was then that they raped many girls. We saw about eight to ten rapes. We saw them strip sixteen-year-old Mehrunissa. They were stripping themselves and beckoning the girls. Then they raped them right there on the road. We saw a girl's vagina being slit open. Then they were burned. Now there is no evidence.'[106]

On 2 March 2002, when mobs attacked houses in Gomtipur, Ahmedabad residents of Patel ni Chali closed the gates to their chawl, and the women kept vigil. The police came led by head constable Narayan Modi. They jumped over the gates, and when the women protested, Modi made them speechless. He and his men pulled down their pants and started abusing the women with filthy language. The mob outside followed the police example. They too started stripping.[107]

The police knocked on Rehana Mansuri's house in Vadodara's Ajwa Road on the night of 1 May as part of the 'combing operations'. Drunk policemen banged on her door. 'I got up to open the doors and the rifle butt hit me on my chest. They also hit my thighs. There are bruises on my chest,' said Rehana. She was pregnant to full term. After the attack she managed to deliver her baby, but could not feed it.[108]

In Bawamanpura, the police hit another pregnant woman with lathis. When her mother-in-law told them she was pregnant, the police said, 'We have to kill it before it happens.'[109]

Such gory and inhuman assaults were unheard of in previous riots. The story of a pregnant woman's belly being slit in Naroda Patiya shocked the nation. Atrocities have occurred in many other places. In rural areas like Dahod, people have remained silent about the rapes—they don't want it to be known for fear of being ostracized.

'I keep thinking of Kupwara (in Kashmir) now,' said seventeen-year-old Shahjahan Kabir Ali from Naroda Patiya, 'for years nobody would marry a young woman from that village.'[110]

The faceless mob

'All Gujarat's Hindus came out on the streets. It was Hindu society's reaction,' Dr Jaideep Patel told me.[111]

But who were the 'Hindus' who went on the rampage? It wasn't Ramesh Pillai in Vadodara, who saved 500 Muslim neighbours and fought back those breaking down their masjid. Nor was it the rabadis from Khokar Kesarpur in Sabarkantha, who saved Muslims from a gang that was stripping the women and were about to set them on fire.

The pattern of the attacks was too similar to suggest that

they were in any way 'spontaneous'. So, who was the 'mob'?

Let's start with the leaders—the instigators. The organizers chalk out the route and the targets to be hit and lay down the ground rules for the attack. Some were visible while others worked behind the scenes, like state ministers Ashok Bhatt and I.K. Jadeja, who took over the police control rooms.[112] The elderly VHP leader Keka Shastri admitted that they made the lists on the day of the bandh itself.[113] Other leaders were more visible. Dr Jaideep Patel and Dr Maya Kodnani were seen instructing local BJP and VHP activists who were creating havoc at Naroda Gaam.[114]

At the local level, several BJP MLAs, councillors and panchayat leaders led the mobs. They rounded up people, weapons, vehicles, petrol, cylinders and coordinated the pogrom on their cellphones. In Mehsana, an MLA supplied arms and went around the town offering rewards for every Muslim killed, guaranteeing no imprisonment.[115] In Jhalod, Dahod district, MP Babubhai Katara's vehicle was doing rounds of the town, making arrangements for vehicles and ammunition.[116] In Vadodara, BJP leaders Pradeep Joshi and Ajay Dave led the attack on Dr Bandukwala's house.[117] Later, they boasted about it in public and canvassed for votes on that basis.

'The organizers are primarily top rank leaders. The majority of them happened to be Brahmin. And more important, they subscribe to the brahmanical ideology of the *varna* (caste) system,' says Ghanshyam Shah.[118] Many judicial commissions have indicted the RSS, its affiliates and/or the Shiv Sena for instigating violence—whether it was the Ahmedabad riots of 1969, the Jamshedpur riots of 1979 or the Bhiwandi riots of 1970. They were also involved in the demolition of the historic Babri Masjid and the violence that followed in 1992, which spread to Mumbai, Patna, Surat, Kanpur, Delhi, Calcutta and Ahmedabad.[119] Certain elements within other parties like the Congress have also stirred communal violence for political ends (like in the anti-Sikh riots in Delhi in 1984). But communalism is not their ideology. For the RSS and its Parivar, it is the very core of their belief.

The second rung are the 'expert mobsters'. They are often a trained, committed cadre, or professional criminals. This cadre works in small groups armed with weapons and equipment necessary to tear down doors and windows, blast walls, start fires and use swords or knives. For example, during the attack in Jhalod village, Dahod, there was a group of men who waited in a truck, and their only job was to reload weapons and hand them back to the attackers. Local hoods are normally patronized and protected by politicians and are mobilized into action at such times. This kind of hooliganism has been a result of unemployment and the general trend towards criminalization in politics.[120] Moreover, the underworld in Gujarat is never out of business since prohibition provides endless opportunities.

The third part of the mob is the 'agent provocateurs' who spread rumours, shout slogans and direct mobs. They are normally activists of the Sangh Parivar. 'They are accompanied by professionals like doctors, advocates, social activists, active members of the Parivar.'[121] For example, in many villages, Sangh activists moved around with front-page pictures of the burning train or photographs of the Godhra victims.

For months, pamphlets were distributed. Some fuelled fear, 'How safe are you in your bungalows? The traitorous, terrorist Muslims will come in truckloads . . .' (from a VHP pamphlet), others called for an economic boycott of Muslims. One pamphlet asked Hindu youth to 'reply in the same language that is used for jehad'. A supposedly 'highly confidential letter of the RSS' was circulated that listed thirty-four ways in which to harm minorities.

Even cable television was used in Vadodara to broadcast VHP leaders' provocative speeches. Often rumours are used to fuel hysteria and insecurity. The most common rumours are of a cow's head thrown into a temple, of water being poisoned, of impending retaliatory attacks by Muslims, of people cheering for Pakistan during a cricket match or of Hindu women being abducted. Certain mass festivals like the Ganesh festival, the Ahmedabad Rath Yatra and Muharram are also used to spark violence. Political rallies like those held during the Ram Janmabhoomi campaign also left behind a trail of destruction.

Many Sangh activists in Ahmedabad, like Harish Bhatt or local Naroda activist Prakash Sevkani, run security agencies. Sevkani distributed swords, knives and trishuls. He admitted this to me in an informal chat while we were waiting outside the Akshardham gate when the temple was under attack. People stocked up on weapons and took turns in keeping night vigils to protect their buildings. A journalist friend told me, 'In my colony, we took turns staying up at night, guarding the neighbourhood. We got swords and knives from the local Bajrang Dal.'

The tail end of the mob is ordinary people who join in. They lose their identity, inhibitions and fear when part of the mob. They loot and throw stones, but are rarely involved in the more gory acts of violence. Those in the general mob could be of any class or caste; it spans the gamut of high society looters sending each other messages on mobile phones to poor migrants who just pick up whatever is lying around in broken homes.

Often local leaders use the poor as foot-soldiers in the mob. In Ahmedabad, Dalits in Gomtipur were used to attack their Muslim neighbours. The first time Dalits participated in communal violence was in the 1985 riots in Gomtipur. Yet, some protected their Muslim friends. The Vaghari community were also enticed with money, liquor and loot. For the first time in Chota Udaipur in central Gujarat, adivasis were mobilized to attack Muslims. They were assured that they could plunder without fear of the police.

The lower castes looted homes, while the elite robbed department stores. March 2002 was not quite a free for all— it was free for some, unbearably costly for many.

Notes

1.   Sujan Datta, 'When Guardians of Gujarat gave 24-hour licence for punitive action', *The Telegraph*, 10 March 2002.
2.   Press Trust of India, 'Singhal justifies Gujarat riots', 3 July 2004.
3.   Interview in Ahmedabad on 26 January 2004.
4.   He was living in the relief camp right until April 2004.
5.   Interview in Ahmedabad on 26 January 2004.
6.   Sujan Datta, 'When guardians of Gujarat gave 24-hour licence for punitive action', *The Telegraph*, 10 March 2002.
7.   Report in *Gujarat Samachar*, 4 March 2002, p. 2.
8.   Sujan Datta, 'When guardians of Gujarat gave 24-hour licence for punitive action', *The Telegraph*, 10 March 2002.
9.   Ibid.
10. 'Modi wanted Godhra bodies to come to Ahmedabad', Times News Network, 22 August 2004.
11. Sujan Datta, 'When guardians of Gujarat gave 24-hour licence for punitive action', *The Telegraph*, 10 March 2002.
12. Ibid.
13. Manu Joseph, 'A plot from the Devil's lair', *Outlook*, 3 June 2002.
14. Former additional chief secretary (home) Ashok Narayan deposed before the Nanavati–Shah commission of inquiry.
     'Modi wanted Godhra bodies to come to Ahmedabad', Times News Network, 22 August 2004.
15. Manu Joseph, 'A plot from the Devil's lair', *Outlook*, 3 June 2002.
16. Ibid.
17. Sheela Bhatt, 'It had to be done, VHP leader says of riots', 12 March 2002, http://in.rediff.com/news/2002/mar/12train.htm.
18. Shyam Parekh, 'Even judges had to run for cover', *The Times of India*, 5 March 2002.
19. Ibid.
20. Interview in Ahmedabad on 4 March 2002.
21. *Crime Against Humanity, An Inquiry into the Carnage in Gujarat,*

vol. 1, Concerned Citizens Tribunal—Gujarat 2002, published by Citizens for Justice and Peace, p. 43.

22. Conversation with a friend of a looter in Ahmedabad, March 2002. He told me his wife got an SMS message from her friend inviting her to come and take some of the goods in the shops, but she didn't go.

23. *Communalism Combat, Genocide: Report on the Violence in Gujarat, Religious and Cultural Desecration*, March–April 2002.

24. The Jagannath Mandir is the most 'sensitive' spot in Ahmedabad. During the Jagannath Rath Yatra every year, there is heavy police security and fear of communal violence. The 1941, 1946, 1969 and 1986 riots were sparked off at the yatra.

25. The Sabarmati river running through Ahmedabad divides the old city from the new suburbs that emerged.

26. Estimates by the Citizens Tribunal, which was organizing relief in refugee camps.

27. Interview in Ahmedabad on 26 January 2004.

28. *Crime Against Humanity, An Inquiry into the Carnage in Gujarat*, vol. 1 and 2, Concerned Citizens Tribunal—Gujarat 2002, published by Citizens for Justice and Peace, p. 36.

29. Interview in Ahmedabad on 26 January 2004.

30. Times News Network, 'Gujarat riots: Revelations thick and fast', 20 August 2004. http://timesofindia.indiatimes.com/articleshow/821212.cms.

31. According to the police charge-sheet for case no. 1002 dated 28 February 2002.

32. According to the police charge-sheet, eight were killed and three bodies were 'missing'.

33. Police inspector K.G. Erda, who held charge of the Meghaninagar police station during the riots, before the Nanavati–Shah commission.
    According to the Nanavati commission, Gulbarg Society was allowed to burn for a week, 'Cop fails to explain why', Times News Network, 25 September 2004.

34. Interview with witnesses in Ahmedabad on 26 January 2004.

35. Interview in Ahmedabad on 26 January 2004.

36. Ibid.

37. Eyewitnesses quoted in Human Rights Watch report, *'We Have*

No Orders to Save You': State Participation and Complicity in Communal Violence in Gujarat', pp. 18–20.

38. '"Newton" Modi has a lot of explaining to do', Times News Network, 3 March 2002.

39. Police inspector K.G. Erda, who held charge of the Meghaninagar police station during the riots, before the Nanavati–Shah commission.

40. Interview in Ahmedabad on 26 January 2004.

41. Police inspector K.G. Erda's deposition before the Nanavati–Shah commission.

42. Ibid.

43. Interview with Tanvir Jafri, Ahsan's son, on 26 January 2004.

44. Professor Bandukwala's press conference in Mumbai, August 2002.

45. People's Union for Civil Liberties (PUCL), Vadodara, and Vadodara Shanti Abhiyan, *Violence in Vadodara: A Report*, p. 62.

46. Ibid., p. 147.

47. Ibid., pp. 80–81.

48. Ibid., p. 7.

49. FIR no. 222/03 filed in Kalol police station by Firdos Yusuf Ghanchi Sheikh on 17 December 2003. Crime Against Humanity, vol. 1, p. 66.

50. *Crime Against Humanity, An Inquiry into the Carnage in Gujarat*, vol. 1, Concerned Citizens Tribunal—Gujarat 2002, published by Citizens for Justice and Peace, p. 73.

51. Interview in Modasa on 20 February 2004.

52. According to Salim Sindhi, interview in Modasa on 20 February 2004.

53. Interview with Mariambibi Sayyed, 4 March 2002.

54. *Crime Against Humanity, An Inquiry into the Carnage in Gujarat*, vol. 1, Concerned Citizens Tribunal—Gujarat 2002, published by Citizens for Justice and Peace, p. 67.

55. Interview with Mariambibi Sayyed, 6 March 2002.

56. Interview in Godhra on 6 March 2002.

57. *Gadar–Ek Prem Katha*: A jingoistic film.

58. Interview in Lunavada on 7 April 2004.

59. Ibid.

60. Ibid.

61. *Crime Against Humanity, An Inquiry into the Carnage in Gujarat*, vols. 1 and 2, Concerned Citizens Tribunal—Gujarat 2002, published by Citizens for Justice and Peace, p. 100.

62. Interview in Jhalod on 6 April 2004.

63. *Crime Against Humanity, An Inquiry into the Carnage in Gujarat*, vol. 1, Concerned Citizens Tribunal—Gujarat 2002, published by Citizens for Justice and Peace, p. 110.

64. Interview with Hafiz Patel in Jhalod on 6 April 2004.

65. Interview in Jhalod on 6 April 2004.

66. Interview in Visnagar on 9 August 2003.

67. *Crime Against Humanity, An Inquiry into the Carnage in Gujarat*, vol. 1, Concerned Citizens Tribunal—Gujarat 2002, published by Citizens for Justice and Peace, p. 117.

68. *Crime Against Humanity, An Inquiry into the Carnage in Gujarat*, vol. 1, Concerned Citizens Tribunal—Gujarat 2002, published by Citizens for Justice and Peace, p. 118.

69. Interview with survivors in March 2002.

70. *Crime Against Humanity, An Inquiry into the Carnage in Gujarat*, vol. 1, Concerned Citizens Tribunal—Gujarat 2002, published by Citizens for Justice and Peace, p. 92.

71. Ibid.

72. Interview at Ismail Nagar camp in Anand on 2 April 2002.

73. Ibid.

74. Concerned Citizens Tribunal, vol. 1, p. 88.

75. Ibid.

76. Interview in Ahmedabad on 29 April 2002.

77. Interview with Gulbarg Society massacre witnesses in Ahmedabad on 26 January 2004.

78. Interview with Mariambibi in Ahmedabad on 26 January 2004.

79. Interview with Nanubhai Maleikh in Ahmedabad on 8 August 2003.

80. Manu Joseph, 'A plot from the Devil's lair', *Outlook*, 3 June 2002.

81. Darshan Desai and Joydeep Ray, 'Dial M for Modi, Murder?', *Sunday Express*, 23 March 2002.

82. Ibid.

83. Ibid.

84. This figure is a gross underestimate. The Gujarat Chamber of Commerce and Industry said that losses were over Rs 11,100

crore within thirty-five days from 28 February to 3 April 2002.

85. Nandini Sundar, 'A Licence to Kill', *Gujarat: The Making of a Tragedy*, edited by Siddharth Varadarajan, Penguin Books India, 2002, p. 82.

86. Vijay Menon, 'Cops admit killing more Muslims', *Hindustan Times*, 3 May 2002.

87. Janyala Sreenivas, 'Who Shot Them Point Blank?', *Indian Express*, 9 April 2002.

88. Praveen Swami, 'Saffron Terror', *Frontline*, 16–29 March 2002.

89. The unofficial death toll for the Mumbai 1992–92 riots is 1500. The official death toll according to the Srikrishna commission report is 900 (575 Muslims, 275 Hindus, 45 unknown, 5 others).

90. *Crime Against Humanity, An Inquiry into the Carnage in Gujarat*, vol. 1, Concerned Citizens Tribunal—Gujarat 2002, published by Citizens for Justice and Peace, p. 123.

91. Ibid., p. 104.

92. Siddharth Varadarajan, *Gujarat: The Making of a Tragedy*, Penguin Books India, 2002, p. 121; Meghdoot Sharon, 'Gujarat minister adds to riot victims woes', 21 March 2002, *Indian Express*.

93. Interview at Dariya Khan Ghummat, Ahmedabad on 29 April 2002.

94. 'Officer discloses how Modi meddled in police transfers', Times News Network, 29 October 2004.

95. Joydeep Ray, 'Police transfers: Gujarat government hits panic button', *Indian Express*, 29 March 2002.

96. 'DGP told me free the rioters; Minister said more Hindu deaths not proper', Express News Service, 31 October 2004.

97. Ibid.

98. Ibid.

99. Interview in Kalol on 7 April 2004, FIR no 222/03 Kalol police station; Navaz Kotwal,'Untold tragedies', *Frontline*, 16–29 August 2003.

100. Interview in Vadodara on 19 February 2004.

101. Ibid.

102. *Crime Against Humanity, An Inquiry into the Carnage in Gujarat*, vol. 2, Concerned Citizens Tribunal—Gujarat 2002, published by Citizens for Justice and Peace, p. 93.

103. Kavita Punjabi, Krishna Bandopadhyay, Bolan Gangopadhyay, *The Next Generation: In the Wake of the Genocide, A Report on the Impact of the Gujarat Pogrom on Children and the Young*, p. 12.

104. Ibid., p. 23.

105. *The Survivors Speak: How has the Gujarat Massacre Affected Minority Women?*, Fact-finding by a Women's Panel supported by Citizen's Initiative, p. 8.

106. Ibid., p. 4.

107. Crime Against Humanity, vol. 2, p. 41.

108. *At the Receiving End: Women's Experiences of Violence in Vadodara*, People's Union for Civil Liberties (PUCL), Vadodara, and Vadodara Shanti Abhiyan, *Violence in Vadodara: A Report*, 31 May 2002, p. 20.

109. Ibid., p. 21.

110. Kavita Punjabi, Krishna Bandopadhyay, Bolan Gangopadhyay, *The Next Generation: In the Wake of the Genocide, A Report on the Impact of the Gujarat Pogrom on Children and the Young*, p. 19.

111. Interview in Ahmedabad on 29 January 2004.

112. Darshan Desai and Joydeep Ray, 'Dial M for Modi, Murder?', *Sunday Express*, 23 March 2002.

113. Sheela Bhatt, 'It had to be done, VHP leader says of riots', 12 March 2002, http://in.rediff.com/news/2002/mar/12train.htm.

114. According to interviews with eyewitnesses who choose to remain anonymous.

115. Crime Against Humanity, vol. 1, p. 91.

116. Interview with witnesses in Jhalod on 6 April 2004.

117. Dr Bandukwala press conference in Mumbai, August 2002.

118. Ghanshyam Shah, 'Caste Hindutva and the making of mob culture', *Economic and Political Weekly*, 13 April 2002.

119. Asghar Ali Engineer, *Communalism in India: A Historical and Empirical Study*, Vikas Publishing House, p. xix.

120. Ghanshyam Shah, 'Caste Hindutva and the making of mob culture', *Economic and Political Weekly*, 13 April 2002.

121. Ibid.

'Strength does not come from physical capacity. It comes from an indomitable will.'

—Mahatma Gandhi

3

Living in a Graveyard:
Refugees

Those who weren't killed landed up in the graveyards.

Javed Sheikh just kept running. He was barely conscious, but survival instinct gave his legs a life of their own. The smoke and the stench of death choked him. He had just seen his family burned alive, a bonfire of bodies just outside their house in Naroda Patiya, Ahmedabad.

Javed had no one to turn to. The police had just led them to their death; he couldn't possibly ask them for help. 'When our houses were being stoned, the police asked us to come out. We thought they would rescue us. Instead, they let the mob surround us on all sides,' said the lanky fifteen-year-old.[1]

In a matter of hours Javed lost everything but his life. 'The mob threw petrol and set people on fire. I hid behind a wall and could see my parents in flames. Someone hit me on the head and I fell unconscious. When I woke up, everything and everyone was in ashes,' said Javed. He didn't know if anyone survived. He lost his parents and sister in the massacre. In all, nine of his relatives were killed.

All he knew was that he had to get out of there. 'I ran to my malik's (employer) house. I used to work as an apprentice mechanic. He took me to the hospital. I was there for a week. Then the police sent me to Shah Alam relief camp.'

Shah-e-Alam Roza is a historic stone dargah situated in south-east Ahmedabad. It has been the centre-point of relief during every communal riot. But this time even old hands at riot relief couldn't deal with the numbers. Hordes of survivors were streaming in, carrying nothing but their grief. All they asked for was sanctuary.

The dargahs and the kabristans (graveyards) are a trusted asylum. As more people flooded in every hour, not an inch of space went unused. The ground was too hot to walk on. Babies cried early in the morning for milk or food but had to curb their hunger until lunchtime. Refugees squatted amongst the long white tombstones. Families took turns snatching a little rest. Living on a grave was better than being in one.

Pregnant women refused to go to the hospital. They delivered in the camp, rather than risk their lives. Snatching a private space was virtually impossible. One woman gave birth in a rickshaw parked outside the camp. Shah Alam camp had more than 9000 people, but just four toilets.[2]

Refugees in rural Gujarat were worse off. When the mobs came, they hid in the wilderness. They camouflaged themselves in fields or fled to the hills and jungles. They lived without food or water for days, chewing on leaves for sustenance. Zainub Buliwala from Mora village hid in a toilet with her daughter for three days. 'My child didn't have anything to eat. I kept begging my neighbours to take us to the police. Finally, the military rescued us,' she said.[3] Camps were in towns quite far from the villages. It was difficult to reach them without police escorts.

Many were in open plots or fields, where people didn't even know they existed. Some didn't have a wall to protect them. In Nepania village, Panchmahal, people lived on a parched field. 'A mob from outside the village destroyed our homes. So we sleep together in the field,' said Noor Khatri, now a refugee in her own village.[4] They borrowed food from their Hindu neighbours, and relief committees from Godhra and Lunavada sent rations.[5]

Farms were dotted with beds. Around twenty-seven Muslim families in Bamanwad village, Panchmahal, lived in the open fields, but the government refused to help these refugees. 'The mamlatdar (local government official) refused to recognize this as a camp and provide rations. Just because he has given seven families compensation. What about the rest of us? Around a hundred people are homeless. Charities in Godhra are supplying us with grains. When that runs out, we have to borrow from the local Patel landowners. How do we pay them back? There hasn't been work for months,' said Ibrahim Khatki, one of the homeless.[6]

There were separate Hindu camps. Eight of the forty-five camps in Ahmedabad were run by the VHP and the government for Hindu refugees.[7] These were people caught in the crossfire—those who lived alongside Muslims and faced a retaliatory attack by Muslims. Some were victims of land grab. Most would be able to return home soon. In Bhilvas, near Shah-e-Alam, around sixty families fled an attack by neighbouring Muslims and sought shelter in the Kankaria municipal school relief camp run by the collector's office.[8] When Mahajan-no-Vando, a Hindu colony in the Muslim-dominated Jamalpur was attacked, its residents stayed in the vando.[9] Since they could not move out during curfew, the Citizens Initiative provided them rations.

It took the government one week before it could supply rations to the relief camps. The administration made no attempt to improve the miserable hygiene conditions until the prime minister decided to visit Gujarat on 4 April 2002. Suddenly, officials got efficient. They organized workers to clean, put up shelters, install toilets and distribute relief allowances (Rs 1250 per family) to refugees.

This flurry of activity was only confined to the places the PM planned to visit. The government stopped distributing cheques midway at Dariya Khan Ghummat in Ahmedabad when the PM cancelled his visit there. Only half of the 1100-odd families received the dole.[10] Even in Shah Alam, cheques disappeared the minute the PM left.[11]

Not a single state minister visited the refugees.[12] It took then prime minister Atal Bihari Vajpayee more than a month to discover the camps; chief minister Narendra Modi didn't visit Shah Alam, the largest camp in Gujarat until he had to escort Vajpayee. The PM visited Gujarat thirty-six days after the violence began.

Soon after the PM left, the Modi administration tried to close down the shelters and get rid of refugees. It didn't matter that most had nowhere else to go. 'On 31 May 2002, the government stopped all supplies—water, electricity, rations,' said Amanullah Khan, organizer of the Vadali camp in Sabarkantha.[13] 'The state has registered all relief sites as 'closed', although most are still running. People can't return to their villages because they face a boycott. Those who tried to settle back home have had to run back.' Refugees were staying at the Vadali and Modasa camps more than a year after the violence.

'Short of throwing refugees out on to the streets, officials are using various tactics to force them into leaving,' said a Citizens Initiative[14] organizer. 'They have stopped ration and water supplies. Monsoon shelters haven't been built. They tell people that they will not get three months free ration, to which they are entitled, unless they leave.' The Gujarat government claimed there were only sixteen camps housing 16,495 people all over the state. In reality, there were thirty in Ahmedabad alone, sheltering as many as 38,200 homeless people, according to a survey conducted on 19 June 2002 by the Citizens Initiative.

'Can the government feed them indefinitely? We have given them cheques to repair their homes and also enough time to construct them,' said S.M.F. Bukhari, the state government's chief coordinator of relief.[15]

Attacks on camps
Relief camps weren't always a safe refuge. None other than a minister, Bharat Barot, instigated the attack on Dariya Khan Ghummat camp. Instead of doing his job and ensuring that refugees got food to eat, the minister for food and civil supplies wanted to get rid of them. He sent a letter to home minister Gordhan Zadaphia asking him to shut down relief at Dariya Khan Ghummat in his constituency. Apparently, it made his 'Hindu voters feel insecure'. 'It is necessary to remove these camps as some of the outsiders living in them have indulged in rioting,' he wrote.[16] Ironically, the camp was situated just behind the Ahmedabad police commissioner's office.

The local police raided the camp on the afternoon of 23 April 2002, claiming that it housed rioters and terrorists. They lobbed tear gas shells into the municipal school, where refugees had taken shelter. The women were sent up to the terrace for protection, but they could still hear the firing. Terrified, an old lady died of shock. After the carnage, this was too much to take.

'Not only have they made us refugees but now we are also accused of being criminals,' said Mohammed Sadiq,[17] a young refugee who was dragged to the police station after the raid. The police filed a case against sixteen from the camp, including relief organizers, accusing them of instigating Hindu mobs to burn Muslim shops. Mohammed was on the top floor of the school, looking after the women when the police took him away. 'They kept asking us, "How many of you are terrorists from Godhra? How many people have weapons?" Finally, they released us at midnight,' he said.[18] 'We get threatening phone calls telling us to shut down or there will be trouble. The minister fears that refugees may try to settle down in his constituency and the number of Muslim voters will increase,' said Haji Ataullah Khan, an organizer.[19]

Then it was the turn of the Rajpur shelter in Gomtipur,

Ahmedabad. It was attacked on 31 March 2002. 'A mob entered while we were having lunch. They even broke the tent for medical check-ups,' said Rashidaben Ghulam Nabi, one of the refugees.[20] 'This is the second attack. The first time was around 15 March 2002, when the Ram temple construction was to start. A few BJP leaders are paying the harijans to do this.'

Families from nearby villages had sought shelter in Dasaj in Sabarkantha. They were attacked on 11 November 2002 at the end of a three-day Goga Mandir pooja held in the village. After a feast in the temple, the crowd attacked the Muslim basti. Two people were killed, fifty injured and sixty-three homes were destroyed. The Patels claimed that they saw people from the Muslim basti running towards them to attack. Actually, some boys were chasing a stray dog out of the basti.[21]

The VHP had started its anti-Muslim propaganda long before. On 18 July 2002 it held a Hindu sammelan. 'During the meeting they said that all refugees should leave. Or else, the number of Muslims would increase. They declared a boycott of all Muslims,' said former sarpanch Hathi Khan.[22]

The entire community was shunned. Landlords threw Muslim sharecroppers off their land. They boycotted Muslim shops and wouldn't sell rations to them. The Patel sarpanch refused school admissions to the children of refugees. The local administration didn't give them permission to construct new homes in the village. 'We didn't like outside Muslims staying here. *Saala!* Their majority keeps on increasing. We stopped any contact with them. Earlier, we were friendly and used to celebrate all festivals together,' Purshottam Patel, a village leader, told me.[23]

A few Gujarati newspapers fuelled resentment against the camps. 'In the name of shelter, migrants from other villages enter city,' a banner headline in *Sandesh*'s Vadodara edition[24] announced. The article alleged that there was 'information about dangerous activities inside the camp'.[25] It said that in the name of riot relief, Muslim leaders used their political connections to set up illegal colonies on municipal land in Tandalja, Wadi and Akota.

The CM spared no sympathy for the refugees. During his Gujarat Gaurav Yatra, he lashed out at them. 'What should we do? Run relief camps for them? Do we want to open baby-producing centres? *Hum paanch, Humare pacchees!* (Us five, our twenty-five). Where does religion come in the way of family planning? . . . We have to teach a lesson to those who are increasing the population at an alarming rate.'[26]

Modi was as good as his word. His government did everything possible to 'teach them a lesson'. After allowing the murder and loot, it kept 1,50,000 refugees on tenterhooks. Compensation was paltry, not enough to rebuild a home. In addition, the government assured them no safety if they went back.

Rehabilitation and compensation

Munnabhai Pathan finally gathered enough courage to visit his home at Avdoot Nagar in Makarpura, Vadodara city's industrial area. It had been fifteen days since he fled when his neighbourhood was attacked. Too scared to live there again, all he wanted to do was pick up whatever was left of his belongings and leave. The police were willing to escort him. That eased his fear.

But they couldn't protect him. On the afternoon of 17 March 2002, while Munnabhai and his neighbours nervously collected the remnants from their broken homes, local goons quickly assembled a crowd. As Munnabhai and his friends drove out in the police vans, they were stopped by a 2000-strong armed mob. Forty-year-old Munnabhai and Nasirbhai Sheikh, twenty-five, were lynched to death. Four others were in critical condition. They never returned to their families who anxiously waited for them back in the camp.[27]

Land grab is another simple tactic to make a return home impossible. Overnight, Waheeda Sheikh's house in Gomtipur disappeared to make way for two temples. 'Whenever we go back to the neighbourhood, the local bootlegger strips in front of us. The local hoods abuse us and threaten to harm us if we try to resettle,' says Waheeda.[28]

The police station is less than a kilometre away, but that didn't offer the Sheikhs any security. The first time they went to file a complaint, the police refused to include the fact that temples had been constructed where their house once stood. 'Whenever we ask them to help us return to our home, they plead helplessness saying that the local Hindus will be upset if the temples are touched. What about us? Aren't we upset? Our life has been totally destroyed,' said Waheeda. The Sheikhs didn't receive any compensation.

Prahladbhai Dantani had fled his hut in Khanpur on the Sabarmati river bank. 'Our Muslim neighbours had run away and yet we were attacked,' he said. For years, the authorities have tried to demolish his slum, located on prime property. Developers and hoteliers want to get rid of the slums along the riverside to make way for the Sabarmati Riverfront Development project. The violence provided a good excuse.

Pavagadh, a village in a pilgrimage site, is strictly off limits. After burning and looting, locals captured Muslim shops. (These shops are located along the route to the temple and have great revenue potential.) They wouldn't let Muslims back into the village, and refugees huddled in rented rooms in nearby Halol town. Some families sent their elders back to look after their homes in Pavagadh, but locals threw stones at their homes and shouted threats at night. Frightened, the seniors returned back to Halol to live with the rest of their family.

Kadval village in Panchmahal district had conditions attached for returning Muslims. At a peace committee meeting, refugees were asked to sign a document with several terms laid out:

- Revoke names of the accused filed in the FIR.
- Muslims cannot attend Hindu marriages or ceremonies.
- If there is any robbery or crime, Muslims will be held responsible.
- They would have to follow the wishes of village elders.
- Apologize for taking out a rally on 3 March 2002 in which they shouted 'Pakistan Zindabad'.[29]

'How could they expect us to sign something like this? The part about the rally is totally untrue,' said Ghulam Mohammad Makrani, a refugee at Baska camp in Panchmahal district.[30] 'At the meeting the deputy collector actually encouraged us to sign. He said, "Sign if you want to go to your village. Otherwise, if you want to go back to Pakistan, we will help you go back."'

'You can't even buy a tin sheet with this money. In a month, the monsoon will start. What will we do?' asked the elderly Noorbanu Sheikh.[31] She was one of the lucky few to receive a compensation cheque, but she returned it to the government. All she got was Rs 500, less than one per cent of all she lost. Her house in Bismillah Nagar, Vatva, in Ahmedabad was totally destroyed. 'We ran with nothing but the clothes on our backs. No one will give us a loan.' After Noorbanu and others in the Jehangir Nagar relief camp at Vatva were treated so shabbily, refugees refused government cheques the next time they were being distributed. Of the 300-odd families there, only twenty-three had received housing compensation two months after the violence.

Hasraben Ghachi had to live under a tree in her village, Mora in Panchmahal district. 'We had a kuccha house. We didn't get any compensation. My husband can't find any work here. So we cook and sleep under this tree. If it rains, we run into another villager's room,' she said.[32] In her village, the elderly Fatimaben Ghachi returned the Rs 3400 compensation cheque she received. 'What can I do with so little? The house is totally destroyed. I sleep and cook outside in the heat,' she said. Her life at home isn't very different from the refugee camp.

Outcasts: The social boycott

'Muslim-free village', proclaimed a poster at Lakshmipura village in Sabarkantha, north Gujarat. The powerful upper castes had declared a social boycott of the minority.

A year after the violence, its outcasts were still living in tents at the Vadali refugee site in Sabarkantha. It was safer than going back home. The local relief committee bought land here and was building homes for the refugees. Four women were attacked when they went back to check on their homes.

A few brave families from Kariadra in Sabarkantha decided to challenge the boycott. 'We are treated like pariahs. The Bajrang Dal threatened the entire village. They have announced a Rs 2000 fine if anyone speaks to us,' said Ismail Mansoori,[33] a tailor. 'No one is allowed to sell us groceries or milk. We buy our rations from Idar town, fourteen km away. They won't buy anything from a Muslim or rent out space to us. I have restarted my shop in another village. I have an MA but I still can't find a job,' said Noor Mohammad Mansoor.[34] Others ran back to the Vadali shelter. 'There was no work. We were only eating milk powder. We are better off here,' said Sakinaben Mansoori.[35]

Tired of being pushed around, some families rented rooms in Muslim neighbourhoods of the closest town. Not only in Vadali, but also in Himmatnagar, Godhra, Kalol, Halol and several other small towns, refugees now seek safety in numbers. Rehabilitation housing has been constructed at the outskirts of these towns, where land is cheaper. That makes these exiles further isolated. The segregation is already complete in cities like Ahmedabad, and now, the ghettoization of rural Gujarat has begun.

Rehabilitation further segregated victims of the violence. Relief committees constructed homes for the victims of

Ahmedabad's two worst massacres, Naroda Patiya and Chamanpura. The new structures are located at Bombay House in Shah Alam and Faizal Park in Vatva—both in secluded plots, far from their places of work.

'My children are not willing to live in our old home,' said Allauddin Mansoori, a mechanic who lived in Naroda Patiya. Like many others here, he enters Naroda for work but doesn't feel safe enough to live there. In the evenings he returns to Shah Alam, a forty-five-minute drive from Naroda, where they have rented a room in a secluded industrial backyard. But many families feel it is worth the effort and additional expenses. They now pay rent for refuge.

The business of relief and rehabilitation

There are stories of relief organizers pilfering rations and acquiring swanky new cars overnight. But, on the whole, the relief business wasn't as lucrative as it was during the Kutch earthquake. Not surprisingly, the relief process also had communal tinges—most of the support came from Muslim charities. A handful of local NGOs, Christian groups and foreign aid agencies chipped in. There was little public sympathy. Either they were afraid, or silently approved of the violence.

The government took a week to respond. It started sending rations only after all the red tape of registration was complete. While it tried to chase refugees out of the camps, it washed its hands off rehabilitation as well and left refugees to their own devices. The groups that did help were Muslim groups like the Islami Relief Committee and Gujarat Sarvajanik Relief Committee.

Modi discriminated while doling out compensation to the families of those killed. While he announced a Rs 2,00,000 compensation for those killed in the Godhra massacre, only Rs 1,00,000 was sanctioned for victims of the post-Godhra violence. It was rubbing salt into the wounds of refugees.

Later, when he was criticized, the prime minister tried to rescue the situation by announcing another Rs 50,000 compensation for victims of the post-Godhra violence.

In all, the government allocated Rs 1500 million for relief and rehab. This is peanuts compared to the estimated Rs 41,000 million suffered in losses.[36] 'The government is giving assistance, not compensation. We can't pay for all the damages,' said S.M.F. Bukhari, government relief co-ordinator.[37] Those who had been given cheques got pathetic amounts starting from Rs 71 and averaging Rs 3000.

After the initial surge of compassion, NGO help also petered out. Money didn't flood in as it did after the Kutch earthquake. NGOs didn't spring up overnight. 'We didn't see the same kind of public sympathy. Post-quake, each house in our neighbourhood made food packets every day to send in trucks to Kutch. This time, relief sites were less than a kilometre away from their homes, but no one came forward to help,' said a peace activist from Vadodara.[38] Several religious charities like the Swaminarayan, Swadhyay and Satya Sai Baba trusts, Ramakrishna Mission, Mata Amritananda Math and several Jain missions, which did a lot of work during the Kutch earthquake, also stayed away from relief. Corporates who rushed in to adopt villages during the Kutch earthquake kept silent. The English press exposed human rights atrocities during the violence, but none of the media companies set up relief funds, as they normally do during other humanitarian crises like earthquakes or floods.

'Not only corporates, but bodies like the Confederation of Indian Industry (CII), Federation of India Chambers of Commerce and Industry (FICCI), and several state governments like Delhi and Rajasthan, who had enthusiastically helped the earthquake victims, were missing. Almost every reconstructed village in Kutch has a concrete gate that proudly screams the name of the donating agency. In contrast, the absence of these organizations in riot rehabilitation shows that they wanted nothing to do with helping the Muslims,' says an NGO relief organizer.[39]

A few took on responsibilities, but didn't deliver. A foreign aid agency had committed to looking after the needs of the last remains of Ahmedabad's refugees. Around nineteen families had been living in a few tents pitched on a dusty field in Jehangir Nagar, Vatva, on the city's outskirts for almost a year. With four families crammed in each tent, they endured heavy rains, sweltering heat and biting cold, and suffered curses as they took a few cans of water from a tap in the neighbouring colony, sometimes sneaking a bath behind a sheet of tarpaulin.

On 10 February 2003, the owner of the plot asked them to vacate. Panic prevailed. Where next? 'We've spent sleepless nights wondering where to go. The aid agency told us to rent rooms until they build houses for us nearby. But we barely have any money for food. Paying for rent and the deposit is impossible. That's why we are here,' said Parvin Banu Memon, one of the refugees.[40] Local aid workers had done little. An independent social worker had to be called to organize rented rooms. The presence of an aid agency doesn't automatically translate into support.

Orphaned in Ahmedabad's most gory massacre, Javed soon became the 'star victim'. Hordes of journalists, donor agencies, government officials, counsellors and researchers descended to interview him. He soon learned how to play to the gallery. In a soft, deadpan voice he repeated his story for every visitor, hoping they would help in some way. His piercing eyes revealed his pain. President A.P.J. Abdul Kalam met Javed during his visit to Gujarat. A photograph of their meeting made it to the front page of newspapers. The president promised Javed that he would make arrangements for his education.

Javed was packed off to a boarding school in his native place in Gulbarga, Karnataka. He came back to Gujarat in two months. He couldn't understand Kannada. The

Ahmedabad collectorate has promised Javed a government job, but only after he completes his school education. The relief committee gave Javed and his uncle (who also lost his entire family) a home at the rehabilitation site in Vatva, but his uncle found a new girlfriend and Javed was thrown out.

Javed's elder brother left his business in Gulbarga and came to Ahmedabad to look after him. But he had to return to Karnataka after a few months. Now Javed lives alone. He wanders between Naroda Patiya and Vatva. He takes up work or a vocational course for some time, but none of it lasts more than a few weeks.

He's back to roaming the streets. Still lost, still grappling with life after.

Kill the patient

Ashraf Khan had barely caught his breath. He had just escaped an attack on the boys' hostel he was a supervisor of and was recovering in Visnagar civil hospital. Zainat and Sayyed Khan had brought him to the hospital. They didn't expect the mob to hound them in the hospital. That evening a gang carrying swords walked down the corridors of the ward, dragged them to the balcony and threw them off the second floor.

The terror squads wanted complete obliteration. They didn't even spare the hospitals. Mobs blocked roads leading to hospitals and crowded the entrances, preventing people from seeking treatment.

A mob inside Ahmedabad's V.S. Municipal Hospital stabbed a young boy in the presence of police guards stationed there.[41] He was in an ambulance carrying a relative who had been stabbed. As he was getting off, Sangh Parivar volunteers attacked him. The saffron activists were demonstrating against the 'partisan attitude' of hospital authorities towards Muslim patients. Outside Kalol Referral Hospital, a mob set fire to a tempo in which Ibrahim Suban was being rushed for treatment after he was injured in police firing. His nephew Hussein managed to escape, but Ibrahim was scorched to death.[42]

Inside the hospitals it was just as dangerous. Shakeel was injured when a crude bomb was thrown at his STD booth in Vatva, Ahmedabad. His family rushed him to V.S. Hospital at midnight. At the entrance they had to contend with a large mob milling around at the entrance. Finally, Shakeel was taken into the operation theatre at 3 a.m., but even the OT was not out of bounds for the miscreants.[43]

While the doctor stepped outside to obtain his father's written consent for the surgery, three men entered the operation theatre. They asked him for his name. When he replied, they held him down by his arms. 'What are you doing?' Shakeel asked. 'We are operating on you,' one of them replied. They tried to choke him with a pillow, but he managed to struggle and throw them off. The gang ran out before the surgeon returned, but he was too scared to tell the doctors about his brush with the death squad.

Similar attacks had occurred in Ahmedabad during the 1992 communal violence. A Muslim patient was thrown off the roof of L.G. Hospital. Since then, hospitals in Ahmedabad have been segregated along religious lines. Muslims don't normally go to hospitals in Hindu areas and vice versa. Generally, Muslims feel that V.S. Hospital is safer for them. During the violence they avoided going to other hospitals fearing that mobs would attack them there as well.

But V.S. Hospital wasn't safe either. A few who made it through the mob outside didn't get treatment easily. Six injured persons from Gulbarg Society were refused treatment because they didn't have a police statement.[44]

Medical staff have also unintentionally internalized the segregation. Doctors feel that patients of the 'other' community should be transferred to 'safer' hospitals. After the violence, Muslim staff in public hospitals were given sympathetic leave, even if they didn't ask for it. A lab technician in a public hospital in a Hindu area was pressured by her colleagues to go on leave. They felt that her presence would endanger her life as well as theirs.[45]

At Sola civil hospital, two BJP corporators were sifting through the hordes of patients streaming in, telling doctors who to treat and whom to turn away.[46] Dr Praveen Togadia even threatened a doctor who was volunteering in the relief camps delivering babies.[47]

The VHP's top functionaries are doctors. Praveen Togadia is an oncologist and owns Dhanvantri Hospital in Ahmedabad. Dr Jaideep Patel, the Gujarat VHP secretary, runs a pathology laboratory in Naroda. The Naroda MLA, Dr Maya Kodnani, is also a doctor. Many medical associations have been petitioning to have Praveen Togadia's medical licence revoked for his role in the Gujarat pogrom.

School's out

'They drive away children from school. They tell us to go home. That's why I haven't gone back to school,' said ten-year-old Shabana Sheikh. After being chased away from school, Shabana worked at a local tea stall earning Rs 15 daily.[48]

Because families had lost everything, the pressure on children to work was greater. After the carnage, jobs were harder to come by due to the economic boycott of Muslims. This made way for another form of employment—child labour. Several children who couldn't return to school after the riots started working, some began labouring while still refugees in the Shah Alam relief camp in Ahmedabad. Others like Shabana took up odd jobs because they weren't accepted back at school.

It took a lot of guts for Shabana's family to return to their home in Naroda Patiya. Shabana still couldn't summon up the courage to go back to school. When she did return, the school wasn't exactly welcoming. 'They told me I wasn't enrolled for the new term. It started while we were still in the relief camp. Now they want my birth certificate to put me back on the roster. But it was destroyed when our house was burned,' says Shabana. 'After the riots, I'm too scared to walk to school. If they start classes inside our chawl, I'll go.'

Azeem Sheikh, eleven, isn't working yet, but he too was refused admission. 'When I went back to enrol myself in school, people didn't even look at me. They just turned their heads the other way,' he says. 'They refused to take me back. They told me to take my leaving certificate after paying eight months' fees.' Azeem is scared to venture the twenty-minute walk to school. 'I saw people being burned. All the way to the relief camp, there were dead bodies on the road. Now, I'm too scared. It's still not safe. Violence still keeps breaking out somewhere in the city.'[49]

Just hours after I spoke to Azeem, his family fled Naroda Patiya back to the Shah Alam relief camp. The Akshardham temple in Gandhinagar had been attacked. Every Muslim feared the worst. The police plainly said that they couldn't protect them against another attack. Azeem's family returned three days later, after the Sangh Parivar decided it wouldn't create any trouble during the bandh it had called to protest against the temple siege.

Why else would mothers prefer to send their kids to boarding schools in Maharashtra and Hyderabad rather than to schools in their own city? A year after the violence, women from Naroda Patiya told me, 'The children refuse to go out now. They are too scared. Can you send them to a school in Hyderabad?'[50]

Yusuf rejoined his class for a few days but then dropped out. 'The teachers tell the other students, "Let the miyas sit separately." They say, "You people don't understand anything. Just copy from other students." I stopped going because I didn't like the way they treated us,' said Yusuf Sheikh, eleven, who studied at the school in the nearby SRP colony.[51] His friend

Shahrukh Mansoori had also ventured back just a week before I spoke to him in February 2003. 'I'm going there only so that I can collect my school-leaving certificate. I want to get admission in a boarding school near Mumbai. My brother is already there,' he said.[52]

'After the riots, four private charitable schools in Naroda refused to accept Muslim students. They asked them to take a leaving certificate. They justify it by saying that they cannot ensure the children's safety,' said Meera Malik, a social worker. 'Some Dalit children are also scared to return to school after seeing so much violence.'

In the more upmarket part of the city, the story isn't very different. Around 200 Muslim students had to leave Ahmedabad's Don Bosco school. The students shifted to the National School in Juhapura, a Muslim ghetto. 'Parents are afraid to send their children to good schools far away from their homes in Muslim localities,' said Professor Abid Shamshi, a retired college teacher.[53] 'So, mediocre schools have cropped up in Muslim areas. They are run in small buildings with incompetent staff. No child from here can dream of getting into a professional career like medicine or engineering. They are condemned to remain second-class citizens.'

Illiteracy rates amongst Muslims in India are much higher than amongst Hindus. In urban India, 30 per cent of Muslims above seven years of age cannot read or write, as compared to 19 per cent of Hindus. Forty per cent of Muslims in cities belong to the lowest 20 per cent income group as compared to 22 per cent of Hindus.[54] In every sphere, Muslims are being further marginalized.

The city is already divided into ghettos. Now the schools are being segregated, and the poorest are being pushed out. With educational institutions closing their doors, more children like Shabana are being pushed to the grind.

Over the edge

It seemed like an ordinary family outing.

Twenty-nine-year-old Jayesh Shukla took his young wife Nita, twenty-five, and son Harsh, four, for a motorcycle ride on the evening of 19 September 2002. They stopped and ate a snack at a local bhel vendor. Then they drove to the railway tracks in Ranip, a suburb in Ahmedabad, and placed themselves in the path of an oncoming train.

Though shocking, such incidents had become common in Ahmedabad. After the communal violence died down in June 2002, nine such suicides occurred in the city between June and September 2002. Almost every week, a new family suicide pact was reported in the local press. Police sources admitted that this was a new phenomenon; no such suicides had been registered earlier. After the violence, the economic crunch spelled disaster for many.

Jayesh, who ran a catering operation, came from a fairly well-off business family and lived in Ghatlodia, a middle-class colony in Ahmedabad. His business saw a downturn during the communal violence. It became more difficult for him to pay back his debts. Jayesh had reportedly borrowed a large amount from moneylenders. A few days before he killed himself, he had an argument with lenders who had visited his home. Jayesh was apparently under great pressure to repay the debts, but his business wasn't picking up. He took another way out.

The police and government deny the suicide phenomenon is linked to the communal violence in any way. But the stories of many families reveal that the recession caused by the riots did lead to their downfall. The police merely state that the family was facing an 'economic crisis', but don't provide more details.

Worst hit were daily wage earners. On the other side of Ahmedabad's Sabarmati river, in the working class ghettos, casual workers came close to starvation. Most couldn't leave their homes for two months due to the curfew. Shankarlal Solanki, a construction worker, was out of work for three months. Barely managing to support his family of five, Shankarlal couldn't afford the medicines for his wife Kailashben's TB treatment. On 5 September 2002 the entire family burned themselves with kerosene in their home in a Bapunagar chawl. Until the violence, Shankarlal had earned a steady income and was able to educate his three children— Ripple (12), Umesh (8) and Dharmesh (5). But work was hard to come by after the bloodshed. That apparently pushed the entire family to take their lives.[55]

They were not attacked, but just as surely destroyed. The after-shocks of the violence pressed people into crises that pushed some to kill themselves.

Others survive, and endure the anxiety silently.

Ordinary heroes

They live in areas engulfed in the thick of the violence, but they didn't run for cover. They were confident that they would be safe. 'While the rest of Gujarat burned, we knew we would remain untouched,' said Hisam Bootwala from Momnavad in Ahmedabad.[56] 'Though we are surrounded by Hindu houses, we were sure we wouldn't be attacked. In the colony just behind us, there were riots, but it didn't affect us.'

Hisam's neighbourhood is in the Shahpur area of Ahmedabad's old city. Over the years there has been bloodshed just across the fence, but not in their basti. 'We have lived together peacefully for almost a century. There have been many riots in Ahmedabad, but not in our colony. Our youth stayed up all night, guarding and patrolling the streets,' says Hisam. 'This time, our Hindu neighbours gave us food because we couldn't leave our homes. They used to remind us to go for namaaz. But we didn't want to venture out because of the curfew.'

Neighbourhoods like Momnavad stood out for their humaneness and wisdom at a time when there were deliberate efforts at inciting hatred and violence. Adversity brought out the best in people. Other localities like Ram Rahim Colony in Behrampura, Ahmedabad also fought back armed mobs who came to attack Muslims. Similarly, in Fatehpur village of Sabarkantha, the sarpanch Taraben Baraiya and ex-sarpanch Daniben Vankar took the lead in ensuring that things remained peaceful.

While other villages had funerals, some celebrated weddings. Daniben organized the nikaah of a girl who was about to get married but fled to Surat fearing that the violence would reach Fatehpur. 'We called her back. The entire village helped arrange the wedding. I was one of the witnesses,' says Daniben.[57] In Devkaranna Muwada village of Gandhinagar district, Ratan Singh Jhala organized the nikaah of his close friend Karim Mansuri's daughter, Nasim. He hosted the ceremony and gave away the bride, which by custom is the role of the mother's brother. Nasim's uncle, who lived in Nadiad, could not make it since his house had been destroyed during the violence, so Ratan Singh stepped in and offered to play the role of the uncle.

Some were courageous enough to risk their own lives to save others. Lawyer Vir Singh Rathod hid sixty-five people in his house in Naroda Patiya for four days. He looked after them until it was safe for them to go to the relief camp in Shah Alam. 'When Muslims were scared to enter Naroda Patiya, my Muslim tenant insisted on staying there. He said he felt safe with me,' says Vir Singh.[58] In parts of Panchmahal and Sabarkantha districts, adivasis and Dalits sheltered Muslims who were fleeing attacks on their bastis. 'Chenwas

(Dalits) hid us in their homes. If it wasn't for them, we might have been killed,' says Sattarbhai Mansoori from Kariadra village in Sabarkantha.[59]

Most villagers report that the attacks were led by Sangh Parivar members, mainly from the Patel community. In many villages, Patels affiliated to the Sangh enforced a social boycott of Muslims. Yet there are exceptions—it was a good-hearted Patel who gave Muslim refugees his land for a relief camp at Vadali in Sabarkantha. 'When the riots began, I called Dr Chagganbhai Patel and asked him if the refugees from surrounding villages could stay in his empty cinema. He sent me the keys to the cinema right away,' Amanullah Khan, a camp organizer, told me. 'The doctor sold the land to us at a low rate, though another buyer was offering him a much higher price. Local Sangh Parivar activists stoned his home. They were angry that he allowed refugees to stay there.'

In many small villages of Gujarat, Hindus and Muslims have helped protect and restore religious places. In Makarba village of Ahmedabad district, both Hindus and Muslims guarded the 500-year-old Sarkhej roza. When rioters attempted to attack this tomb of the Sufi saint, the Hindu sarpanch fought them back. Muslim villagers in Hatkeshwar, Kutch, helped organize the restoration of a temple in their village, worshipped by the Nagar community. They even hosted pilgrims who arrived from outside for the first idol worship after the temple was rebuilt.[60]

In the communal madness that swept Gujarat, these villages were islands of calm. Common sense and humanity overcame the hatred and insanity.

Business first

'Why have you come to us? Don't you know that we give

donations to the BJP?' That's the puzzling reply a group of professors from the Indian Institute of Management (IIM) got when they went to meet the local branch of the CII to ask them to be part of a peace lobby group. The business community seemed like an obvious section to advocate peace. Commerce is all-important in Gujarat. However, pleasing the powerful is also essential for business.

When it came to donations for relief, Gujarat's business community was not particularly forthcoming. Not many companies came forward to help, wanting to remain 'neutral'. A few donated secretly.

'There was no need for us to donate. The government had set up relief camps,' Kalyanbhai Shah, the then president of the Gujarat Chamber of Commerce and Industry (GCCI) told me.[61]

Finally, corporate bigwigs from outside the state broke the silence. Deepak Parekh, chairman, HDFC, and Anu Aga, chairperson of Thermax, spoke out expressing concern about the law and order situation in the state. After her statement, the GCCI would not let Anu Aga speak at a meeting in Gujarat.

Almost a year after the violence, Rahul Bajaj, chief managing director of Bajaj Auto and Jamshed Godrej, chairman, Godrej and Boyce, asked the chief minister 'to create a proper environment for business by taking care of all sections of society'[62] at a CII meeting in Delhi.

The angry CM didn't show up to inaugurate a CII conference in Ahmedabad after confirming that he would attend. Instead, he released a statement blaming the CII for 'insulting five crore Gujaratis'. The Gujarat CII was in a tizzy and immediately apologized.

Even one of the oldest business dynasties in Gujarat, the Sarabhai family, was not spared. Mallika Sarabhai, one of the family's members, is a petitioner for a case in the Supreme Court asking for an independent investigation into the communal violence and for proper rehabilitation for the victims. She too was harassed for her stand.

Sarabhai's Darpana Academy, a performing arts institute in Ahmedabad, was accused of cheating students by promising to help them to illegally immigrate to the US masquerading as performers in her dance troupe. Sarabhai said the government was behind the false case, because it wanted to get back at her for speaking out against its role in the pogrom.

But the Sarabhais were an aberration. Most of Gujarat's business community preferred to remain silent. 'The government did whatever they could to help us. During the violence, two ministers would sit in my chambers every day and arrange security for anyone who needed it,' the affable Kalyanbhai Shah told me. 'Every time we (Hindus) suffered, this time we came out forcefully. What could the chief minister do?'

As Kalyanbhai says, his role is 'to maintain a good rapport with the government'. And indeed, did his job well.

Notes

1. Interview in Ahmedabad on 30 April 2003.
2. As on 8 March 2002, data from Citizens Initiative. After the PM's visit on 4 April 2002, Shah Alam camp had more than 13,000 people, but just thirty-eight toilets. Interview on 31 April 2002 with relief camp organisers.
3. Interview at Dawoodi Musafir Khana camp, Godhra, March 2002.
4. Interview at Nepania camp on 16 April 2002.
5. The government started supplying rations to the camp only on 15 April 2002, a month and a half after the attack on the village.
6. Interview in Bamanwad on 15 April 2002.
7. According to district collector's records as on 13 March 2002, from Stalin K., documentary film maker.
8. Interview by Stalin K., documentary film maker, on 8 March 2002.

9.   Ibid.

10.   Interview on 31 April 2002 with relief camp organizers.

11.   Only 1400 of the 2200 families got the living allowance. Interview with camp organizer on 31 April 2002.

12.   Then union defence minister George Fernandes (from the Samata Party) visited the 'riot-affected' areas of Ahmedabad on 2 March 2002 and in Surat on 4 March 2002.

13.   Interview in June 2002.

14.   Citizens Initiative is a group of NGOs involved with relief work in the camps.

15.   Telephone interview in May 2002.

16.   Siddharth Varadarajan, *Gujarat: The Making of a Tragedy*, Penguin Books India, p. 121. Meghdoot Sharon, Gujarat minister adds to riot victims woes, 21 March 2002, *Indian Express*.

17.   Interview in Ahmedabad on 2 April 2002.

18.   Ibid.

19.   Ibid.

20.   Ibid.

21.   Interview with Hathi Khan, former sarpanch of Dasaj on 23 November 2002.
      'Tension prevails in Mahudha, Dasaj', Times News Network, 12 November, 2002.

22.   Interview in Dasaj on 29 September 2002.

23.   Interview in Dasaj on 23 November 2002.

24.   People's Union for Civil Liberties (PUCL), Vadodara and Vadodara Shanti Abhiyan, *Violence in Vadodara: A report*, 31 May 2002, p. 156.

25.   Ibid.

26.   Siddharth Varadarajan, *Gujarat: The Making of a Tragedy*, Penguin Books India, 2002, p. 318.

27.   Interview with refugees in Tandalja Road relief camp and with Makarpura police in March 2002.

28.   Interview with Waheeda Sheikh on 8 June 2002 at Madhavpur Mill compound camp.

29.   Interview on 15 April 2002 with refugees in Baska camp.

30.   Ibid.

31.   Interview on 30 April 2002 at Jehangir Nagar relief camp, Vatva.

32.   Interview on 9 June 2002 at Mora.

33. Interview in Kadiadra on 5 August 2002.
34. Ibid.
35. Interview in Vadali camp on 23 November 2002.
36. According to the Gujarat Chamber of Commerce & Industry (GCCI) estimates.
37. Interview on telephone in June 2002.
38. Interview in Vadodara on 15 March 2002.
39. Interview via e-mail in July 2004.
40. Interview on 9 February 2003 at Jehangir Nagar, Vatva.
41. *Carnage in Gujarat: A Public Health Crisis*, Report of the Investigation by Medico Friends Circle, 13 May 2002, p. 1.
42. FIR no. 36 of 2002, Kalol police station.
43. *Carnage in Gujarat: A Public Health Crisis*, Report of the Investigation by Medico Friends Circle, 13 May 2002, p. 35.
44. *Crime Against Humanity, An Inquiry into the Carnage in Gujarat*, vol. 2, Concerned Citizens Tribunal—Gujarat 2002, published by Citizens for Justice and Peace, p. 119.
45. *Carnage in Gujarat: A Public Health Crisis*, Report of the Investigation by Medico Friends Circle, 13 May 2002, p. 43.
46. *Crime Against Humanity, An Inquiry into the Carnage in Gujarat*, vol. 2, Concerned Citizens Tribunal—Gujarat 2002, published by Citizens for Justice and Peace, p. 119.
47. Ibid., p. 118.
48. Interview on 8 February 2003 in Naroda Patiya.
49. Ibid.
50. Ibid.
51. Ibid.
52. Ibid.
53. Interview in Ahmedabad on 12 September 2003.
54. C. Rammanohar Reddy, 'Deprivation affects Muslims more', *The Hindu*, 12 September 2002.
55 Based on information provided by the Ahmedabad police to the author and to journalist Atul Dayani and published in his articles in *Gujarat Samachar*.
56. Interview in Ahmedabad on 8 February 2003.
57. Interview on 8 February 2003.
58. Ibid.
59. Ibid.

60   Based on stories in the book titled *Path of Humanity* written and published by Charkha—Development Education Network, Ahmedabad.

61. Interview in Ahmedabad on 10 August 2004.

62. Dev Chatterjee, 'No, Mr Narendra Modi, we won't do it again', *Sunday Express*, 12 February 2003.

'An error does not become truth by reason of multiplied propagation, nor does truth become error because nobody will see it.'

—Mahatma Gandhi

4

We Didn't Start the Fire:
Godhra and Other 'Terrorist' Attacks

Twice bitten

Ramol, Ahmedabad

'They (local VHP members) haven't shown us their faces after my husband's funeral. He was their worker. They talk of protecting Hindus. It's ironic that two of our family died because they were involved in their work,' said Bela Rawal.[1]

Her husband Ashwin, forty-two, a VHP activist, was stabbed during the riots. Their family suffered a double blow in Gujarat's violence. Bela's seventy-five-year-old mother-in-law, Sudhaben, was one of the kar sevaks who died when the Sabarmati Express was burned on 27 February last year.

Sudhaben went to Ayodhya as part of the VHP delegation from Ramol in Ahmedabad. The trip was a religious junket. Each VHP worker sent a family member as part of the kar sevak contingent. Around eleven Godhra victims were from Ramol itself. The neighbourhood remained peaceful during the VHP bandh. Six weeks later, on 16 April, Ashwin and his VHP friends were ambushed and killed by a mob while walking home from work.

'The police are also to blame. Why did they let the violence continue for so long? If they wanted to, they could have done something to prevent it,' said Dr Girish Rawal, Ashwin's father.[2] 'More than a week before Ashwin was killed, I called the police to tell them that trouble could break out here. But they did not respond.'

With the family's main breadwinner gone, Bela and her two daughters rely on Dr Rawal's pension. 'After Godhra, there was a flood of sympathy. NRIs sent huge donations to the VHP. Where has all that money gone? Nothing has reached us. All we got from the VHP was one month's rations,' said Dr Rawal. Their family got the Rs 1,50,000 government compensation.

'Politics is very dirty. They should not mix religion with politics and use it to gain votes,' said Bela. Her neighbour, Bharatbhai Panchal, who lost his wife in the Sabarmati Express tragedy, agreed. 'The BJP utilized this opportunity very cleverly to win the election. They took advantage of public sympathy,' he said.

'They haven't stopped, they continue to stir up trouble. Just a few days back at a meeting for the municipal elections (which were to be held on 16 February 2003), someone gave a speech saying that we must retaliate for what happened in Godhra. That's all that they did for the past year. Now they should let us live in peace,' said Bharatbhai.

The families of those who died in Godhra didn't want revenge. Why was the Sangh Parivar so keen on it?

Godhra: The trigger

'It (the burning of the Sabarmati Express) was a pre-planned act. The culprits will have to pay for it. It was not communal violence. It was a violent, one-sided, collective terrorist attack by only one community.'

—Narendra Modi, Gujarat's chief minister, press statement during his visit to Godhra on 27 February 2002.[3]

In a matter of hours, the chief minister had pronounced his verdict. But how the S6 compartment of the Sabarmati Express actually caught fire, killing fifty-nine people, still remains a mystery. The investigation itself raised more serious questions than it has so far answered.

On 27 February 2002, the Sabarmati Express stopped at Godhra station at 7.42 a.m. Within a matter of minutes, the S6 compartment was in flames. The sequence of events, according to the first charge-sheet dated 14 March 2002, based on statements by the police and witnesses before the Nanavati-Shah commission, was as follows:

7.43 a.m.: The Sabarmati Express arrived at Godhra station. Some kar sevaks got down to buy tea and snacks from the platform vendors. The kar sevaks got into a fight with a Muslim vendor over the payment for the tea.

7.47 a.m.: The train departed from Godhra. While getting on to the train, some kar sevaks tried to pull into the compartment a girl standing on the platform with her mother, but she managed to break free from them.

7.48 a.m.: The emergency chain was pulled, as many kar sevaks were still left on the platform. Stone throwing started between the kar sevaks and some local Muslims gathered behind the Parcel Office.

8.00 a.m.: The train started moving again.

8.05 a.m.: The train stopped again, this time when the vacuum brakes were applied. Local Muslims, armed with weapons, rushed to catch up with the train, crowding in separate groups outside the compartment. They started pelting stones and shouting slogans. Coach S6 caught fire.

8.25 a.m.: Police arrived at the scene and fired to disperse the Muslim mob.

Desperately trying to corroborate the CM's statement with evidence, the Special Investigation Team (SIT) arrested 100[4] people. Modi and Advani announced that Pakistan's Inter Services Intelligence (ISI) was involved in this 'premeditated attack'. With every new arrest and with every new charge-sheet filed, the SIT's story kept changing.

At first, investigators started out with the theory that terrorists torched the train from outside. That story fell flat after the Forensic Science Laboratory (FSL) report[5] concluded that the fire started inside the compartment with at least sixty litres of petrol.[6] Then they modified their story and said that six terrorists jumped on to the train and torched it from inside. The first charge-sheet that the Gujarat government filed in the court did not charge the accused under the Prevention of Terrorism Act (POTA), but under other laws such as the Indian Penal Code, the Indian Railways Act, etc. But in the second chargesheet, many of the accused were accused under POTA. Later, in May 2005, the Central Review Committee on POTA ruled that the tragedy was not a terrorist conspiracy and the accused should not be charged under POTA, but under other sections of criminal law. The committee was formed to safeguard against the arbitrary use of the terrorist act against innocent people. Although the review committee directed the Gujarat government to apply for the withdrawal of POTA charges against the accused, the Gujarat government has refused to do so and maintains its stand that they were terrorists.

The official line as it stands today is based on the testimony of one of the alleged conspirators, Zabir Bin Yameen Behra, a known criminal who deposed before the chief judicial magistrate in Godhra. In his statement, Behra supposedly spilled the beans on the conspiracy, revealing details of how the plan was hatched. Later, Behra went back on his testimony, and told the POTA court that he gave the statement under duress.

'The conspirators stored around 140 litres of petrol used to torch the train in Aman Guest House, which is owned by

Razak Kurkur. He is leader of a local gang involved in railway crimes, and organized meetings of the conspirators in his Guest House,' said Rakesh Asthana, head of the SIT.[7] They brought the petrol to a masjid near the railway tracks in a rickshaw and then waited for four conspirators who jumped on to the train to pull the vacuum brakes from four different places, Asthana said. 'The actual operation was conducted by six people who cut open the vestibule and entered, opened the closed doors of the compartment, poured 120 litres of petrol (each supposedly carried a 20 litre jerrycan) and jumped out. Then, burning rags were thrown in through the windows in the middle of the compartment. Zabir is one of those who entered the train.'

But there are holes in the SIT's story. If it was pre-planned, why didn't they burn the train when it halted at Godhra station? Was the fight on the platform between kar sevaks and Muslim hawkers a mere coincidence? How did they get 120 litres of petrol into the train in such a short span of time? Not one of the witnesses saw people pouring any fluid down the aisle. Not a single railway official present saw anyone enter the compartment. Is it possible that the petrol was already stored inside the compartment? 'We have ruled out that possibility since the owner of a local petrol pump said he sold the petrol to Kurkur the day before,' said Asthana.[8] What was the motivation for the attack? Asthana still doesn't have an explanation.

Investigators suspect that there are conspirators higher up in the chain, but have not been able to identify them. The SIT's attempts to prove the involvement of the ISI and the Students Islamic Movement of India (SIMI) have fallen flat.[9] After the police initially arrested Haji Bilal, an independent municipal corporator, as one of the key accused, they claimed that he had a second passport with which he travelled to Pakistan. But they failed to come up with any fake passport or evidence of an ISI link.[10] Two SIMI activists, Haseeb Raza and Firdaus Ansari, were arrested. The SIT claimed that both were in touch with local leaders Mohammed Hussain Kalota and Haji Bilal, and were on the railway platform on 27 February. They were released after the police found no evidence against them.[11] Now, all the SIT has to cling on to is the 'local conspiracy' theory.

Earlier, investigators named Mohammed Hussain Kalota, a Congress corporator from Godhra, as one of the main accused. The BJP government created a huge media campaign when he was arrested, claiming it was proof that the Congress supported terrorists. Now, they don't consider him part of the main group of around twenty 'core conspirators', but merely a part of the mob.

On their journey to Ayodhya too, kar sevaks had created trouble when the train stopped at Rudauli station in Uttar Pradesh on 24 February 2002. They beat up people who entered the train at Rudauli, jumped on their chests, stabbed them with knives and tridents. 'First, they attacked the women sitting in burqas . . . They kicked and beat me very badly and jumped on my chest. They kept lifting me by the legs and threw me on the ground. They kept telling me to say '*Jai Shri Ram*'. I said it properly. But they didn't let me go,' said Mohammed Siraj, who boarded the train at Rudauli.[12]

During the return journey, several passengers with reserved tickets complained they were harassed by kar sevaks who travelled ticketless and took over the reserved compartments, packing them to three times their capacity. They threw out ticket checkers who tried to enter the compartment. At every station, they shouted slogans.

At Godhra station they refused to let a passenger buy tea from a Muslim vendor and pushed him out of the coach while abusing him. Sophiya Sheikh, eighteen, a resident of Vadodara, was on the platform waiting for the train with her mother and sister. Both saw the kar sevaks get off the train. One of them grabbed Sophiya from behind, put his hand over her mouth and dragged her towards the train. He let go after her mother screamed for help. The police recorded Sophiya's statement soon after the incident occurred, but did not include it in the first charge-sheet. Eventually it was part of the second charge-sheet.

The statements of eyewitnesses contradict the police's findings. None of the passengers mentioned in their police statements that they had seen anyone entering the compartment. They all said that the mob set the coach on fire. Some kar sevaks in S6 and adjoining compartments, interviewed by the *Indian Express*[13] also denied that the mob could have entered the compartment. They said that the doors were bolted from inside.

Investigators refute the accident theory. 'There was no fuel inside the train,' said one officer. He dismissed the idea that the kar sevaks could have been carrying fuel for cooking on their journey. Grain was also found inside the compartment. However, the official said a family travelling to their village for a wedding had taken the grain.

Is there enough evidence to prove that it was a 'pre-planned' or a 'terrorist' attack? The police story rests on Behra's testimony before the open court, in which he gives details of the conspiracy plan. But he later backtracked on it, saying he was forced to testify. The police claim that forensic tests and testimonies by three other witnesses corroborate Behra's statement.

Local railway officials who deposed before the Nanavati–Shah commission say that the Godhra incident occurred after a spontaneous fight between local Muslims and kar sevaks travelling on the Sabarmati Express. Assistant station master Rajendraprasad Mina testified that no crowd was waiting for the train to stop. It gathered after the train stopped for the second time. He said that people did not arrive in a mob. Groups of ten to fifteen persons collected, including women and children. The railway police constable at Godhra, Mohan

Yadav, also said that he did not see any suspicious movement throughout the route between the 'A' cabin and his office before the arrival of the train. Raju Bhargava, Panchmahal district's superintendent of police said that when he arrived at the station he saw passengers sitting on the tracks. He also saw many kar sevaks with saffron scarves shouting anti-Muslim slogans. Bhargava also said that he did not smell any inflammable fuel like petrol, diesel or kerosene.

Survivors were injured on the upper parts of their bodies. If the petrol was poured down the aisle, how come most injuries were on the upper, not the lower, part of their bodies? Investigators argue that they were burned by ricocheted flames from the other end of the compartment.

In his deposition before the Nanavati–Shah commission, the first investigator of the Godhra case, K.C. Bawa, said there was no evidence that it was premeditated or that a 'foreign hand' was involved.[14] He said that the incident started as a fight between kar sevaks travelling on the train and Muslim hawkers on the Godhra station platform. He later ruled out the conspiracy theory being floated by the SIT.

After the public disclosure of the FSL report which said that the fire started from inside coach S6, the Congress accused the Sangh Parivar of masterminding the tragedy. 'The report shows that someone inside the train set it on fire. No one from outside could have entered the compartment. That too with sixty litres of petrol. The criminal mentality of the VHP leadership is such that they are even capable of killing their own kar sevaks for gain. Believe me, I know them very well,' alleges Shankarsinh Vaghela, a Congress leader who defected from the BJP.[15] He adds that no one could have entered the already crammed compartment unnoticed. The kar sevaks, who were behaving in an aggressive manner throughout the journey would not have let a Muslim enter, Vaghela points out.

Neither the Gujarat police nor the railway police were aware that the kar sevaks were supposed to come back that morning.[16] Intelligence agencies had not received any information about their return from Uttar Pradesh, although there were tight security arrangements made when they left amidst much fanfare from Ahmedabad on 22 February 2002. If the police did not know of their return, then how would the supposed 'conspirators'?

The SIT's method of investigation has raised doubts. A year after the tragedy, still groping for evidence, the team tried an easy way out. In February 2003 they decided to charge the 135 accused in the Godhra case under POTA. (Immediately after the massacre, the police had applied POTA, but they withdrew it on 22 March 2002[17] on advice from the government's legal department.) This would make it easier for the prosecution to prove its case. They took this decision soon after they obtained Behra's testimony. It is only under POTA that confessional statements recorded by the superintendent of police are admissible in a court of law. These are not considered evidence under other criminal laws. Moreover, POTA allows investigators to use electronic interception devices like telephone tapping and videography.

The decision to use POTA was taken after the arrest of Maulana Hussain Umerji from his home in Signal Falia, Godhra on 6 February 2003. His arrest bolstered the SIT's claims. Investigators allege that he had masterminded the plan to torch the train. 'We have evidence that a core group of around fifteen to twenty people were involved in the conspiracy. Umerji gave them instructions to torch S6,' said Rakesh Asthana, who heads the SIT.[18]

The Muslim community in Godhra observed a bandh for five days after Umerji's arrest. There was panic—if a community leader like Umerji could be picked up, what would be the fate of ordinary Muslims? He is a trained maulvi, respected social worker and businessman. He was actively involved in social and relief work during the riots and the Kutch earthquake. After his arrest, many relief organizers stopped work, fearing that they too would be targeted.

The main evidence was never properly collected or preserved. The victims' bodies were not photographed or sent for forensic tests. Several people were allowed inside the compartment before forensic tests were done or the FIR was made. These included chief minister Narendra Modi, home minister Gordhan Zadaphia and VHP leader Dr Jaideep Patel, along with media crews and VHP volunteers. The evidence was trampled over. The compartment should have been sealed until police investigations were completed. In fact, Dr Jaideep Patel proudly told me that he entered the burnt compartment even before the police did.[19] Can evidence collected after the coach was messed up, or even tampered with, be admitted as evidence in court? Two years after the massacre, the S6 coach remained at the far corner of the Godhra railway station. It had become a kind of tourist landmark, attracting visitors from nearby towns.

The use of 'truth serum' while questioning the accused also stirred up a controversy. Some of the accused were injected with sodium pentathol, a dangerous drug commonly known as 'truth serum' in order to get those being interrogated to speak more freely. This is internationally considered a method of psychological torture. According to the *Yale Herald*, 'it is a short-acting barbiturate that depresses the central nervous system, slows heart rate and lowers blood pressure. In the relaxed state produced by the drug, subjects are more susceptible to suggestion and are therefore easier to interrogate. However, the drug does not actually guarantee that prisoners will tell the truth. Often it makes subjects "gabby" without revealing any important information.'[20] The investigators justified its use, saying that they took court permission and that it was carried out under the supervision of an expert medical team. That still doesn't detract from the fact that it is a human rights violation.

For more than two years, the 'terrorist conspiracy' theory

was the only one accepted by government and public opinion in Gujarat. After the Congress-led United Progressive Alliance (UPA) came to power at the centre in May 2004, union railway minister Lalu Prasad Yadav ordered a high-level committee headed by Justice U.C. Banerjee to get to the root of the cause of the fire. Just before the state elections in Bihar, Justice Banerjee released his interim report, which said that there was no proof of the 'terrorist conspiracy', and the train caught fire accidentally. It was the first government response that contradicted the SIT's findings.

The Banerjee committee said an inflammable liquid did not cause the fire, as first there was a burning smell, followed by smoke and flames, which would not be the case if an inflammable fluid had been used. 'The inflammable liquid theory gets negated by the statement of some of the passengers who suffered injuries on the upper portion of the body and not the lower body, and who crawled towards the door on elbows and could get out without much injury,' said the Banerjee report.[21] 'The committee has found it unbelievable that kar sevaks (90 per cent of the total occupants) armed with trishuls would allow themselves to be burned by miscreant activity like a person entering S6 coach from outside and setting it on fire.'

It also severely criticized the entire hierarchy of the Western Railways for pre-judging the cause by describing the fire as 'miscreant activity' without even conducting a preliminary inquiry. Even later, no statutory inquiry into the fire was carried out. Neither the railway minister nor any members of the Railway board visited the site of the accident or the injured passengers. Moreover, the railway administration did not try to preserve the evidence. The S7 coach, despite some damage to it, was allowed to travel onward to Ahmedabad, even though it was a crucial piece of evidence.

A committee of engineering scientists from the Hazards Centre in New Delhi also released a report on the Sabarmati

Express fire, with the same findings, on the same day as the Banerjee committee.[22] They concluded that the accidental fire probably started in the region between cabins 8 and 9, and started by burning the lower berth first. Dismissing the SIT's findings, they said, 'It is highly unlikely that the fire could have started on the floor of the passage of the floor outside the toilets by throwing of inflammable liquid.' The scientists also believed that from the time the dense smoke was first seen, it would have taken 20–30 minutes for the entire coach to be on fire.

Justice Banerjee also dismissed the 'miscreant' theory and eliminated the possibility that the fire could have ignited after the fight that erupted between the kar sevaks and hawkers at Godhra station, and local hawkers gathered a mob which allegedly threw stones and burning rags at the kar sevaks inside S6. 'The committee has noted the forensic laboratory's experiment and verified its conclusion that it was impossible to set fire to the train from outside,' Banerjee concluded.

Eliminating the 'petrol' theory, the 'miscreant' theory and the possibility of an electrical fire, the committee concluded that the case of the burning was an 'accidental fire'. But it gave no reasons as to what could have caused the 'accident'. Moreover, it totally ignores the fact that a fight did flare up at the station platform, and continued when the train stopped twice a few minutes after it pulled out of Godhra station. A huge mob did gather, which hurled stones and burning rags at the compartment. It is hard to see how the committee believed that a fire happened 'accidentally', just when a brawl occurred at the same location.

So what evidence does that leave the SIT with? A confession by Behra in which he says he was under duress, a few other statements by those who helped transport the petrol, eyewitness statements that contradict the conspiracy theory and no clear motive established.

The 'truth' about the Godhra fire seems to alter when governments change. Railway minister Lalu Prasad Yadav used the committee report to please the Muslim vote bank in Bihar, and also as a game of one-upmanship with the BJP and Sangh Parivar, who had exploited the tragedy for their own political ends, regardless of the cost to human life. Once again, the Godhra tragedy was being used as an election issue, this time to appeal to Muslims.

The real truth about the burning of the Sabarmati Express may remain a mystery. Many powerful Hindutva leaders had already written the script, as well as the 'reprisal reaction' that followed on the day of the tragedy itself.

Akshardham: The backlash?

Sumitraben Chauhan could never have imagined that her visit to the Akshardham temple would end in Ahmedabad civil hospital, being treated for shrapnel wounds. She certainly couldn't have thought that her two infant children would be killed during a family outing to the temple. When I met her, Sumitraben was still dazed, trying to come to terms with the 24 September 2002 terrorist attack on Akshardham. 'We heard an explosion. There was smoke and then the shrapnel hit us,' she said.[23]

The storming of the temple complex in Gandhinagar, which claimed thirty-seven lives and injured eighty-one, shocked everyone. But no one was surprised; in a sense, the real surprise is that the tragedy didn't happen sooner.

Sumitraben may not have expected the temple to be attacked, but the police did. As early as March 2002, intelligence reports had warned of a backlash to the Gujarat carnage. Soon afterwards, the Delhi Police picked up terrorists it claimed were planning to kill leading politicians of the Hindu Right, including Modi. Many feared revenge attacks similar to the bomb blasts after the 1992–93 Bombay riots. Police reports had warned that places of worship were vulnerable targets, but despite police warnings, the BJP government refused to cancel its Jagannath Rath Yatra in July 2002. Politics, not professional policing, was the Gujarat government's main concern.

VIP victory

Within hours of the Akshardham siege, deputy prime minister L.K. Advani reached Gandhinagar. He brought along with him the nation's top anti-terrorist squad, the Black Cats.

The then prime minister Atal Bihari Vajpayee immediately cut short his visit to the Maldives. He flew straight to Gujarat within twenty-four hours of the militant attack. But after the pogrom that started on 28 February 2002, he arrived on the scene thirty-five days later, after more than 1000 people had been killed and 1,50,000 were left homeless. Advani reached Gujarat three days after the Sabarmati Express tragedy in Godhra, which killed fifty-nine people and preceded the communal violence. By then, Sangh Parivar mobs had already ravaged the state with attacks on the Muslim community. But within three hours of the temple siege, Advani made his way to the Akshardham complex. Both leaders raced to the temple, scrambling to claim the Akshardham 'victory'. The victims of communal violence didn't receive the same VIP treatment.

L.K. Advani hailed it as 'a victory over terrorism for India' soon after National Security Guard (NSG) commandos ended the siege by killing two militants. He asked the tired commandos to stand up and chant *'Bharat Mata ki Jai!'* (Victory to Mother India!). Many within the BJP were planning to evoke jingoism and the fear of the 'Muslim terrorist' during the state election campaign. Akshardham and Godhra provided the fodder.

Whodunit?

By immediately blaming 'the enemy', Pakistan, for the siege

of the temple, Advani tried to deflect attention from the fact that it was a revenge attack. The militants apparently wanted to avenge the state-supported mayhem in Gujarat.

At Akshardham, a note found in the pockets of the dead militants from the Tehriq-e-Kasas[24] (Movement for Revenge) stated, 'This is a gift to Modi and Advani.' The deputy prime minister lost no time accusing Pakistan in an effort to deflect attention from the BJP's hand in inciting the attack.[25] Even before investigations began, chief minister Narendra Modi had declared that the terrorists were from outside the state and it was not a revenge attack.[26]

Initially, investigators were able to establish little about who carried out the attack, and why. After almost a year, in August 2003, the Gujarat police arrested five local Muslims who were apparently led by Ahmedabad cleric Mufti Abdul Qayoom and claimed that they had solved the mystery of Akshardham.[27] They were part of the Tableeq Jamaat, an orthodox religious group. The police said that Qayoom had planned the attack and also provided shelter to the assailants, who came from Pakistan. In early September 2003, the Gujarat crime branch changed its Akshardham story when the Jammu and Kashmir police arrested Chand Usman Khan, a Lashkar-e-Toiba (LeT) activist who allegedly confessed to being part of the Akshardham conspiracy.[28] Until then the Gujarat police had not found any link with Kashmiri terrorists, but now they rushed to Kashmir to find the connection.

Chand Usman Khan's statement to the Jammu and Kashmir police did not fit in with the Gujarat police's story. After the Gujarat police gained custody of Khan, his testimony changed. Earlier he told the Jammu and Kashmir police that he did not know anyone in Ahmedabad, but in his statement to the Gujarat police, he mentions the five locals caught by them.

According to the Gujarat police, Khan left Anantnag on 17 September 2002 with his family, Yasin (another LeT member) and the two fidayeens, Shakeel and Abdullah. When they reached Bareilly in Uttar Pradesh, Khan left his family with his in-laws and met up with one Ali Ahmed, who helped carry the weapons to Ahmedabad. He assigned Yasin the task of escorting the fidayeens.

In Ahmedabad they stayed at the Gulshan Guest House in Kalupur, behind the railway station. The plan was already in place. A day before the attack, the fidayeens did a recce of the Akshardham temple with Khan.

Later that day, the fidayeens went with Qayoom to pray at the Haji Shakki-ni-Masjid, near the Char Wat area of Ahmedabad's old city. After prayers, the duo asked the mufti for special blessings so that they would attain martyrdom and entry into Heaven. Qayoom, the Gujarat police say, asked them their real names to ensure that they would be correctly received at the gates of Paradise; they told him that their names were Hafiz Yasir of Lahore and Mohammad Farooq of Rawalpindi.[29]

On the morning of the siege, one of the fidayeens, Abdullah, gave Khan Rs 7500 and sent him home, as his task of transporting weapons was over. He heard about the attack on the news, while travelling back home.[30]

Qayoom apparently gave the assailants the revenge letters that were found in their pockets. Investigators found that the letters were in his handwriting. According to the police, the Ahmedabad conspirators did not know much about their colleagues from outside. The team worked in sub-groups which had assigned tasks and did not know much about the others in order to maintain secrecy. The Jaish-e-Mohammed (JeM) and the LeT jointly planned the operation. The LeT provided finance, weapons and fidayeens, and the JeM provided local support, the police said.[31]

The six accused are still in custody. There are twenty-six accused still wanted by the police. And there are still many missing links in the chain.

Was the investigation at a dead end? Was Chand Usman Khan used as the convenient terrorist to tie up the case? Who was the mastermind? And what was the motive? A lot about the Akshardham attack remains a mystery.

It isn't hard to see why terrorists would want to target the Akshardham temple. The complex is close to chief minister Narendra Modi's residence. It is also near the Gujarat police's headquarters, a force charged with complicity in the pogrom.

Spread over twenty-three acres of land, the elaborate Akshardham complex was built in 1992, and is centred around a temple with a gold statue of Lord Swaminarayan. Its main attractions are its multimedia shows, exhibition hall, cafes and a vast landscaped garden—a kind of Disneyland of religion. 'Several foreign dignitaries have visited Akshardham, including Bill Clinton and Prince Philip. Any attack on it would invite international attention,' said a police officer. The complex attracts two million visitors every year.[32]

The Swaminarayan sect is one of the most powerful in Gujarat, with a strong following among the Patel community and Gujarati NRIs. Sections of the Patel and NRI communities are BJP supporters, which might also have made the Akshardham complex a target for a terrorist attack.

The siege within

When terror struck at 4.45 p.m., the state police were caught off guard. By the time they reached Akshardham at around 5.10 p.m., the terrorists had already opened fire.

The fidayeens climbed over the wall next to gate 3 and immediately opened fire. They lobbed a grenade into an exhibition hall, killing twenty people. Visitors panicked and rushed towards the nearest exit. In one exhibition hall, around seventy people sealed all entrances to ensure their safety. BJP MLA Hirabhai Solanki emerged from the temple with his clothes drenched in blood, proudly brandishing his pistol. He claimed to have shot at the terrorists. He was in Mantralaya, the government headquarters nearby, and rushed to the site when a friend informed him of the attack. Temple employees acted promptly, warning others on the intercom so that the gates to the main temple could be shut before the assailants reached there. Nearly forty people locked themselves inside the main temple.

Outside, there was little coordination between different police units. Some group leaders had mobile phones, but networks were jammed due to a system overload. Most squads had no radio handsets and this lack of contact may have caused several preventable injuries. 'We were instructed to break the cordon and go forward. The terrorists saw us and lobbed a grenade at us. Ten of us were injured and one died,' said a wounded constable. 'The inspector leading us had a mobile phone, but could not get through to anyone for almost an hour. Finally, we established contact with the group next to us. Then, it took another hour for the rescue team to come.'

Gujarat police commandos were later instructed to suspend their operation and wait for the arrival of NSG units from New Delhi. What exactly happened after the NSG commandos arrived at 10.30 p.m. remains unclear, but their failure to capture at least one of the terrorists alive raises questions. NSG teams are equipped with specialized non-lethal equipment like stun-grenades, so that suspects can be caught rather than killed. The use of such weapons forms a key part of the NSG's training.

On the night of the attack, I met Gordhan Zadaphia at the temple gate and asked him whether there were any efforts on to negotiate with the terrorists. 'Why should we negotiate?' he told me. 'There are no hostages. People are safely locked inside the halls. We will fight the terrorists till they are finished.'

Meanwhile, a jingoistic crowd had been allowed to assemble, further obstructing security operations. In the midst of the chaos, BJP, Bajrang Dal and RSS members were let inside the temple complex. While the siege was on, Dr Jaideep Patel said that he had been inside the complex and had spoken on the intercom to sadhus locked inside. A Bajrang Dal member from Naroda who was waiting near the gate boasted to me, 'Even at Naroda Patiya, I was present. I was one of those who stood on top of the masjid. I also went to the Ram temple in Ayodhya. My name has appeared in the papers as one of the people who distributed swords during the riots.'

At the hospital, RSS volunteers in khaki shorts swarmed around, breathing down the necks of the staff who were supervising arrangements. Each injured person was assigned an activist to help them. When I tried interviewing the patients, the RSS volunteers would interfere, trying to oversee the conversation, objecting if they disagreed with what the injured victims said, sometimes even coaching them to say otherwise. While injured policemen told me about the lack of coordination between various units during the operation and the fact that one unit did not have a clue what the other was doing, the volunteers quickly shut them up. When I persisted, they made me leave the ward. The hospital staff had no say in the matter. The khakhi brigade had taken over.

The 'reaction'

Following the BJP's cue, the VHP also used the anti-Pakistan line. Praveen Togadia demanded a war to 'break Pakistan into forty pieces' at a press conference in Ahmedabad in September 2002. The VHP's call for a national bandh struck fear in Gujarat. Their previous bandh after the Sabarmati Express incident started the pogrom. This time round, Muslims who had just returned to their homes fled back to relief camps. 'We feared another onslaught. The police advised us to leave our homes. They couldn't offer us protection. So we left late at night in a truck organized by the relief committee. We spent the night in a school and then made our way here,' said Ershad from Naroda Patiya.

Fortunately, there was not much violence in this bandh. Still, two people were stabbed in Surat and riots broke out in Ahmedabad, Bhuj, Bharuch, Palanpur and Valsad. Conflicts continued in Vadodara and Bhavnagar up to two weeks after the bandh. The Sangh Parivar chose restraint. Perhaps this time the fear of President's Rule being imposed and elections getting delayed if violence erupted again prompted the Sangh to control its cadre. The BJP probably didn't feel the need to stir trouble this time—it sensed that it was already riding a strong Hindutva wave.

The VHP offered a somewhat different explanation. Praveen Togadia said that the bandh was peaceful this time because the state responded effectively to curb the terrorists.[33] Narendra Modi's explanation was, 'This time, pseudo-secularists behaved and did not make statements against the majority community.'[34] The Congress tried to beat the BJP at its own game, using the Akshardham incident to appeal to Hindu voters. It pre-empted the VHP by calling for a bandh on the day after the siege. However, it didn't manage to instill the same kind of fear as a VHP bandh.

The BJP's image as the self-proclaimed protector of Hindus may have taken a beating. It failed to safeguard one of the largest temple complexes in the state belonging to the powerful Swaminarayan sect. When Modi went to meet the head of the Swaminarayan sect, Pramukh Swami Shri Narayan Swaroop Dasji, hoping he could convince him to make a statement condemning Pakistan for the Akshardham attack, the swami refused. Instead, he told Modi to 'show restraint'. Chiding the chief minister the swami said, 'Whatever has happened at Akshardham has happened. Whoever has done it, we don't want to blame anyone. There is no need to drag any names into this now. And I think you should also stop referring to the ISI and Miya Musharraf and make efforts to maintain peace.'[35]

Before the Akshardham attack, several Hindu and Jain priests were already angry with the BJP government. The Jain muni (priest) Acharya Mahapragya had asked Narendra Modi to call off the BJP's Gujarat Gaurav Yatra to prevent violence in the state. A delegation of sants had called on the CM with a list of their problems which they felt were being ignored by the BJP government.

The day after the tragedy, the then prime minister Atal Bihari Vajpayee visited Akshardham. The PM expressed grief that terrorists had entered a religious place. But there had been no similar expression of sorrow when his cadre destroyed around 230 masjids and dargahs during the pogrom.[36]

Just outside the Ahmedabad police commissioner's office in Shahibaug, some vehicles swerve suddenly while speeding down the busy road. They are trying to avoid driving over the sacred tomb of the eighteenth-century Sufi saint Wali Gujrati, which stood here until 1 March 2002. Overnight, it was destroyed by the mobs that took over the city. The Ahmedabad Municipal Corporation built a tarred road over the ruins, leaving no trace of the historical monument. The tomb may no longer exist, but its sanctity remains for many drivers whizzing down the street. In Vadodara too, the tomb of Hindustani music maestro Faiyaz Khan was destroyed and wreathed with burning tyres. The stone mosque of Malik Asin in Ahmedabad, a protected monument built in the fifteenth century, was levelled with bulldozers. The mosque of Muhafiz Khan in Ahmedabad was also destroyed.[37] There was never any talk of punishing the 'terrorist' mobs behind the attacks on these holy places.

The convenient 'terrorist'

Who was really behind the Akshardham attack? Was it really a revenge attack? After the pogrom, many within the administration feared reprisal attacks. A month after the communal violence in Mumbai abated, a series of bomb blasts were triggered off on 12 March 1993 at key places across the city, killing 257. Many expected a similar backlash in Ahmedabad. The only two incidents of post-riot terrorism were the Akshardham massacre and the Tiffin bomb blasts in Ahmedabad on 29 May 2002, in which crude bombs exploded in three buses, injuring twelve.[38]

With every new outbreak of violence, politicians counted the votes while ordinary people counted deaths.

Dead men tell no tales

He was the man who knew too much. Haren Pandya was Narendra Modi's nemesis—the only minister who dared to disagree.

Haren and Naren were natural born rivals. Haren was former chief minister Keshubhai Patel's blue-eyed boy. The state home minister, he was second in line. When the BJP high command suddenly decided to oust Keshubhai in October 2001, they brought in Modi as chief minister. Modi had not been part of Gujarat politics for three years. Haren, among other hopefuls, was rebuffed. He remained a minister, but was brought down to size as minister of state for revenue.

Tensions between the two leaders surfaced soon enough. Modi wanted Pandya to give up his Ellisbridge constituency in Ahmedabad so that he could contest a by-election from there. Many other MLAs were keen to oblige Modi and get into his good books, but Pandya refused. Finally, Modi had to stand from Rajkot.

In the first five months of Modi's tenure, they were on an even keel, but the violence ruptured the truce. Some ministers within the BJP government disagreed with the manner in which the CM had dealt with the situation. Haren was one of them. Not that Haren was exactly a clean-cut politician himself. Many saw him in the mobs in his constituency. But after a few days of mayhem, perhaps he felt that the violence had gone too far and was shocked by the brutality of the massacres.

There were 'moderates' like him within the BJP who felt that the initial 'reaction' was justified but shouldn't have continued for more than three days. That was bad for business. Besides, some Hindus were also killed and later, a few Sangh cadres were arrested too. That wasn't good for local party morale. Besides, Modi's brusque, egoistic and authoritarian style of functioning didn't go down well with some of his colleagues.

Later, *Outlook* magazine published an article[39] that ruffled Modi's feathers. It alleged that an unnamed senior minister had deposed before the Citizens Tribunal (an independent body of retired judges) with details about the chief minister's role in abetting the riots. The evening after the Godhra incident, Modi apparently instructed the state's director-general of police, K. Chakravarthi, and the Ahmedabad police commissioner P.C. Pandey not to 'obstruct the Hindu backlash'. There were other ministers present during the meeting. Modi suspected that Haren was the turncoat who deposed before the tribunal. He did everything he could to sideline Haren and refused to attend party meetings in which Haren would be present. He was adamant about getting him out.

Gujarat BJP president Rajendrasinh Rana wrote a public letter to Pandya, asking him to explain why he deposed before the tribunal. In a public reply to Rana's letter, Pandya denied making any such deposition and resigned as minister. 'I don't want the party to suffer because of one person's whims,'[40] he said. After that, he was totally isolated within the party.

It didn't end at that. There was more drama when the time came to distribute tickets to contest elections. The BJP announced all the nominations except for Haren's old constituency, Ellisbridge, which was kept hanging till the last day. Modi threatened to withdraw his nomination if Haren was given a ticket to contest elections. To prove how serious he was, Modi even admitted himself into the hospital for a day during the election campaign. At the last minute, the BJP high command had no choice but to give in to his demand—it was the end of Pandya's political career. After that, he led a semi-retired life playing golf, exercising, reading and spending time with his family.

But not for long. Ironically, his death pulled him back into the limelight. On 26 March 2003 at 7.40 a.m., two assassins shot five bullets at him when he went for his morning walk at the Law Gardens in Ahmedabad. His body lay in his car near the park for two hours. Pandya's family started worrying when he did not return home. His personal assistant, Nilesh Bhatt, went to check on him. He found him lying dead in his car. Just before his death, Pandya's political career was about to be revived; there had been talk of the BJP high command appointing him to the party's national executive.

Haren's death was the first blow to Naren's popularity. More so because his main election promise was safety and security—'*Bhaymukt Gujarat*' (Gujarat free of fear). People felt that if this could happen to a BJP leader in broad daylight, it could happen to anyone. The CM had to duck for cover when he visited the hospital where Pandya's body was taken. BJP activists shouted slogans against him.

There was a showdown at the funeral. BJP leaders were speechless when Haren's father, Vithalbhai, refused to let the CM garland the last remains of Harenbhai. 'Why have you come here with your security and gunmen? You couldn't even protect my son. We don't need your sympathy,' he told Modi. His family blamed the CM for failing to provide Haren with any security after he resigned. 'If you couldn't protect my son, what security are you going to provide the rest of Gujarat?' Vithalbhai asked Modi.

Deputy prime minister L.K. Advani and BJP national president Venkaiah Naidu were scheduled to arrive in

Ahmedabad on the day of the killing, but they delayed their visit to the next day after sensing the strong resentment against the party leadership. When Vithalbhai Pandya proclaimed at a public prayer meeting that Haren's assassination was 'a political murder', the BJP leaders were red in the face. Advani was forced to concede that an injustice had been done to Pandya.

The next day Advani blamed the Dawood Ibrahim gang for the murder. His announcement surprised police officials in charge of the case—they had barely started their investigation. In order to deflect any accusations of interference, Modi handed over the investigation to the CBI. The then prime minister Atal Bihari Vajpayee also came to his rescue, ruling out the possibility that the killing was due to 'political enmity'.

Since then, Ahmedabad's Muslim areas have faced the brunt of this crime. In the middle of the night, police teams raided homes in search of 'ISI agents'. Soon after Advani's prophecy the Ahmedabad police's crime branch arrested five suspected 'ISI-trained terrorists' on 3 April 2003, who were allegedly involved in the plot to kill Pandya. Later, the CBI arrested five more youths in Andhra Pradesh. Of them, Asgar Ali is allegedly the one who pulled the trigger.

The CBI arrested eight persons from Andhra Pradesh suspected to have been involved in the Haren Pandya killing. The Ahmedabad police said that the mastermind, Maulana Mufti Sufian Patangia, was still at large. He was apparently coordinating with Rasool Parti, now in Karachi, who was once part of the infamous Latif gang in Ahmedabad.[41]

Maulana Sufiyan Patangia used to run the Waliullah seminary next to the Lal Masjid—officially called the Hafizi Masjid—in Kalupur in the old city area of Ahmedabad. He is hiding in Riyadh, according to intelligence sources.[42] Patangia's seminary apparently had funders in Saudi Arabia. The preacher had organized relief operations after the Bhuj earthquake.

The cleric supposedly had two parallel sources of funding. 'Two Saudi-based Jaish-e-Mohammad fund-raisers of Hyderabadi origin, Farhatullah Ghauri and Abdul Rehman, had been energetically raising funds for the victims of the Gujarat pogrom at a series of public meetings for Muslim expatriates from South Asia. Salim Sheikh and Rashid Ajmeri, both Ahmedabad residents who had long been living in Saudi Arabia, put Patangia in touch with the fund-raisers,' says a report by Praveen Swami.[43] Investigators say that Rs 5,00,000 was transferred in October 2002 through hawala channels to organize and fund Pandya's assassination. But who paid for the killing? The police haven't been able to answer that.

His other backer was the JeM in Karachi, say investigators. Rasool Khan 'Party' (Ahmedabad slang for wholesale contractor or businessman) had once been a key lieutenant of top city mafia lord Abdul Latif Sheikh.[44] He went underground after Latif was arrested and killed, and reportedly lived in Hyderabad. 'In May 2002, say the CBI and the Gujarat Police, the Khan brothers met Patangia in Mumbai. Rasool Khan, incensed by the communal violence of the past months, reactivated his Karachi links. The road led directly to the JeM's Karachi-based commander, Abdullah Shah Mazhar,' says Praveen Swami's article. 'He, however, wanted evidence that Patangia was serious—and evidence was duly provided on 29 May 2002, when five low-intensity bombs went off on public transport buses in Ahmedabad, injuring twenty-six people.'

The police said Patangia had sent eight boys from Ahmedabad for training to the JeM in Pakistan in December 2002.

When the boys returned in March, ready to avenge the Gujarat killings, the plan was to target Sangh Parivar leaders involved in the communal attacks, destabilize Gujarat and embarrass Modi. They were instructed to wait for orders from

Pakistan; however, Sufiyan, under pressure from his Saudi financiers, decided to act immediately. Sufiyan's gang first attempted to assassinate VHP leader Jagdish Tiwari on 10 March 2003, the police said. After the practice run, they were successful in killing Haren Pandya thirteen days later. The preacher's plan backfired, as all the boys he had trained were arrested soon after.

The Gujarat police's raids struck terror in Ahmedabad's already-petrified Muslim community. 'They bang on doors in the middle of the night, barge into homes, rummage through their belongings and arrest people without giving the family any information,' said Nazneen Bastawala, a corporator from Kalupur, Ahmedabad.[45] She organized a protest of women whose sons and husbands have disappeared. Bastawala claims that the police have detained more than twenty-five men illegally. There is no record of their arrest. 'For days, we didn't know where they were. A week later, the police released them. Luckily, the police let off many without filing a false case against them,' said one of the women.

When the police came looking for Arif's younger brother, Salim, he wasn't home. So instead they arrested Arif, his father, and his other brother. 'They wouldn't let us go until we told them where Salim was. But I really didn't know where he had gone. The interrogations were like mental torture. They let my brother go home after two days. My elderly father, who has a heart problem, fell unconscious twice. But they weren't bothered,' said Arif.[46]

Finally, Arif and his father were released after a week. But Arif was soon arrested again because he wasn't able to trace Salim. 'They even sent me to Mumbai to look for Salim. But they caught him in Ahmedabad on the day that I left for Mumbai,' said Arif. Several others narrated similar stories about brothers or fathers of wanted youth being illegally detained.

The raids continued till the end of April 2003. Women

went rushing to lawyers, asking them to help trace their husbands. Those who traced their sons and husbands in custody are afraid they could be killed in fake 'encounters', a notorious police technique.

'Why are all Muslims branded terrorists? Why is POTA applied only to the Godhra accused and now to these youth? Why not against those who killed so many during the communal massacres in Naroda Patiya and Gulbarg Society? Why are they out on bail? Why is there selective justice?' asked one of the women who protested against the arbitrary arrests.[47]

Even Haren Pandya's family was wary of the arrests. 'I am of the firm opinion that this was an intentional political murder. This talk of a terrorist plan is absolutely absurd,' said Vithalbhai Pandya, Haren's father. 'The murderer may have killed because of money. But the real political culprit must be arrested. No real inquiry can be made until the person in power steps down. They are making arrests just to show people that action is being taken. Everyone knows what is happening. But no one can speak.'

Modi managed to silence the questions for a while, but Haren's ghost could still come back to haunt him. He was the man who knew too much. Ironically, in death too, he remained a thorn in Modi's side.

Guilty by faith

A case of mistaken identity cost Abid Husain Sheikh eleven months in jail.

Abid, a young lawyer practising in Godhra, was in court on the day of the train massacre. 'We saw the news on TV in the lawyers' room. Some of the judges called me to their chambers to update them on the news,' he told me.[48] 'I left the court at around 3 p.m. While I was going home, one of the judges even offered to arrange for a police van. I thought it would be quicker to walk.'

He reached safely and was sitting in the mohalla, when a friend's brother-in-law approached him for help. 'My friend's shop was burned. He had gone to the police station to lodge a complaint, but had not returned after several hours. His brother-in-law asked me to accompany him to the police station to help find him,' said Abid.

At the police station, Abid told the inspector that he was looking for his friend. 'They took me inside saying, "Okay, come and meet him," and pushed me in the lock up,' he said. They lodged a case of rioting against him. After four days they framed him in the Sabarmati Express case, and named him Habid Karim. He was accused of being someone else. 'They didn't even check my identity. After the train burning, the atmosphere was such that anyone who was Muslim could be arrested for no reason,' Abid explained.

Did the police make an innocent mistake, or were they out for revenge? A few months before, Abid had lodged a case on behalf of a client against three policemen for wrongful detention. They got Deepak Soni, who had previously been his opponent when Abid stood for municipal elections, to testify that he saw Abid on the train platform.

On the morning of the incident I was present in the court of the same judge who denied me bail, said Abid. 'No one helped me even though they all knew I was innocent.' Eleven months later the Gujarat High Court granted Abid bail, but he isn't a free man. The case against him still stands. He has yet to prove that he is not a terrorist.

Many others like Abid were arbitrarily picked up and accused of burning the train. These include a blind man and a government clerk who was on duty on that day. Inayat Jhujara was on his way home from the government office in which he worked when he was arrested for violating the curfew. Before he knew it, he was charged in the train burning case. His boss is willing to testify that Inayat was working that day, but the police haven't yet taken down his statement. They arrested the blind Ishaq Mohammed Mamdu at his home in Godhra two months after the incident. Ishaq's bail applications have been rejected. The tension of his confinement killed his mother.[49] Until January 2005 both Inayat and Ishaq were still in jail.

If you are a Muslim in Gujarat, there's a prevalent fear that the police can barge in at any time, raid your home or pick you up from the street, arrest you without evidence, torture you for a confession and then label you a terrorist. Soon after the Godhra incident, several youth and old men were arrested as suspects. Since then, arbitrary arrests have continued. Young boys in Ahmedabad vanished for weeks, and their families became ill with worry, not knowing where they disappeared. Cases were registered many days, or even weeks, after their actual arrest.[50]

Abu Baker was sitting in his office in Bhopal when the Gujarat police suddenly rushed in and arrested him on 28 October 2002. They kept him in jail for nine months. He was accused of being part of a conspiracy to assassinate Narendra Modi. A passport agent, Abu Baker was charged with helping Samir Khan Pathan, the supposed brains behind the conspiracy, obtain a fake passport to travel to Pakistan for training from militants in January 1998.

Abu doesn't remember meeting Samir Khan Pathan. 'There are so many people who apply for passports. We just help them fill in and submit the forms. It's the duty of the passport office to check their files before issuing the passport,' Abu told me.[51] Samir Khan Pathan had a previous criminal record. He was arrested by the police and then killed in a supposed 'encounter'. The entire Modi assassination conspiracy case rests on a confession that Samir supposedly gave to the Ahmedabad crime branch. Twelve others like Abu were also arrested on that basis, but none of them were charged under POTA.

Both the sessions court as well as the high court dismissed

the case before charges were even framed. There was no evidence against them—the case rested solely on a dead man's supposed confession. Those arrested were released, but only after they had been through hell in jail, their families ruined.

After the Godhra incident, nine cases have been registered under POTA. All the accused are Muslim. The police did not hesitate to apply POTA in these cases, some of which are based on little or no evidence. But not a single accused in the post-Godhra massacres has been charged under POTA, although some of the attacks were equally barbaric.

POTA was enacted in 2002 to make it easier to prosecute terrorist crimes. It is different from normal criminal law, as it allows confessions before a police officer to be considered as evidence in court. The act also has very strict provisions for getting bail. The police can use POTA to keep people in custody for a long period of time and extract a confession which will be admissible in a court of law. In normal criminal trials, only statements made in a courtroom are considered evidence.

Post 9/11, after US president George W. Bush announced his 'War on Terror', several countries enacted very harsh counter-terrorism laws. In the US, the Patriot Act was introduced, which allows the government to detain foreigners indefinitely on charges of terrorism. Not just the US, but nations across the world used the mass hysteria of that time to introduce more authoritarian laws and procedures. It helped leaders project their states as 'strong'.[52]

In Gujarat, POTA served a dual purpose. It terrorized Muslims long after the violence, and kept the public on tenterhooks as they would read about new arrests of 'Muslim terrorists trained by the ISI' in the newspapers. It fed their prejudices and fears, and helped Modi project himself as the 'Hindu hero'.

Gujarat has had no terrorist attacks before 2002. The main targets of terrorism in India have been the states of Jammu and Kashmir, Nagaland, Manipur, Bihar and Andhra

Pradesh. In Jammu and Kashmir, extremist Islamic groups have killed thousands. All Muslims have subsequently been stereotyped as terrorists because of the Kashmir problem. Few realize that the victims of terrorism in Kashmir have mainly been Muslim. In 2003, there were 801 civilians killed in Kashmir, of which 712 were Muslim and 89 were Hindu.[53]

Anyone listening to Modi's speeches during the state election campaign would have believed that Gujarat is a hotbed of terrorism; that Pakistan is out to get us. But the same question pops up—where are the terrorists?

'Notorious'

> 'The anti-national history of Godhra will definitely form part of the charge-sheets to tighten the noose against the culprits (of the Godhra massacre).'
> —Gordhan Zadaphia, Gujarat's home minister.[54]

'Just look! All India's mosquitoes live here,' says Mohsin Pathan, a motor parts shop owner. 'People are constantly falling ill. At a time when they have no money for food, we are paying expensive medical bills. I just recovered from malaria three days back. The municipal workers don't come here to clear the garbage or the drains. We are living in a gutter.' Mohsin lives in Signal Falia, the now-notorious neighbourhood in Godhra where a mob assembled to attack the Sabarmati Express.[55]

Ever since then, all Signal Falia's residents have been branded 'criminals'. It's been tough living with the label. 'The municipal authorities don't bother to clean up this neighbourhood. There's hardly any water supply. We have to fill water from a hand-pump three kilometres away. For the last ten days, we have got only two or three hours of electricity. When I called up the electricity board to complain, they said "Go back to Pakistan. What are you still doing here?" This is our condition today. They want to harass us, destroy our businesses. They want us to leave,' says Mohsin.

'For months on end, people have been starving,' says Anwar Kurkur, a twenty-seven-year-old computer operator at a local maternity hospital.[56] 'Most people in the neighbourhood are daily wage earners. They were scared to go out for fear of being arrested. People have stopped coming to our shops. If this continues, the local economy will collapse.'

Frequent raids and arbitrary arrests have made the local youth experts in the art of the quick escape. 'When the police come, all the men have to run into the nearby bushes. We never had to flee like this earlier. Now the entire neighbourhood has been blamed. Politicians have spoiled our name,' says Anwar.

Godhra has had a history of communal discord. In the nineteenth century, the business rivalry between the Ghanchi Muslims and Hindu Banias split the town. In the 1900s both communities sought support from fundamentalist groups to legitimize their local rivalry.[57] However, since 1992 the town remained free of violence. Business ties between the large Ghanchi Muslim and the Bania and Sindhi trading communities had strengthened until the burning of the Sabarmati Express in 2002.

Within Godhra, ghettoization is complete. 'Most of my friends are Hindu. But we can't go to each other's houses any more. I hardly meet them. Sometimes I bump into them on the street,' explains Anwar. 'For months I haven't been to the main market, which is a Hindu area. Muslim children have been shifted out of schools in Hindu localities.'

Prejudice hasn't affected only Muslims, but the entire

town. Even Hindu businessmen are feeling the pinch. 'Godhra has been divided into two parts. It wasn't like this twenty years back. In the last year, the division has been total. Fights still keep breaking out at the smallest excuse. People and traders from outside have stopped coming here. It's bad for everyone,' says Babubhai Mavar, a restaurant owner.[58]

Godhra's residents are still trying to brush off the tar that has tarnished them all. And the mosquitoes.

Notes

1. Interview in Ramol on 8 February 2003.
2. Ibid.
3. Reported in *Sandesh* on 28 February 2002.
4. According to the SIT as on September 2004. Thirty-five others are still absconding.
5. Signed by M.S. Dahiya, Assistant Director, Forensic Science Laboratory, Ahmedabad, dated 17 May 2002.
6. The FSL report has ruled out the possibility that the compartment was set on fire from outside by the mob. 'No inflammable fluid had been thrown inside from outside the coach.' It also rejects the possibility that any inflammable liquid was thrown through the door of the bogie. The report concludes that someone standing between the compartment and the northern side-door of the bogie threw around sixty litres of inflammable liquid.
    Working on the assumption that the fire was caused by an inflammable liquid, the FSL team conducted an experiment at the spot of the incident, recreating various ways in which it could have been ignited. From the railway platform, the FSL team threw buckets of water into the coach, whose window was seven feet from the ground. Only ten to fifteen per cent of the water entered the compartment. If the inflammable liquid was thrown from outside, the FSL report noted, then most of it would fall around the track outside and the resulting fire would cause damage to the bottom of the outer part of the coach. But since this part of the S6 coach was not severely burned, the report ruled out the possibility that

the mob threw inflammable fluids from outside.

7.   Interview in Vadodara in February 2003 and 9 August 2004.

8.   Ibid.

9.   Rohit Bhan, 'Godhra: 6 months later, nagging doubt: Whodunit?', *Indian Express*, 5 September 2002.

10. Ibid.

11. Ibid.

12. *Godhra Tak: The Terror Trail*, a documentary film by Shubhradeep Chakravorty.

13. *Indian Express*, Ahmedabad Newsline, 6 July 2002.

14. Deposition before the Nanavati–Shah commission on 30 June 2004.

15. Interview in Ahmedabad on 11 July 2002.

16. K.C. Bawa's testimony on 30 June 2004 and state intelligence official R.B. Sreekumar's affidavit before the Nanavati–Shah commission.

17. POTA revoked in Godhra case, rediff.com, 22 March 2002.

18. Interview in Vadodara in February 2003 and on 9 August 2004.

19. Interview in Ahmedabad on 11 July 2002.

20. Yale Herald, 'A closer look at the grim methods of modern torture', http://www.yaleherald.com/archive/xxxii/11.09.01/news/p3gray.html.

21. Interim report of the High-level Committee on Incident of Fire on 9166 Sabarmati Express at Godhra Station, 17 January 2005.

22. An inquiry into the reasons for the burning of coach S6 of the Sabarmati Express, by the Hazards Centre, New Delhi, January 2005, by A.K. Roy, Professor Dinesh Mohan, Professor Sunil Kale and S.N. Chakravarty.

23. Interview at Ahmedabad civil hospital, 25 September 2002.

24. Until then, this terrorist group had never been heard of.

25. Manas Dasgupta, 'Temple siege ends', *The Hindu*, 26 September 2002.

26. 'Attack not a revenge: Modi', *The Hindu*, 27 September 2002.

27. Manas Dasgupta, 'Akshardham Attack: "There was a standby terrorist"', *The Hindu*, 30 August 2003.

28. Praveen Swami, 'Akshardham: A search for truth', *Frontline*, 11-24 October 2003.

29. Ibid.

30. Gujarat police crime branch press note.

31. Ibid.

32. www.akshardham.com

33. Press conference at VHP headquarters in Ahmedabad on 25 September 2002.

34. 'Pseudo-secularists behaved this time, says Modi', *The Times of India*, 26 September 2002, http:/timesofindia.indiatimes.com/articleshow/23397397.cms

35. 'Akshardham head to Modi: Behave', *Sunday Express*, 29 September 2002.

36. Communalism Combat, *Genocide: Report on the Violence in Gujarat, Religious and Cultural Desecration*.

37. Ibid.

38. 'Blasts in 3 Ahmedabad buses; 12 injured', Times News Network, 29 May 2002.

39. Manu Joseph, 'From the Devil's lair', *Outlook*, 3 June 2002.

40. 'Haren flays state BJP chief for sending show cause', Times News Network, 5 August 2002.

41. Interview with crime branch officials in August 2004.

42. Praveen Swami, 'A circle of hate', *Frontline*, 11-24 October 2003.

43. Ibid.

44. Latif was Ahmedabad's biggest don. He had connections within the government, police and with Dawood Ibrahim.

45. Interview in Ahmedabad on 28 April 2003.

46. Ibid.

47. Ibid.

48. Interview in Godhra on 9 August 2004.

49. Interview with Ishaq's brother Shabbir in January 2005.

50. According to the law, once a person is arrested, he/she has to be produced before a magistrate within twenty-four hours and a case must be made out against him/her.

51. Interview on 29 January 2004.

52. 'In the Name of Counter-Terrorism: Human Rights Abuses Worldwide', a Human Rights Watch briefing paper for the 59th Session of the United Nations Commission on Human Rights, 25 March 2003.

53. Home ministry, Government of India statistics.

54. 'Latest from Gujarat: Godhra anti-national, it will help our case',

The Indian Express, 30 April 2002.

55. Interview on 10 February 2003.
56. Ibid.
57. David Hardiman, 'Passing blame on Godhra muslims', *Economic and Political Weekly*, 11 May 2002.
58. Interview on 10 February 2003.

'If intolerance becomes a habit, we run the risk of missing the truth.'

—Mahatma Gandhi

5

No Peace Without Justice

She still has to hide behind closed doors—no place is safe. Her attackers are free, but Bilkis is on the run.

Village leaders, who raped her and killed fourteen of her family, remained unpunished. Bilkis Yakub Rasool testified against them in her police statement. She was afraid they would harm her before the trial.

'There's a rumour that they have announced a Rs 5,00,000 reward to kill me. They are all roaming around freely and can track us down anywhere,' said Bilkis.[1] When I met her for the second time in February 2003, a year after the attack, she didn't move out of the house. A thin, slender girl, she hid behind her dupatta and spoke hesitantly, poker-faced, completely exhausted by the pain. After leaving the Godhra relief camp in July 2002, her family had lived in over twelve residences, and moved between them over twenty times in the span of two years.

The seventy-odd Muslim houses in her village, Randhikpur, in the dry, rocky parts of Dahod district, were attacked on 1 March 2002. In the mob there were people from her village as well as outsiders. Bilkis's entire family fled towards the hills. She and her sister-in-law Shamim were pregnant and found it difficult to run, but fear moved their feet.

They made it to Chundagi village, 5–6 km away, where local MLA Bijal Damore gave them shelter. But the next day, he asked them to leave because the mob could hunt them down. They hiked through remote and rugged terrain, and at the next village, Kuajher, they found shelter in a mosque. Here Shamim gave birth to a baby girl, but had no time to catch her breath. The mobs were targeting mosques, so the entire family was back on the road the next day.

Shamim limped to the next village, Kudra, without food or water. There adivasis looked after them for the night. The next day they moved on. Their hosts escorted them to the next village, Chhaparvad, from where the family headed to Panivela.

As they approached the village, the roar of a vehicle winding down the dirt track broke the silence of the wilderness. Their hearts were in their mouths. Was their game up? Were their three days of escape futile, or was help at hand? People poured out of the truck. Some were familiar faces—men from their village. Death had caught up with the Yakub family.

'They pulled my two-year-old baby from my arms, and threw her down. I saw them raping my sisters, my cousins, and my aunts. They did not even spare my mother. They raped and killed all of them, then set fire to my family,' said Bilkis. 'I was next. One after the other three of them were on me. I was screaming. My thoughts ran to my child, Saleha, who had been killed, and to the one inside me. I lost my senses.'[2]

Mistaking her for dead, the mob let Bilkis lie there. When she regained consciousness, the first thing she saw was the dead bodies of her family strewn all around her. The next morning, she started walking. She had no clue where she was going. After trekking for at least six hours, she came across a team from Limkheda police station. At the police station, they recorded her complaint and treated her injuries. Then they took her to a relief camp in Godhra.

There was no harm to her unborn child. Six months later, she gave birth to a girl while still living in the Godhra relief camp.

Her husband was in the fields during the attack—he fled

to another village and was missing for several months. He traced his family many months later. Fearing that his wife's attackers could get to him, he avoided going out to look for work. Even one year after the incident, they lived on the generosity of local relief committees.

Some refugees from Randhikpur have returned to the village, but not to their homes. They live in the nearby Devgad Baria village and go to Randhikpur for work. 'It's too dangerous. I will stay far away so that I can testify against them,' says Bilkis,[3] her diffidence hiding her dogged determination. 'I named more than ten people in my police statement. But not one of them has been arrested. They are all big people in the village—doctors, lawyers, and panchayat members. Some are from the VHP.'[4]

Ironically, the police said there wasn't enough proof against the accused. 'We haven't arrested anyone because there is no evidence. Bilkis gave contradicting statements at different points in time,' said D.R. Patel, police superintendent of Dahod district.[5] Bilkis denied making inconsistent testimonies; it was the police who were trying to cover up the mass murder.

In the FIR, Somsinh, the Police Station Officer (PSO) of Limkheda, refused to write the names of the accused. He did not even record the rape of Bilkis. The cops closed the case, saying it was 'true but undetected'. Bilkis, the main witness, was called 'unstable'.

Human rights groups took up the case, and supported by the National Human Rights Commission (NHRC), petitioned the Supreme Court for an impartial investigation by the CBI. The court agreed. It was the first and only post-Godhra violence case that was handed over to the CBI. In two months, the CBI did more than the Gujarat police had done in two years.

Skeletons came tumbling out—literally.

The CBI found that six policemen and two doctors deliberately destroyed evidence and conspired to shield the accused. In the FIR, the local police had recorded all fourteen dead bodies as 'missing'. CBI investigators uncovered the remains of five bodies. In a hurry to bury the proof, the police had brought two doctors to conduct a farcical post-mortem at the site itself. Normally, bodies are sent to the hospital for a post-mortem. The police made panch witnesses bury the corpses and added sixty kilos of salt, so that the bodies would disintegrate quickly. By law, the police is supposed to hand over the last remains to the families of the dead. Instead, they destroyed the evidence.

Although Bilkis named her attackers, the police didn't conduct an identification parade. They didn't arrest any of them; evidence like hair, blood or nail samples was never collected for forensic examination. When Bilkis reached the police station, they did not even conduct medical tests to establish rape. They did not get her clothes tested for blood or semen stains. Photographs of eight dead bodies were hidden.

The CBI charge-sheeted all twelve accused, including six policemen. Among those arrested were district BJP president Sailesh Bhatt and Ramesh Chandana, the former PA of Jaswant Bhabor, a minister in Modi's previous government. By digging up the dead, the CBI exposed the Gujarat police's complicity. The conspiracy to bury the truth and deny her justice came to light.

Convinced that Bilkis would not get justice within Gujarat, the Supreme Court ordered that the trial take place in Mumbai, following the precedent set in the Best Bakery case. Charges were framed against nineteen accused, including the six policemen.

Bilkis's case is not an aberration. The police closed 2120 riot cases as 'true but undetected'. That's half of the total 4252 FIRs filed. The reason—insufficient evidence.

No one bothered to ask why until August 2004, when the Supreme Court instructed the Gujarat police to form a grievance committee to review all these cases, and open those in which investigations were not properly conducted. The court responded to an application made by advocate Harish Salve, the *amicus curiae* (friend of the court) appointed to help the Supreme Court in the petitions relating to the Gujarat violence. Salve pointed out that all petitions before the Supreme Court indicated that the investigative machinery had failed to carry out proper investigations, and that the pathetic conduct of trials had resulted in the large-scale granting of bails and acquittals. The Supreme Court said that steps were needed to ensure that riot victims felt that justice is being done. Till the end of January 2005, the police had reviewed 1521 cases and reopened 518.[6]

Where the worst violence occurred—places like rural Vadodara, Banaskantha, Mehsana and Dahod—more cases were closed than the number actually charge-sheeted. For instance, in Sabarkantha district, 289 were closed, while charges were framed for only 178. Only 15 per cent of the cases registered in Bhavnagar were investigated one year after the massacres.

But the large number of closed cases only begin to tell the story. Cases with damning proof are being closed; names have disappeared from charge-sheets. Many witnesses are still trying in vain to get the police to record their testimonies. While noting down their statements, the police have left out names or vital facts. Those who testified against powerful politicians have been put in jail, while the real criminals roam free.

Speaking up against the powerful carries a price. Twelve people from Naroda Gaam in Ahmedabad testified on the role of Dr Maya Kodnani and Dr Jaideep Patel in the attack on their locality. Six months later, in September 2002, the police jailed all twelve as accused in a murder case which occurred in March 2002. When the case was filed, the names of neither the deceased nor the accused were known.

Those unlucky enough to have been wounded and in hospital were accused of rioting. Women injured in police firing have been jailed. Sairabanu[7] from Bangali Vas in Chandola, Ahmedabad, was at her doorstep when a police bullet mowed her down. 'The police surrounded our basti from all sides. They were standing on people's roofs and shooting down. I peered out of our home to see what was happening, when a bullet hit my thigh. My neighbour was also hit in the neck and died,' says Sairabanu, a widow.

After spending a month in hospital, she and her five children stayed at the Shah Alam camp for a few months. Soon after she returned to build a new home, Sairabanu was arrested, accused of rioting with intent to kill. 'I was in Sabarmati jail for a week for participating in the rioting. How could I? What would happen to my five children?' she says.

Sairabanu, a daily wage earner, had no money to pay her Rs 3000 interim bail. Luckily, her neighbours collected the money to get her released. Barely managing to earn enough to feed her children, she had to borrow another Rs 2000 for the final bail amount. 'The police filed rioting cases against anyone who was admitted into hospital with bullet injuries in police firing. They assumed that they were all part of the mob. That's why Sairabanu was arrested,' says her lawyer. Several others like Sairabanu were jailed.

Only a few cases made it to court. In Panchmahal district, twenty-six were tried in court.[8] In all of them, the accused were acquitted, said Narsimha Komar, district superintendent of police.[9] In Pandharvada village, where twenty-seven people were murdered, all the fifteen accused were acquitted. In two different places—Sapadia and Limbadia Chowkdi—two tempos filled with people fleeing Kidiad village were attacked on the road, and seventy-three people[10] were killed. All the accused, including local BJP leader Kalubhai Malivad, were found not guilty by the district court. In the December 2002 state elections, he was elected as an MLA. His defence lawyer was the BJP MP Bhupendra Solanki.

Yet, when the indicted are acquitted in court, it is the victims who are blamed. 'It's very difficult to prove riot cases. Witnesses turn hostile. They have to live in their villages. Even people who lodged FIRs have gone back on their initial statements,' says Komar. But the police and the public prosecutors did nothing to make sure that witnesses felt safe enough to testify.

In Gujarat, the VHP has a strong support base among lawyers. Vadodara's Bar Association filed a contempt of court case against the NHRC for insulting the Gujarat High Court's acquittal judgment in the Best Bakery case by describing it as 'a miscarriage of justice'.

The public prosecutor in the Best Bakery case 'appears to have acted more as a defence counsel than one whose duty was to present the truth before the Court,' said the Supreme Court. State counsel in other cases behaved similarly. Many were affiliated to the VHP. Witnesses of the Sardarpura massacre in Mehsana, in which thirty-three were burned alive, didn't trust the public prosecutor. They asked for a special public prosecutor to represent them. The current district public prosecutor is Dilip Trivedi, who is general secretary of the local VHP. In Ahmedabad, Chetan Shah has been appointed district government pleader. He was acquitted in a 1986 communal riot case in which eight people were burned alive in Meghaninagar.[11]

The VHP ensured that 'their boys' were properly represented. Soon after the riots, it appointed a team of lawyers to bail out the accused. It even made sure that home-cooked meals reached those activists who were jailed.[12]

There was a glaring difference in the zeal with which the police investigated the Godhra case and its apathy in bringing the riots accused to book. 'If the government really wants to, it can do a lot. It can seal the property of all the accused who are "absconding", like they did in the Godhra case,' said lawyer Mihir Desai, who fought for Zaheera in the Supreme Court.[13] 'Why should witnesses turn hostile? Why can't they ensure their safety? The law allows judges to threaten hostile witnesses with a jail sentence. They can make use of this as well. But what justice can one expect when the prosecutors, many of whom are VHP members, are siding with the accused?'

No conspiracy case has been filed in the Naroda Patiya or Chamanpura cases. More people died in these planned attacks than in the Sabarmati Express burning at Godhra. 'The fanatics who spread violence in the name of religion are worse than terrorists and more dangerous than an alien enemy,' said the Supreme Court.[14] But only the Godhra case was considered a terrorist act and charged under POTA.

Many of the post-Godhra attacks were premeditated. Yet, the police never thought of investigating the conspiracy behind these attacks, nor has there been any talk of arresting the brains behind the pogrom.

The one single individual who all riot witnesses blame, but whose name has never appeared in a single charge-sheet is none other than the universally accused—Narendra Modi. In any conversation with the riot affected, they always mention the chief minister's invisible hand in allowing this to happen, giving the mobs a free rein, directing the police not to act and then shielding the culprits. Modi's own minister acknowledged that he instructed the police not to act.[15]

In parliament, the opposition called for his resignation, but it was waved aside because the BJP's allies, while condemning the attack, didn't support the demand for his resignation. However, the pleas for Modi to step down continued. At the BJP's national meeting in April 2002, the matter was resolved in a well-enacted drama where Modi offered his resignation. The party didn't accept it, and asked him to dissolve the assembly and go in for elections instead—killing two birds with one stone. They were eager to convert the communal fervour into votes. That is the story of how Modi got away and got his way.

In previous communal massacres too, the main culprits have escaped without punishment. Congress MPs like H.K.L. Bhagat, Jagdish Tytler, Kamal Nath and Sajjan Kumar, who allegedly led mobs in the anti-Sikh pogrom in 1984 after the assassination of Indira Gandhi are still to be punished. An appeal against Sajjan Kumar's acquittal is still pending in the Delhi High Court. Several other cases filed against him were closed by Congress governments at various points in time.[16]

After instigating the 1992–93 violence in Mumbai, Shiv Sena leader Bal Thackeray and his lieutenants like Madhukar Sarpotdar, who was caught by the police carrying arms in a truck, got away. There were cases against Bal Thackeray for his inflammatory writings in *Saamna*, his party's newspaper. No action was taken against him. Later, when his rival Chaggan Bhujbal became Maharashtra's home minister, he opened up one of the eleven cases against him. He was arrested and immediately taken to court on 25 July 2000, but the Bhoiwada metropolitan magistrate court dismissed the case saying it was 'time barred',[17] ending the drama.

After the 1984 and the 1992–93 pogroms, the Congress swept the national elections and the Shiv Sena was voted to power in Maharashtra for the first time—victories drenched in blood.

The NHRC and other civil liberties groups in the country have been monitoring the Gujarat riot cases carefully. With no hope of justice within the state they approached the Supreme Court, which responded with unprecedented orders like the transfer of cases outside Gujarat, reinvestigation by the CBI and the review of acquittals.

Yet, not a single case was filed against the political

masterminds. Instead, Narendrabhai became Gujarat's Hindutva hero. He was invincible; even more so after his election victory vindicated his bloody politics.

Across the ocean in the United Kingdom, the Dawood family couldn't file a case against Modi and his cronies in the International Court of Justice for the pogrom against Muslims because India is not a signatory to the Rome statute of the International Criminal Court. Their two sons, their childhood friend and an Indian driver were killed on the highway near Pratinj, Sabarkantha, North Gujarat, while they were travelling from Agra on 28 February 2002. Only one family member travelling with them survived. The Dawood family has filed a civil suit in a Gujarat district court against Modi and the Gujarat government asking for damages.

Such legal action against senior political and government officials is unprecedented in Indian courts, and will highlight the specific roles played by political leaders and state officials in the carnage. It also holds the CM responsible for the 'acts of commission and omission committed by his officers in the command structure' for violence that constitutes 'genocide, torture, crimes against humanity and violation of the fundamental rights of life and liberty'.[18] In 2003, lawyers in the UK were demanding a warrant of arrest for Narendra Modi under Article 1 of the International Convention Against Torture and Section 134 of the UK Criminal Justice Act of 1988. However, it is difficult to acquire evidence that proves Modi's direct complicity in the mass killings.[19]

Until the big fish are caught, people like Bilkis may have to keep hiding. She is still hoping that the day will come when there will be a role reversal, when criminals will be put behind bars and it will be safe for her to walk the streets again.

The riot commission

Imagine that you're Narendra Modi. After the riots, the heat is on you—the nation and the world are pushing for your dismissal. They accuse you of being biased during the violence. What do you do?

Easy—appoint a judicial commission that can't punish, and can only recommend action. Restrict the commission's terms of reference only to the Godhra incident. Then, if human rights activists kick up a fuss, agree to include the post-Godhra violence. Anyway, the commission can't do much, but at least you will have shown the world that you believe in justice—as long as it's in your favour.

That was the birth of the Shah Commission to inquire into the Godhra incident and the violence that followed. With the world breathing down his neck, Modi appointed Justice K.G. Shah to head the commission. Again, human rights activists created a ruckus and accused him of being biased.[20] He silenced them by including Justice G.T. Nanavati, a retired Supreme Court judge who was heading the Delhi riots commission.

Even if the commission does indict the government or the Sangh Parivar, the government is hardly going to punish itself or its party members. It isn't even likely to go for the small fish who brought them to power—the VHP and Bajrang Dal goons.

But for now, the commission has to justify its existence. So, it starts working slowly and steadily. It held hearings in all the affected districts. Here is a sampling of the proceedings.

A conference room in the Circuit House in Vadodara, with tables all around. The witness sits in the centre with Vadodara's top police brass seated behind the tables, looking on. Outside, the compound is swarming with police jeeps and policemen who can't get in. The city's police station chiefs are there in full force.

Would you step into this room? Even if you dared to, would you tell the truth? Would you complain that the police did nothing to save you and refused to take down your statement?

Just to make doubly sure that they weren't embarrassed, the police went knocking on people's doors the night before, asking them to attend the hearing and testify about how the police helped them. That's a request no one would dare refuse.

They landed up at Aminaben's[21] house at 10.30 p.m. 'Two policemen came and asked me to report to the police station the next morning. They told me to attend the hearing,' Aminaben told me. The next day they took all potential witnesses to the police headquarters. 'There was a large meeting. The government lawyer Arvind Pandya told us, "Forget what has happened in the past. You should keep good relations with everyone. If you support or don't support the police, you will need their help later. So it's better if you speak in their favour. Tell the commission how they helped you and rescued you during the riots . . . Don't do what I say, but what you feel is best." He spoke sweetly but with an underlying warning.'

Aminaben didn't testify before the commission. 'They took us to the Circuit House. But I left before my name was called.' She saw people protesting outside, calling for a boycott of the commission and readily agreed to join them. 'Why should we be the police's advocate? They didn't help us at all when our houses were being burned. They allowed the mobs to kill and loot. This commission is totally one-sided,' she said.

Those who stayed to testify were mainly 'friends' of the police, locals who work in tandem with the cops, also called police khabris (informers). Not surprisingly, the police proudly boasted that 201 of the 204 witnesses from urban and rural Vadodara spoke in their favour.[22] But Vadodara's police commissioner, Sudhir Sinha, denied that they had arranged any meeting to influence witnesses. Who would dare to disbelieve the police commissioner?

'This Nanavati commission is a banavati (fake) commission,' said Jitubhai Pandya, owner of *Newsplus* channel, and also a local Shiv Sena leader.[23] 'Almost all the witnesses were brought by the police. It was stage managed. People from the worst riot-hit areas spoke as if nothing had happened there. Then how did more than a hundred people die? Did they commit suicide?'

The next stop for the commission was Ahmedabad. Here, there was a new master of ceremonies—one of the main accused in the Naroda Patiya massacre—Mangubhai Maharaj, a local Bajrang Dal goon. A self-confessed Muslim hater, Mangubhai stood outside the courtroom while the hearings on Naroda Patiya were on. He brought his Bajrang Dal witnesses to drown out the voices of actual riot victims. Outside, he told the media, 'Muslims are like a disease in India, like diabetes. And we, the VHP, Bajrang Dal, RSS, we are the doctors.'[24]

It is a system that lets anyone who is powerful off the hook. What happened during the Delhi riots? Eight commissions looked into the anti-Sikh riots that killed 2733.[25] None of the guilty have been punished so far.

And so the commission continues with its work. We don't know when or whether it will reach any conclusion.

Zaheera: From Heroine to Villain

Zaheera Sheikh—a young girl whose defiant eyes staring out of a burqa made it to the covers of magazines all over India. A girl who was intent on emerging triumphant from a tragedy, come what may. Like many victims who were swayed by the flood of promises and offers made to them after the crisis, Zaheera's confused family also wavered from one extreme to the other, from challenging the government to becoming its puppet.

The media was the first to judge her. From heroine to villain, Zaheera Sheikh's decline was swift. Her dramatic swings in court and outside made the Best Bakery case one of the most controversial and publicized cases of the Gujarat carnage. Initially, the media glamourized her as the star witness, but soon after she was portrayed as a greedy manipulator. In the media uproar, the dilemma she was caught in was overlooked. No one stopped to think that Zaheera's family had to choose between justice and safety.

Zaheera lost her younger sister and uncle when a mob burned down their Best Bakery in Hanuman Tekri, Vadodara, killing fourteen people. Her neighbours and workers in the bakery (some of whom were Hindu) were also killed in the attack. From the terrace above the bakery, Zaheera saw the culprits, many of whom lived close to her, reduce them to ashes. The police FIR was based on her testimony. She was a high-profile witness, and frequently gave interviews to the press.

But when the case came up in the sessions court, she turned turtle, and so did the rest of her family—her brother Nafitullah and her mother Sehrunissa. They said they couldn't see anything that night. Zaheera said the police had concocted her testimony, even though she had given three police statements naming the accused. She had also narrated the same story to an NHRC team that had visited Vadodara soon after the violence.

When the Sheikhs went back on their police statements, there were no questions asked in court. The public prosecutor didn't cross-examine her; Zaheera hadn't even met him until the day of the trial. He had not even bothered to brief his main witness. Zaheera left the court in BJP MLA Madhu Shrivastav's car. People smelled something fishy; some suspected that they had struck a deal. A lot of questions were left hanging in the air, and Zaheera disappeared from Vadodara. The press couldn't track her down.

After the court acquitted all the accused, her family decided to speak up. Her mother spoke first to the *Indian Express* and admitted to lying in court because Madhu Shrivastav had threatened them. 'Several times he sent threats through others. He called to threaten us as well. He warned that if we told the truth in court, we would be killed and that Zaheera would not be allowed to reach court. In fear, we retracted our statements.'[26]

In the next few days, Zaheera was brought to Mumbai by the Citizens for Justice and Peace, a group brought together by Javed Anand and Teesta Setalvad of *Communalism Combat* magazine. 'I was intimidated by BJP MLA Madhu Shrivastav and his cousin, Congress councillor Chandrakant "Bhattu" Shrivastav. He threatened to kill our family if I spoke the truth. I want the case to be tried again outside Gujarat,' Zaheera now said at a press conference.

'The atmosphere in court was very dangerous. There was a big crowd. Everyone was staring at me. The court was packed with Bajrang Dal activists and people from our neighbourhood, Hanuman Tekri. They had killed and burned our family and home. Madhu Shrivastav was standing opposite me while I was in the witness box. Seeing him, I got even more nervous. I didn't know who he was then, but he looked very dangerous. The lawyer was also not mine. I didn't know whether to speak the truth or not. Two questions kept coming to my head. One was the safety of my family. And the other was to get the culprits punished. Between the two, I had to choose my family's lives.'

Just before the trial began, Madhu Shrivastav's cousin Chandrakant Shrivastav waylaid Zaheera. 'When I was entering the court, Chandrakant "Bhattu" Shrivastav saw me downstairs and said, "Decide now: do you want to save your family's lives or do you want these people to be punished? Even now, you have time to think." I didn't believe him at that time. Even then, I thought, 'No, I'll fight.' But later when I was in the witness box, I got scared.'[27]

Why did she leave in Shrivastav's car if he was threatening her? 'My brother told me to go. I asked him whose car it was but he didn't reply. He (Madhu) was not in the car with us,' she replied. Apparently, Nafitullah had met Shrivastav before the trial. Shrivastav had sent threats to the family through Lal Mohammed, whose timber shop opposite Best Bakery was also burned in the riots. Lal Mohammed had arranged the meeting.

Many speculated about whether they had struck a deal. Even if they did, you could hardly blame the Sheikhs, considering their dilemma—their lives were under threat, and they had no support from the prosecution lawyer or the police. Everything seemed to favour the accused. Testifying truthfully would not necessarily guarantee them justice, or safety.

Zaheera approached the Supreme Court asking for a retrial outside Gujarat. This embarrassed the Gujarat government's prosecution, and to extricate themselves from the quandary, they filed an appeal in the Gujarat High Court against the judgement. But the high court also acquitted the accused due to lack of evidence.

The Supreme Court delivered a landmark judgment ordering a retrial outside Gujarat. Such a move is extremely rare. Its judgement[28] said that truth had become a casualty in this case, and a retrial was essential 'to save and preserve the justice delivery system from vested interests'.

Extremely critical of the role of the Gujarat judiciary, the state government, the police and the public prosecutor in averting a fair trial, the Supreme Court said, 'The justice delivery system was being taken for a ride and literally allowed to be abused, misused and mutilated by subterfuge.'

The Supreme Court also condemned the state government. 'The modern-day "Neros" were looking elsewhere when Best Bakery and innocent children and women were burning, and were probably deliberating how the perpetrators of the crime can be saved or protected.'

Sympathetic to Zaheera's plight, the Supreme Court ruled that even though she had taken different stands, 'it was obligatory for the Court to find out as to what is the correct stand and real truth which could have been decided and examined by accepting the prayer for additional evidence.'[29]

'The public prosecutor was not acting in a manner befitting the position held by him,' the Supreme Court said. He did not take any steps to protect Zaheera, the star witness, even though four witnesses who testified before her had turned hostile, the Supreme Court observed. Nor did he request for an in-camera trial to shield his witnesses. The Supreme Court reiterated the high court's observations that 'the police manipulated in getting false witnesses to rope in wrong people as the accused.'[30]

Criticizing every branch of the administration, the Supreme Court said, 'The investigation appears to be perfunctory and anything but impartial without any definite object of finding out the truth and bringing to book those who were responsible for the crime. The public prosecutor appears to have acted more as a defence counsel than one whose duty was to present the truth before the (High) Court. The Court in turn appeared to be a silent spectator, mute to the manipulations and preferred to be indifferent to sacrilege being committed to justice.'[31]

But it wasn't a happy ending—the battle had just begun. While the retrial was under way, the Sheikh family turned hostile once again. Just before her testimony was due to begin, Zaheera did a complete somersault. In November 2004 she suddenly appeared at a press conference in Vadodara (while she was supposed to be under police protection in Mumbai) and said she would lodge a police case against activist Teesta Setalvad and her associate Raees Khan because they forced her to lie before the Supreme Court and identify accused whom she had never seen. She said that they had threatened her and kept her confined in Mumbai.

Who are the lawyers who brought Zaheera back to Vadodara to file a case against Teesta Setalvad? Who are they linked to? Atul Mistry, the lawyer representing Zaheera, is a junior of Rajendra Trivedi, who defended the Best Bakery accused in the Vadodara sessions court. Jal Unwala, another lawyer supporting her in the Vadodara press conference, is a junior of Gujarat High Court lawyer K.J. Sethna, whose older brother Justice B.J. Sethna upheld the acquittal of the Best Bakery accused by the sessions court.

Was there a deal being struck? Who was funding this deal? In December 2004, while Zaheera was testifying in court, *Tehelka* magazine added to the drama by releasing tapes that contained conversations recorded on a spycam with BJP MLA Madhu Shrivastav and his cousin Bhattu Shrivastav, whom Zaheera alleged had threatened her and made her turn hostile in the Vadodara sessions court. Both politicians admitted on tape that Madhu paid Zaheera Rs 18 lakh to go back on her police statement in court.[32] Both Zaheera and the Shrivastavs vehemently denied the contents of the tapes.

But what happened during her second U-turn? Were the Sheikhs threatened to keep their silence, or bought off? The story behind the Sheikh family's constant shifts between fact and fiction seems to be not just money, but also a tussle between their quest for justice and the risk to their own lives if they spoke against those who have the upper hand. They have to keep quiet if they want to return home, and yes, money is needed to rebuild a life that has been burned to cinders.

The grand irony would be if in this tangled mess of contradictions, the accused are freed and the Sheikhs are finally jailed for perjury.

Camouflaging crimes

Being gang raped was just the beginning of her nightmare.

After that Sultana Sheikh had to fight with the police to acknowledge the crime. The police refused to record her complaint and denied it ever happened.

It took two months of pestering the police, repeating her story, and reliving her trauma before she got them to record the fact that she was raped.

When a mob attacked the Muslim basti in her village, Delol, on 28 February 2002, they all ran into the fields. As they moved from field to field, two boys were killed on the way. The next day, Sultana jumped into a tempo crammed with nineteen others and fled. They made it to the road near Ambica Society in Kalol, where a mob stopped them, overturned the tempo and killed ten people. Sultana managed to escape. But she was third time unlucky—three from the mob chased her, gang raped her and left her lying among the dead. Sultana's husband Firoze and four other family members were burned inside the tempo.[33]

Sultana kept going back to the police station, asking them to take down her statement. Each time she had to repeat her story, reliving her trauma, only to be told at the end that a complaint had already been filed. One callous constable told her to forget it—a separate FIR would not be filed for 'simply rape'. They had already recorded the tempo attack on their own.

Two months later they agreed to attach her statement to an existing FIR. Sultana's story remained a forced appendage and the Kalol police didn't take down all the details. They did not record her rape in the statement they took down, which only said that when she woke up she was without clothes. She was sent for a medical examination forty-five days later and the report, of course, did not confirm rape because the examination should be conducted soon after the crime; preferably before the victim has a bath.

Imagine what it's like to see your parents, your wife and child being killed by a crazy mob, and then the police refuse to take down your complaint. It's already been filed, they tell you. But they won't give you a copy of the document.

Yunus Ismail Sheikh was also with Sultana in the ill-fated tempo. He lost his entire family in a matter of hours. He recognized the killers; he even knows their names. He went to the police, but he was turned away. The complaint has already been filed, they told him. But why wouldn't they include his story? Or show him a copy of this complaint? How was it filed without taking down a statement of a single eyewitness?

On that same day, 1.5 km away, the police watched as Imran Yusuf Ghodawala was caught by a mob, dragged into the Rabbani Masjid, hit with sticks and swords, rolled in a carpet and burnt alive. They did nothing to save him. All they did was fire from a distance—not at the murderers, but at Muslim victims. Imran's brother Idris went to the Kalol police to register his brother's murder and recover his body. They didn't give back the body and refused to record his statement. There was no need, they told him, they had already filed an FIR.

Hussein Suban was given the same reply when he tried to register his uncle Ibrahim's murder. A police bullet hit Ibrahim Suban while he was running away from a mob in Kalol. Hussein put him into a tempo and rushed him to hospital. A mob attacked them in the compound of the Kalol Referral Hospital and set fire to the tempo. Hussein could escape but his injured uncle couldn't, and was burned to death.

What links together these unfortunate people besides inconsolable grief? The police have registered all the crimes they suffered separately under one common FIR: no. 36/2002. In Boru village (6 km away from Kalol), only the violence, but not the murders, is recorded in the same FIR. They happened in four separate places—within a 10 km radius. The only thing linking these crimes is that they occurred on the same day and under the jurisdiction of the same police station. So one clever policeman decided to record his version of these events in one single FIR, without taking down any eyewitness statements.

Sultana, Yunus, Idris and Hussein didn't ever imagine that all their complaints had been clubbed together. They discovered this when they demanded the police show them their FIRs. There it was—all in one.

Here's the police's version of what happened, as written in the FIR:

- There was no mention of Sultana's rape.
- They counted only ten killings in the tempo instead of thirteen. A few more dead bodies make no difference, do they? They did not name any accused. Yunus could have provided the names.
- They did not record Imran's murder, only the destruction of a mosque in the same area. Do mosques matter more than men?
- They did acknowledge Ibrahim's death, but he was a nameless Muslim killed by a faceless mob.

After the witnesses pestered the police to record their statements, the charge-sheet named four accused who murdered the passengers in the tempo—Sheetal alias Tikudo, J.P. Shah, Jaggubhai Paanwala and Vijay Thakore. Guess who else were named as accused? Imran and Ibrahim. The dead victims were held responsible for rioting. Moreover, two of the prosecution witnesses are none other than the brothers of two of the accused.

In December 2003 an independent police officer, Neerja Rao, ordered a proper investigation into all these cases and asked for a new charge-sheet to be filed. In August 2004, sub-inspector R.J. Patil, who filed the group FIR, was arrested for tampering with evidence by burning the bodies of those killed in the tempo.[34]

With investigations in this state, it is hard to blame the judiciary entirely. The police know how to bury a case with the dead even before it reaches court.

Missing persons

It took Yakub Sheikh twenty-two months just to get his FIR registered.

Until then, the police refused to acknowledge the death of seven in his family. 'I would go to the Kalol police station twice every day. But they refused to record my statement. The policemen told me that they could not register the FIR because they did not find the dead bodies,' Yakub explained.[35]

But they were all hacked and burned. What proof could he produce?

Yakub's village, Delol, was attacked on 28 February and 1 March 2002. On the first day, his house was ransacked. After spending one terrifying night in what remained of their home, Yakub and his family ran into the fields when the mob returned to obliterate the Muslims. By the evening, the men in saffron bands had started searching the fields for the survivors.

They caught up with Yakub's family, who were hiding in a bush. Yakub saw the mob hack his parents and five other family members to bits and set them ablaze with petrol. There was little he could do except gather his wits and walk on. He walked for two hours in silence, still reeling from the shock of seeing his dear ones butchered. Finally, he reached Godhra.

Firdos's family also fled Delol. While they were on the run, the mob accosted them at the Goma river. Firdos and his two nephews, Ijaz, eleven, and Javed, nine, hid in the bushes.[36] From there he saw them butcher ten people. They grabbed Ijaz's mother and slit her neck. Ijaz couldn't remain silent any longer, and he ran to save her. They caught him and made him walk around a bonfire of the dead bodies. Then, they threw him into the blaze too.

After escaping the attack, Firdos ran to Godhra and then to Kalol. Both Firdos and Yakub would do the rounds of the Kalol police station every day, but the police refused to file the complaint until they found the 'missing' bodies. Three months later, Firdos and Yakub insisted on taking the police to the site of the slaughter, but by then, most of the remains had been cleared from the site. Totally, twenty-four people were killed in Delol village.[37]

They lost everything—their families, their loved ones, their homes, their shops. After three months, they received the Rs 1,50,000 compensation due to them for each family member who had died. A government order demanded that the penniless refugees must pay Rs 4,50,000 in collateral for each dead member, just in case they turned up alive in the future. After several arguments with government officials, they finally agreed to drop that condition.

These murders would have gone unreported if Neerja Rao had not entered their lives, even if it was twenty-two months too late. Rao, known to be an efficient police officer, was brought in as an additional investigator to probe the sixty-five murders in Kalol. She immediately made sure their FIRs were recorded properly and the charge-sheet filed. But during the investigation, Rao was suddenly transferred to the Gandhinagar Women's Cell.

Yakub and Firdos are not sure whether any action will be taken on their complaint, but at least they got their FIRs registered before Neerja was sent away. Will it take another few years for the next step towards justice?

Unlucky survivors?

For two years, Salim Sindhi had no address. He was still living in a tent at a relief camp at Modasa.[38] When I went to visit him, he told me, 'I'll come to fetch you on the main road. You won't be able to find the campsite where we live. It's in the middle of nowhere.' True to his word, Salim was waiting on his motorbike at the side of the road, ready to direct us to his campsite, keen for us to hear his story.

He's one of the lucky survivors of the massacre at Limbadia Chowkdi. Salim fled his burning village, Kidiad (Sabarkantha district) on 2 March 2002. He and his brother Ayub crammed people into two tempos, and escaped as their houses went up in flames.

'At many places on the road there were people throwing stones. The windows were broken. One stone hit my brother Zakir's four-month-old son. He died instantly,' said Salim.

Up ahead, the road was barricaded, so they stopped and got down near Sapadia. 'Everyone ran into the bushes near the river. My wife was with some of the women. They couldn't move that fast. A mob caught up with them and killed five of them,' Salim said. A motorbike was trailing their tempo. The bike riders brought people from the nearby village to attack them, he explained.

The other tempo was stopped by a mob at Limbadia Chowkdi in Panchmahal district. The young men sitting on top ran off, but the mob wouldn't let the women and children sitting at the back get off. They poured petrol inside and set them on fire.

Nothing remained of the sixty-two who were burned to death inside the two tempos. The police have listed them as 'missing'. A total of seventy-three people were killed, of which thirty-two were children. Only eleven bodies were found.

Arzubibi Sindhi and her husband Ayub were the main witnesses in one of the FIRs, but she was too scared to speak the truth. They had already dodged death twice. Arzubibi didn't want to take any chances again. So she lied in court.

Kalubhai Mariwad, a local BJP activist, is one of the accused. Later, he was elected an MLA in the elections. None other than the Panchmahal BJP MP Bhupendra Solanki, a practising lawyer, defended him in court. Mariwad and the other accused were acquitted. Before the trial they heard rumours of threats to burn down Kidiad's neighbouring village, Karanta, if witnesses testified in court. Arzubibi chose to protect lives rather than punish the guilty. In court, she testified that she was unconscious and didn't see anything.

But Ayub was bolder. In his police statement, he named all the ten people he identified. He is determined to get them punished. 'I was driving the tempo. I saw the people who attacked us. They are all locals of Limbadia Chowkdi. I ran a transport business and travelled there often. That's how I knew who they were,' said Ayub. The police listed them as 'absconding'.

The court testimony was an ordeal for Arzu. 'A huge, intimidating crowd packed the courtroom. Arzu was scared they would kill us. When we left the court, we drove back on a diversion route and stayed that night at Balasinhore. She was so scared they would come after us,' Ayub recalled.

She had every reason to be afraid. Two years after the carnage, they were still living in tents at the Modasa relief camp. There is no one to protect them except the other 200 refugees living there with them. All sixty families have sold their agricultural land to local Patels. They hoped to move into houses in Modasa built for them by the Islami Relief Committee.

'These houses are so tiny compared to our homes in the village. Eight of them would be equal to the size of my old home. But this is all we can hope for now,' said Salim, the amiable sarpanch of his village, now fighting for justice. Tall and well built, Salim has a towering presence and still keeps the faith despite the tragedy he has been through.

Around half of the families haven't yet received a single paisa as compensation from the government.

The lucky survivors of the Limbadia massacre haven't had much luck after the incident. They are still struggling to survive, looking for some way out of the camp.

Playing with fire

Do you dare to call political leaders criminals? You'll be framed and jailed for the same crime you accuse them of—murder.

Nanubhai Maleikh, a witness in the Naroda Gaam case in Ahmedabad, was actually imprisoned for four months. In his police statement he said that Dr Maya Kodnani and Dr Jaideep Patel had directed the mob that went on a rampage, killing thirteen people and burning his entire neighbourhood to dust.

Nanubhai's testimony has conveniently disappeared. There is no police record of it. He keeps writing to various police officials and political leaders pleading for his statement to be recorded and for the guilty to be punished, but the police have not yet acted on his requests.

The only action they did take was to frame him for murder. During the riots, the body of a Hindu, believed to be part of the mob, was found. The police case didn't list any accused. Six months later, the police named twelve residents of Naroda Gaam as the murderers. They were in jail for four months. 'After my complaint, top leaders were in trouble. That's why the police framed me. I have been working in the peace committee for more than twenty years,' said Nanubhai.[39] 'How could we kill anyone? Our lives were in danger. There was a huge mob out to get us. All we could do was take our families and run for cover.'

The elderly Nanubhai was still a refugee. He still hadn't returned to Naroda Gaam. His entire family, with sons and grandchildren, lived in a tiny room opposite a bubbling sewer in the bylanes behind the Shah Alam camp. His friend had given him a room to live in. 'Earlier, we had pitched a tent here. We made friends with the local people. One of them felt sorry for us and gave us this room. Twelve of us are squashed in here. Our house in Naroda had five rooms. Even my shop was burned. Since then, I've been unemployed. Not one of the accused is in jail. How can we go back?' asked Nanubhai.

His statement naming political leaders is not the only one that has vanished; another less controversial one is also missing. 'When the police came to the Shah Alam camp to take down complaints, Medinaben and I had made an FIR about five of her family who were burned alive. I managed to rescue her from the flames. But the FIR doesn't exist any more. I keep writing to the police commissioner asking him to file the case,' he said.

In his other 'missing' police statement, Nanubhai had named eleven people including Dr Maya Kodnani, Dr Jaideep Patel, BJP corporators Vallabh Patel and Ashok Patel, and other local VHP leaders. 'What else can you expect? The police were with them. The police station is barely 30 metres from our neighbourhood. We went to ask them to save us. But no one came. People from the mob were even drinking water from the tap at the entrance of the police station. Later, a tanker was parked outside the police station to provide them water. VHP leaders walk freely in and out of the police station,' he alleged.

Isn't he scared of speaking out? Especially after being jailed for being outspoken? 'What is fear for people who are dead? I am lucky to have the chance to get these criminals punished,' he replied. Nanubhai still wants to play with fire, even though it destroyed his entire life.

Notes

1. Interview in Godhra on 10 February 2003.
2. Navaz Kotwal, 'Untold Tragedies', *Frontline*, 16–29 August 2003, http://www.flonnet.com/fl2017/stories/20030829007601300.htm
3. Interview in Godhra on 10 February 2003.

4. These people were arrested two years later, when the CBI took over the investigation. When I interviewed Bilkis, they were still free.

5. Interview in February 2003.

6. www.riotcell2002.gujarat.gov.in

7. Interview on 28 February 2003.

8. As on March 2003.

9. Interview in February–March 2003.

10. But only eleven were reported dead, the remaining sixty-two were considered 'missing'.

11. Crime register no. 304 of 1986, Shahibaug police station, 12 July 1986. Acquitted in court of designated judge, Ahmedabad city as Terrorist case no. 1/1987. Acquitted on 10 September 1990.

12. Radha Sharma, 'VHP cooks up a treat for riot accused', Times News Network, 12 September 2002. http://www1. timesofindia. indiatimes.com/cms.dll/articleshow? art_ID=21998732

13. Interview in March 2003.

14. Supreme Court judgement dated 12 April 2004 by Justice Doraiswamy Raju J. and Justice Arijit Pasayat.

15. Manu Joseph, 'From the Devil's lair', *Outlook*, 3 June 2002.

16. *Tehelka*, 'Justice delayed, denied', 1 May 2004.

17. Syed Firdaus Ashraf, 'Court throws out case against Thackeray', Rediff.com, 25 July 2000.

18. Dawood, Criminal case against Modi, Independent Media Center, 26 May 2004. http://india.indymedia.org/en/2004/05/209432. shtml

19. Legal action to arrest Narendra Modi, chief minister of Gujarat, for torture, 21 August 2003, Awaaz—Projects and Campaigns http://www.awaazsaw.org/awaaz_camp.htm

20. Justice Shah had sentenced to death several Muslim accused in the Dabgarwal Laliwala case in the 1985 riots. Later, the Supreme Court acquitted the accused and strongly criticised Shah's judgment.

21. Interview in Vadodara on 24 June 2003.

22. Interview in Vadodara on 25 June 2003 with police commissioner Sudhir Sinha.

23. Interview in Vadodara on 24 June 2003.

24. Interview in Naroda, Ahmedabad on 12 September 2003.

25. According to the government-appointed Ahooja committee to determine the official death toll, in 'Justice delayed, denied', *Tehelka*, 1 May 2004.

26. Abhishek Kapoor and Ayesha Khan, '*Kaanpte kaanpte jhoot bola tha court mein*' (Trembling with fear, we lied in court), *The Indian Express*, 6 July 2003.

27. Dionne Bunsha, 'I want the case to be reopened', *Frontline*, 19 July–1 August 2003.

28. Supreme Court judgement dated 12 April 2004 by Justice Doraiswamy Raju J. and Justice Arijit Pasayat.

29. Ibid.

30. Ibid.

31. Ibid.

32. 'The shame of Gujarat', *Tehelka*, 22 December 2004.

33. Interview on 26 June 2003 and 7 April 2004.

34   The details of this story are based on information provided by Navaz Kotwal from the Commonwealth Human Rights Initiative, which supports the witnesses in their fight for justice.

35. Interview in Kalol on 7 April 2004.

36. Ibid.

37. According to eyewitnesses and residents of Delol.

38. Until April 2004. Later, proper houses were built for them close to the relief site.

39. Interview on 8 August 2003.

'The machineries of government stand between and hide the hearts of one people from those of another.'

—Mahatma Gandhi

6

Divide and Rule:
Elections

'If you repeat a lie often enough, it becomes the truth.'
—*Joseph Goebbels, Propaganda minister in Hitler's
government.*

What's the easiest way to win an election?
Simple—start a riot. Fuel hatred. Divide people. Make them fear each other. Keep the terror brewing.

Then project yourself as the saviour of the larger vote bank.

Voters should stop blaming you for their problems, so give them a scapegoat.

A sure-fire formula for victory. That, in a nutshell, was Narendra Modi's strategy.

The violence worked. In the state elections held in December 2002, the BJP's greatest gains were in riot affected areas. It captured fifty-two of the sixty-five riot affected constituencies.[1] But Gujarat's people paid the price. Over 1000 lives were lost, 1,50,000 were made refugees and peace was ruined.

Before the pogrom began on 27 February 2002, the BJP's popularity seemed to be on the downslide. The Congress had swept the district and taluka panchayat elections in 2000.[2] It continued to win every subsequent by-election.[3] A nervous BJP central command brought in hardliner Narendra Modi as chief minister to rescue the sinking ship.

On the evening of 27 February 2002, when the Sabarmati Express was burned, the BJP saw it as an opportunity to engineer an election win. The next day, Sangh Parivar mobs unleashed a pogrom. Mainly Congress strongholds in north and central Gujarat were targeted during the violence. However, Ahmedabad, a BJP stronghold, experienced the worst carnage.

In the 1998 state elections, there were ninety-six seats where the Congress and the All India Rashtriya Janata Party's (AIRJP—a party formed by BJP rebel Shankarsinh Vaghela) combined vote was greater than the BJP vote. Later, Vaghela scrapped his party and merged it with the Congress. The BJP was scared of losing those seats because of the combined strength of its rivals. The places where the Congress–AIRJP combine would have won (Mehsana, Banaskantha, Kapadvanj, Dahod, Godhra, Kheda, Anand and Chotta Udaipur) are precisely the places that were targeted during the communal clashes. The only other places affected by riots which still showed a BJP lead were Ahmedabad and Vadodara. Even in the local government elections in 2000, the BJP lost heavily in central Gujarat—Kheda, Vadodara, Panchmahal. These were the areas worst hit by the 2002 riots.

Right until election day—12 December 2002—the Sangh Parivar built and sustained a climate of prejudice and paranoia. Local cadres kept intimidation and insecurity brewing in villages and ghettos. After Godhra, they kept instilling the fear of Muslim terrorists and criminals through rumours, pamphlets and meetings. In some villages affected by the communal violence, Sangh activists enforced a boycott of Muslims. Modi's Gaurav Yatra played on irrational fears of terrorist attacks. The propaganda was all-pervasive.

The strategy of hate and violence paid off. The BJP won the state elections in December 2002 decisively with 126 of 181 seats, improving on its previous tally of 117 seats. Its vote percentage increased from 44.81 per cent in the 1998 assembly election to 49.8 per cent this time.[4]

Close to Godhra, in central Gujarat's Panchmahal, Dahod and rural Vadodara, where the worst carnage occurred in rural Gujarat, the BJP won all the seats. The Congress didn't win a single seat in what was until now considered its main stronghold—the adivasi areas. In Ahmedabad, which also saw the most ghastly violence, the BJP got ten of twelve seats in the city. In all the BJP got forty-two of the fifty seats in central Gujarat and thirty-five of the fifty-two seats in north Gujarat, the two regions most affected by the communal violence. In the highly controversial Godhra seat, the BJP nominated former Bajrang Dal chief Haresh Bhatt, who defeated the sitting Congress MLA Rajendra Patel.

In places untouched by riots, the BJP lost ground. In Kutch, it got only two out of six seats as compared to four in the previous election. A reflection, perhaps, of the anger with the corruption and inadequacy of earthquake relief. Kutch is also perennially drought prone, and in 2002 it was suffering the fourth successive year of water shortage. But the BJP government hadn't yet started drought relief work, although people were desperate. In Saurashtra, where the water crisis is acute, the BJP slipped from forty-eight of fifty-two seats in 1998 to just thirty-seven in 2002. This region is also former chief minister Keshubhai Patel's stronghold. Patel voters here were upset that Modi had ousted their leader. In south Gujarat, both the Congress (eleven seats) and BJP (ten seats) got an almost equal number of constituencies. Here, the Congress gained seats as compared to the last election, a hint of an anti-incumbency vote.

Another indication of people's disgust—seventy-six seats changed hands between this and the previous election.[5] Nine ministers including the speaker of the assembly lost their seats.[6] These include Modi's close aide and cabinet spokesperson Purushottam Rupala from Amreli, finance minister Nitin Patel from Kadi, industries minister and former chief minister Suresh Mehta from Mandvi in Kutch. Congress stalwarts Naresh Raval, who was leader of the opposition in the previous assembly, and senior MLA Dinsha Patel were also defeated in this election. Shankarsinh Vaghela's son Mahendra also lost from Sami in north Gujarat.

The Congress defeat was not surprising considering that its cadre had been virtually non-functional. Over the years, the Sangh has been systematically setting up a wide network of shakhas throughout the state. Even the Congress's tried and tested KHAM formula failed this time, mainly because the party didn't take a very firm stand against the violence. It spread itself too thin. The Congress played a defensive kind of soft Hindutva to counter the BJP. It didn't work. The Congress's choice of Vaghela as leader also worked against the party. He is seen as a discredited politician after his defection from the BJP, and has had allegations of horse-trading directed at him.

Only in the last few weeks before election day did the Congress get its act together. Until then, rival camps were squabbling over ticket allotments. Their election campaign had no clear direction and was badly organized. On the other hand, the BJP's campaign of hate stretched over ten months. People were overwhelmed with Godhra propaganda—posters, T-shirts, advertisements, banners, SMS messages, video clips. Gujaratis weren't allowed to forget the burning train even if they wanted to. Chief minister Narendra Modi would talk about it at every public meeting.

While Modi kept on harping about terrorism, he didn't mention the Sangh terrorists who planned and executed the riots. Who would protect the people from them?

Immediately after the BJP victory was announced, Modi forgot Godhra. It was now time to switch to talking about development, an issue totally sidelined in his campaign. 'The victory is not that of any political party, but of Gujarat's self-respect. We will try to live up to their expectations and work for the welfare of the common man,' said the victorious CM at a press conference. 'Whoever tried to spread venom has been defeated . . . People have given their verdict and now it is the turn of the media to accept the truth and be accountable for its false propaganda in the past ten months . . . For God's sake, stop dividing Gujarat,' he said.[7]

Yet, the violence continued. Two people were killed— one in Rajkot and another in Vadodara—when BJP victory processions passed through Muslim areas and allegedly shouted provocative slogans. A cameraman was assaulted outside the BJP office after results were announced. On election day curfew was imposed in Jambusar, Vadodara district, and conflicts also broke out in Godhra, Anand, Mehsana and Kheda.

The victory celebrations were full of bravado. Hardliners within the BJP and VHP were extremely chuffed. 'The Hindutva laboratory has started functioning . . . the BJP has won all the three seats in Rajasthan assembly by-elections too. A Hindu Rashtra can be expected in the next two years . . . we will change India's history and Pakistan's geography by then,' said Praveen Togadia.[8] Togadia has been trying to replicate the Gujarat experiment in Rajasthan. 'When madrasas in various parts of the country can train jehadis, why can't the VHP set up its Hindutva laboratory? Gujarat has turned out to be a graveyard for secular forces,' he said.

The Congress camp, on the other hand, conceded defeat. Gujarat Congress president Shankarsinh Vaghela accepted responsibility for the downfall. At a press conference, he said, 'People did not accept our offer of "Peace, Happiness, Prosperity and Security". Instead, they opted for "*Maro, Kato, Jalao*" (Attack, Hack, Burn). In the coming days, the youth who voted for them will ask for jobs. People in drought-hit areas will ask for relief works. Will the BJP be able to provide it?'

The day after—Lok Sabha elections
His rival's words proved prophetic. As the communal frenzy fizzled out, voters sobered down to confront everyday realities. Narendra Modi didn't seem to be the larger-than-life king any more. There was more hype than action. His publicity blitz promised several new irrigation and development schemes, but delivered very little.

Modi's most unpopular decision was to hike electricity tariffs for farmers. Already an expensive proposition, the government made agriculture even less profitable by announcing an almost threefold hike in power—from Rs 350 per horsepower (hp) to Rs 1050 per hp. The BJP's farmers wing, the Bharatiya Kisan Sangh (BKS), was the first to turn against him.

With cultivators furious, the BKS launched an eight-month-long agitation against the power hike. After months of animosity, the government agreed to reduce the rate to Rs 750 per hp, still more than double the original rate. Lalji Patel, a senior RSS leader and BKS founder, went on a hunger strike against Modi's adamant stand. Finally, a settlement was reached in which the chief minister budged by reducing the rate by a further Rs 50 per hp. BKS members were livid not only with Modi, but also with their own leaders for caving in so easily.

The BKS is dominated by Patels, a powerful farming community that comprises around 16 to 20 per cent of the population. They have played an influential role in the state's politics. Ousted chief minister Keshubhai Patel supported the BKS struggle from the sidelines. The BJP in Gujarat paid the price for displeasing farmers and the Patel lobby in the Lok Sabha elections of May 2004.

It just about managed to retain its edge over the Congress, winning fourteen of the twenty-six seats. In the previous Lok Sabha elections in 1999, it had gained a thumping majority with twenty-one seats. The BJP's downturn came as a surprise even for the Congress, which more than doubled its previous tally.

Soon after the Lok Sabha verdict, BJP MLAs turned against Modi and demanded his removal. Many were fed up with his autocratic style of functioning. The only thing holding back the rebellion backed by the Keshubhai Patel camp was the BJP's central command. Several of the BJP's allies in the central government like the Shiv Sena, the DMK and the Telugu Desam Party (TDP) also felt that Modi's complicity in the Gujarat communal violence had contributed to their defeat.

Former PM Atal Bihari Vajpayee told the media that the Gujarat violence was one of the factors that led to the party's rout from the central government.[9] It sounded like an excuse. What was Mr Vajpayee doing when Gujarat was burning? Why did it take him forty days to visit? Why did he let Narendra Modi remain in power when many were demanding his dismissal?

Was the violence really a deciding factor during the Lok Sabha elections? Not really. The vote across the country, including Gujarat, was against policies of a government that had failed to protect the poor.

During the 2002 state elections, Modi pursued an aggressive communal campaign to divert attention from real problems and squelch the simmering discontent against larger economic policies. In the parliamentary elections discontent returned—voters seemed to have wisened up. Many were still reeling from the economic after-effects of the violence. Narendra Modi hadn't delivered much more than gimmicks and propaganda. Water scarcity and unemployment were the two major problems affecting people.

'If they had not raised the communal issue, the BJP would have lost the state elections. Now, people realize that they were fooled. The BJP governments at the state and centre have done nothing about the unemployment and law and order problems,' said Shankarsinh Vaghela, leader of the Gujarat Congress.[10]

The BJP government in Gujarat will have to focus on rural problems which have been ignored for too long. As one farmer put it, 'If they can build so many highways, then why can't they also start constructing canals?'[11]

The gaali yatra

Halol, 11 November 2002. This weary industrial town had never hosted such a spectacle. The bright lights and saffron flags attracted restless crowds. They waited anxiously to catch a glimpse of the chief minister, but they were in for a long wait. His chariot was stuck in the mud.

Modi's new-age rath—a custom-made luxury bus fitted with hydraulic lifts and its own hi-tech acoustic system—was stopped in its tracks by a punctured tyre. It was 10.30 p.m., and the crowd had been hanging around for more than two hours. The only ones happy with the delay were local food vendors who had set up shop outside the school ground.

Local musicians and comedians tried desperately to entertain the crowd. After the musicians had exhausted their repertoire and the comedian had run out of NRI jokes, local BJP workers started with their speeches. 'We are so happy our chief minister Narendra Modi is coming here. It's like raining gold,' announced a local BJP leader. As he kept singing praises of '*Gujarat no sher*' (lion of Gujarat), a party pooper shouted, 'What are you going to do for the unemployed? So many factories here are closing. People like me with an M.Com. cannot get jobs.' Immediately, local BJP leaders jumped out of the 'VIP enclosure' and whisked him away.

'On 12 December, there will be a war. We will be the soldiers in that war,' said a local BJP leader. Even those ranting speeches ran out of breath. Then, there was just silent anticipation. The commander in chief's chariot finally drove in. Music blared from the speakers attached to the rath. Narendrabhai sat in the front, waving at the crowd. When the chariot stopped, two doors opened and a stage emerged carrying the 'sher'. Unfortunately, we missed the spectacle of seeing Modi appear in the hydraulic lift dome at the top of the bus. It was out of order. There were chants: *'Dekho, Dekho kaun aya! Gujarat ka sher aya.'* (Look who's come! The lion of Gujarat). The magic show over, the theatrics began.

In an electronically engineered fierce tone, Modi made digs at and threatened his Congress rivals and, ridiculously enough, 'Miya Musharraf'. He said, 'Miya Musharraf wants to kill us. Miya listen—you can kill one Narendra Modi but 1000 Narendra Modis will rise then.' With that threat, his stage folded back, the doors closed. The music started as the rath left, with children running after it.

All the Gaurav Yatra stops didn't wrap up as peacefully. One meeting at Morbi in Surendranagar ended with a shower of chappals (slippers).[12] The crowd, which had endured Modi's spiteful speech so that they could hear the local Mahesh–Naresh orchestra play at the end, suddenly turned violent. All hell broke loose. They flung chappals and chairs. Some flying objects broke the halogen lights, making it more difficult to see in the darkness. A fire ignited on the stage, caused by a short circuit. Frightened orchestra musicians hurled a huge speaker into the crowd. The local legislator, who organized the show, flung a microphone into the crowd in a fit of rage. One of the CM's aides slapped a volunteer. He claimed he was trying to 'disperse the crowd'. The police lathi-charged the audience in an effort to break up the brawl.

Even before it was flagged off, Modi's Gujarat Gaurav Yatra was the source of much amusement, histrionics, conflict and controversy. It was a Yatra to 'restore Gujarat's pride'. Actually, it was election campaigning before polls had even been announced. Scheduled to start in July 2002, the chariot was kept waiting in the wings because the Election

Commission and NHRC were against it, fearing it would vitiate the atmosphere in the state.[13]

Once the NHRC/EC obstacle was cleared, Congress rival Vaghela put a spoke in the wheel. He organized a counter puja at the Bhattiji temple in Phagvel, from where the yatra was to be flagged off, on the same day. The stage was set for a confrontation. There were rumours that the villagers, strong Vaghela supporters, would not allow the chief minister to enter. Finally, Modi backed down and started off his Gaurav yatra a few days later.

Even as some incidents of violence continued to spark off from time to time, Modi continued with his yatra. As a part of the chest-thumping exercise, he mostly spewed his venom at the places where violence occurred—Pandharvada, Dahod, Godhra. In Kalol, he held his public meeting at Ambica Society, the place where thirteen were burned in a tempo. In Lunawada, he gave a speech at the same street corner where a jeep full of people was burned. Fearing trouble, Muslims shut their shops along the route that the yatra passed through.

There was also a fair share of tokenism. A BJP MLA at Mendarda, near Junagadh, made the local Sunni Muslim Samiti organize a welcome programme for Modi. Five of its members stood by, their heads shaved, with lotuses painted on to show 'solidarity with the BJP'. An hour before the yatra arrived, the BJP media cell had called up newspapers and told them about the unique welcome.[14]

There were meetings held specially for women. Dressed in saffron saris, women garlanded the chief minister. Getting carried away with their own publicity drive, a BJP public relations officer told me, 'Never before has any chief minister been so popular. Not only is he hero-worshipped, but the women also see him as some kind of sex symbol. People have even started discussing his clothes, his spectacles, his image.'[15]

Children were also roped into the circus. They were made to abandon school, wear saffron flags and cheer Modi en route. Schoolchildren carried BJP flags and pots with slogans like '*Aapnu kaun? BJP.*' (Who's there for us? BJP.) In Kalol, about 300 girls from KGM School waited for Modi for two hours in the sun, balancing pots on their heads, and in Dhamasana village, boys from H.S. Patel High School were doing the cheering and waving. Local BJP leaders had instructed the teachers to enlist their students in the cheering squad. One teacher complained that despite promises that students would get 'biscuits and water' they got nothing.[16]

Modi kept feeding the media regular doses of quotable lines. He made digs at '*Italy ki beti*' (Italy's daughter), Lyngdoh and 'Miya Musharraf'. At Bechraji (Mehsana district), he made a speech saying, 'We must teach a lesson to those who multiply like this.'[17] The state IB suggested filing a case against the chief minister for instigating communal feelings. Soon after, R.B. Sreekumar, an IB official, was transferred.

Although it was criticized by the national media, the NHRC and the EC, there is no doubt that Modi's yatra struck a chord with people. Using theatrics to manipulate fear and insecurity, he became the 'Hindu hero'. Moreover, he was probably the only politician who travelled extensively throughout the state for months before the elections. Even if he didn't deliver on the state's development, at least he provided excitement.

The only safe bearded man in Gujarat

During the communal riots, a joke doing the rounds was that the only bearded man who was safe in Gujarat was Narendra Modi. Since then, Modi has created a cult of personality around himself. The fifty-four-year-old chief minister fashioned himself as a Hindutva hero, a saviour. Hardline Hindutva was in vogue, and it was all thanks to the bearded former RSS pracharak.

This larger-than-life personality grew up in Vadnagar, a small town in Mehsana, north Gujarat. His family is from the Ghanchi community (traditionally, oil millers; an OBC caste). He left Vadnagar to study political science in Gujarat University, Ahmedabad. As a student, Modi worked at his brother's canteen at the city's state transport bus depot. He also got involved in student politics and was an active member of the Akhil Bharatiya Vidyarthi Parishad (ABVP), the student wing of the BJP. At some point he got married to Jashodaben, but they separated soon after the wedding. Jashodaben is now a primary school teacher in a village near Vadnagar.

Modi left the ABVP to join the RSS, where he became a pracharak. He lived and worked for several years at the RSS headquarters in Maninagar, Ahmedabad, which is now his constituency. While in the RSS he was also a leader of the Gujarat Lok Sangharsh Samiti in 1972, which was initiated by Jaiprakash Narayan and was part of the anti-corruption Navnirman Andolan. Modi participated in the anti-Emergency movement in 1975.

Later, his RSS mentors sent him to the BJP. In 1985, Modi worked with Shankarsinh Vaghela in the Gujarat BJP, now his greatest rival in the opposition Congress. While Vaghela was the president of the Gujarat BJP, Modi was the General Secretary. Modi was involved with strategy and campaign planning, while Vaghela built the BJP's grassroots cadres. It was Modi who was the main organizer of L.K. Advani's Ram Janmabhoomi rath yatra in 1989.

After Keshubhai Patel was made chief minister in 1995, he ensured Modi's swift transfer out of Gujarat, sensing that he could create trouble. Modi left for New Delhi to work in the all-India BJP. He was responsible for building the state units of Haryana, Punjab, Chandigarh, Himachal Pradesh and Jammu and Kashmir. 'Whichever state he has gone to, Modi has created dissidence within the party, and trouble with coalition partners. Wherever he has gone, state units have asked for his removal,' says a BJP insider.

Modi was suddenly sent back to Gujarat as chief minister in October 2001. This came as a rude shock to Keshubhai Patel, who is still sulking about this. Patel was seen as a non-performer. The BJP had lost all elections after the 1998 assembly elections, and in 2000, the BJP was totally routed, losing twenty-one of twenty-three seats in the Panchayat elections. Later it lost two assembly by-elections, including the Sabarmati seat, located in L.K. Advani's parliamentary constituency, Gandhinagar. Fearing a similar disaster in the assembly elections, the national command decided to send Advani's man to Gujarat. Modi had never contested a single election before. He was elected from Rajkot-II constituency with a reduced margin of 14,000 seats, much less than the BJP's previous 28,000 lead.

Known for being rude, arrogant and egoistic, Modi upset several MLAs soon after becoming chief minister. He especially insisted on the resignation of former home minister Haren Pandya, who was close to Keshubhai Patel.

Just after Modi was elected CM, a BJP insider told me, 'So far he has had it easy. He hasn't had to deal much with MLAs. Even in that short span of time, he antagonized many. Now will be the true test of how he manages to keep MLAs happy. Knowing his autocratic style of functioning, Vaghela may not need to engineer defections. Modi may drive them away himself.'

He was right. In June 2004 Modi faced a crisis of confidence within the Gujarat BJP. Unhappy MLAs were demanding his dismissal, and former prime minister Atal Bihari Vajpayee indirectly supported the dissidents by blaming the Gujarat violence as one of the factors responsible for the party's Lok Sabha defeat.[18] Once again, his mentors within the BJP high command came to his rescue and contained the embarrassment.

As chief minister, Modi has not pleased the electorate. This was a major reason for the BJP's loss of seven constituencies in the Lok Sabha elections in 2004. His governance is more hype than actual work. Modi announced several new schemes and always has his picture splashed across posters and advertisements. However, he hasn't done much to address the main problems faced by people—water shortages, unemployment, the agriculture crisis, industrial closures.

Yet, his public functions and speeches full of bravado made him '*Gujarat no sher*'. Modi also likes to call himself '*Chotta Sardar*' (Little Sardar) after Sardar Patel, the freedom fighter who became India's first home minister. With time, however, his popularity has abated. Because of his authoritarian ways, there is growing opposition to him. His roar is not as loud any more.

Modi-isms

- 'If Congress wins, they will burst firecrackers in Pakistan. If the BJP wins, India will celebrate Diwali. You choose.'[19]
- 'It is not an election for MLAs or choosing a chief minister. It is an election related to religion.'[20]
- 'This is the deciding moment. If you want to save the state from the clutches of fundamentalists and jehadis you must all vote . . . If you want to sleep well till 2007, wake up on December 12 and vote. Come out in large numbers and kick the jehadis and the fundamentalists out. I assure you that if you keep awake for one day on Thursday I will keep awake for you for five years.'[21]
- 'This is a fight which will decide who is the protector of Hindus . . . When we talk of protecting Hindus, there's objection from certain quarters who talk of "Hindu militancy". Hindus can never be militants. And militants cannot be Hindu. If some day a group of Hindus becomes militants, they will rule the world and Pakistan

will be wiped out.'[22]

- 'Before you vote, think for a moment: you have a car, you have everything under the sun but what if your son does not return home alive in the evening? Until there is no security, there is no progress.'[23]

- 'If all the destinations where Lord Ram travelled between Ayodhya and Lanka are joined, they will all pass through the tribal areas of India. So the tribals are the original Hindus who are being abducted by the Swarn Mrigs (golden deer) who are roaming freely in the jungle.'[24]

- 'We do not want to continue to run relief camps to produce children. We wish to go towards family planning. But for some people that means "*Hum paanch, hamare pacchees*" (Us five, our twenty-five).'

- 'They keep on giving birth to long queues of children, who keep repairing cycle punctures everywhere. We must teach a lesson to those who multiply like this.'[25]

- 'We brought Narmada waters during Shravan but the Congress would have wanted it in Ramzan.'

- 'I would like to specifically tell the Muslims of Signal Falia that instead of sheltering the antisocial elements responsible for the Godhra carnage they should have isolated them at that time. But they failed to do so and today their heads are down in shame.'[26]

- 'Congress has always been supporting criminals and anti-social elements. Even when the Muslims of Godhra killed a Sindhi family they did not condemn it.'[27]

- 'Musharraf should remember that if he tries to create any problem with the people of Gujarat then the Hindus would become terrorists who will remove Pakistan from the world map.'[28]

- 'I have been to Godhra. I have seen the bodies, the shrunken, charred, shrivelled bodies of the women and children and boys. I cannot forget Godhra. For me, Godhra is not an election issue. It is an issue that concerns humanity. I swear to you that the criminals of Godhra will not go unpunished. How the women, children and men must have shrieked when they were being burnt. Can man be so evil? And I am asked to forget Godhra. How can I?'[29]

• 'Congress men cannot see Gujarat's Gaurav because they are wearing Italian spectacles.'[30]

• 'Is Lyngdoh from Italy? He and Sonia Gandhi could be meeting each other at church.'[31]

Voting for survival

Just getting to the voting booth was an achievement. Huddled in a truck, refugees from Delol went back to their village to cast their vote. They had a police escort, but they didn't want to set foot inside the village, just to the polling booth and back into the truck. Women dared not step down from the truck. 'It's still very tense. So many were killed,' said Rabiaben Sheikh, from Delol village, whose son was murdered in the violence. 'Our farm is here. But it isn't safe for us here. It's better for us to stay in Kalol,' she said.[32]

They feared violence, but were determined to participate in the polls. 'We were the first at the booth,' said Bismillahbibi Kazi from Pavagadh village in Panchmahal. 'They had threatened that there would be riots if Muslims vote. So we went early before they could start any trouble. Our vote shouldn't be wasted.'[33]

'I'm getting a sinking feeling in my stomach,' said Shehnaz Sheikh as we walked through her village, Pavagadh, in Panchmahal. She hadn't yet returned home after the communal riots in March. Pavagadh is a religious site visited by several pilgrims and tourists. Muslim stalls en route to the temple were burned and captured. Local goons still threw stones at Muslim homes and shouted insults at the few who had returned to their homes. 'The Bajrang Dal boys don't want us back. They can do anything; they could rape us,' said Rashida, Shehnaz's sister-in-law. But they braved the threats to cast their vote. 'We won't stay long. We'll just see our house and go back to Halol,' she said.[34] Their family lives in a rented room in the nearby town.

Others were too afraid to even sneak a peek at their houses. 'What's there to see? We'll just sit in the jeep and rush back to Halol,' said Hameeda Sheikh, a widow. She didn't have a husband to escort her. 'They drove us out and captured my tea shop. I can't support my kids any more. We are still living off rations given by the relief committee,' she said.

While some went back home, others fled their homes on election day. In Naroda Patiya, people left for their relatives' homes. 'See, almost all the houses are locked. People will return only after the results are announced. Some have stayed on to vote early. Then, they will also leave,' said Irshad Sayyed, a young resident. Relief committees had arranged to bring refugees from Naroda Patiya who had now been rehabilitated in Vatva back to the booth to vote.

The EC took every precaution to ensure that the ballot was accessible to Muslims. Its efforts seemed to have paid off; Muslims were determined to go out and vote. Muslims comprise 9 per cent of Gujarat's population. A community that was persecuted during the communal violence now wanted to make its voice heard.

'Even if the Congress puts up a crook, we will elect him, and if the BJP nominates a God, we will chase him off,' said Rashid, a paan vendor from Maninagar.[35] 'The BJP has sown so much poison and destroyed so many lives that even little kids feel the Hindu–Muslim divide,' he added.

However, some in central Gujarat's tribal belt, a traditional Congress stronghold, were wary of the party. But they were left with no other choice. 'The BJP started it all. But Congress leaders here did nothing to protect us. It makes no difference who we give our vote to. No one helps us,' said Rafiq Gudala, a shopkeeper in Fatehgunj, Dahod district, whose house and shop were burned during the violence.[36] Many Muslims were in a dilemma similar to Rafiq's. Although unhappy with the Congress, it was their only choice. For instance, in Godhra, several Muslims didn't want to support the Congress candidate, sitting MLA Rajendrasinh Patel. Many of them alleged that he participated in the riots. But pitted against the BJP candidate, Haresh Bhatt (the local Bajrang Dal chief), who was the lesser evil?

During the polls, even refugees in relief camps were attacked. Two were killed when violence broke out on 11 November 2002 in Dasaj village in Mehsana district. Local Patels were determined to drive away the hundred-odd families from other villages who took shelter here. While both communities blame the other for attacking first, the reason for the clash is clear. 'We don't want outside Muslims to settle here. Their majority keeps increasing. Around 184 new Muslim voters are now registered here,' said Hasmukh Patel, a local landowner. 'In July, we held a Hindu sammelan in the village, during which we decided to cut all ties with them. We took back the land that we had given them to till as sharecroppers. Maybe that's why they decided to get back at us.'

The Muslims, whose houses were burned, had a different story to tell. 'They had been planning this for a long time,' said Sattarbhai Khatri, a refugee from Unjha village.[37] 'We were attacked at the end of a three-day festival organized for the installation of a temple in the village. Thousands of people had come from outside.' Sajid Khan, a long-time Dasaj resident,[38] added, 'The local rabadis (lower castes) had warned us that we would be attacked at 9 p.m.' Houses were burned during the attack, mainly in the basti where refugees had settled. 'Refugees have been registered here. But Muslims will only vote if the collector's office organizes a separate booth. We cannot go into their basti. It's too dangerous. Our children can't even go to the secondary school which is located there,' said Sajid.[39]

The EC found that around 4,00,000 voters had shifted after the communal riots. Of these, it was not yet clear how many were displaced due to the riots and how many migrated for other reasons. Around 1,71,000 had been traced to their new homes, while 2,29,000 were yet to be found.[40] Those who were traced, like the refugees in Dasaj, were registered in their new neighbourhood. Even those living in relief camps were listed as voters in the location of the relief camp.

At the relief camp at Vadali in Sabarkantha district, refugees were added to the electoral rolls. 'We have asked for a special booth here,' said camp organizer Amanullah Khan Pathan. The camp houses around 150 families who have been prevented from returning to their homes in Khed Brahma, Lakshmipura, Kariadra, Derol and surrounding villages. 'It's not safe for us to go back. Even those who returned to their homes keep running back to the camp whenever there is any rally or Gaurav Yatra. They even chased away a charitable trust that wanted to rebuild our houses,' said Nooriben Mansoori from Lakshmipura.[41] The fear that the smallest provocation could spark trouble was felt both in the cities as well as the villages. The attackers still seemed to have the upper hand, and had managed to keep the fear alive.

Some involved in the riots were even rewarded with election nominations. The most prominent was Dr Maya Kodnani. Several victims had named Kodnani in their police statements, but her name has not been mentioned in the FIRs. Another controversial BJP candidate was Jitu Vaghela, who was behind bars for more than a month for rioting in Gomtipur. Bajrang Dal leader Haresh Bhatt was also nominated to stand for election from Godhra. His 'boys' had executed several attacks.

Right until the end of the election campaign, the BJP kept insecurity brewing. It capitalized on an advertisement issued by the All India Muslim Ulema Council[42] appealing to 'secular-minded people to vote for the Congress to defeat fascist forces'. Calling it a 'Muslim fatwa', the VHP published a counter-campaign saying, 'Now is the time for the Hindus to become decisive for their safety . . . vote 100 per cent.' The BJP kept reminding people to counter the 'fatwa'. The mention of the word 'fatwa' annoyed many Hindus; making them more determined to defeat it. The BJP's strategy worked.

As Rashid from Maninagar put it, 'This time, we don't care. Even if our houses are burning, we will go to take part in the election.'[43]

The minorities' will to vote was not driven by any fatwa. It was pure survival instinct.

Notes

1. Yogendra Yadav, 'The patterns and lessons', *Frontline*, 3 January 2003.
2. Ghanshyam Shah, 'Contestation and negotiations: Hindutva sentiments and temporal interests in Gujarat elections', *Economic and Political Weekly*, 30 November 2002.
   In the September–October 2000 local government elections, the BJP lost its hold over all 19 district panchayats (in the 1995 elections, it won 18 of 19 district panchayats.) In the taluka panchayats, the BJP got only 33 per cent of the seats (earlier, it had held 67 per cent of seats.) In the municipal elections, the BJP lost 5 out of 6 municipal corporations, including Rajkot, which it had held for more than twenty years.
3. In the 2000 by-elections held for one Lok Sabha and one assembly seat, the Congress won both. After Modi came to power, by-elections were held for three assembly seats, including his own. While he won the Rajkot-II seat, the BJP lost the other two seats.
4. Yogendra Yadav, 'The patterns and lessons', *Frontline*, 3 January 2003. www.floonnet.com/fl1926/stories/20030103007901000.htm
5. Ibid.
6. 'Nine BJP ministers, assembly speaker meet their Waterloo', Press Trust of India, Ahmedabad, 15 December 2002, http://www.

hindustantimes.com/news/5905_120512%2C000900040003. htm

7. 'For God's sake, stop dividing Gujarat: Modi'. http://www.rediff.com/election/elecmain.htm
    Defeat for pseudo-secularists: Modi, http://www.rediff. com/election/elecmain.htm
8. '"Hindu Rashtra" in two years: Togadia', Press Trust of India, 15 December 2002, http://www.rediff.com/election/2002/dec/15guj13.htm
9. 'A month later, Vajpayee admits: Gujarat a reason', *Indian Express*, 12 June 2004.
10. Interview in May 2004.
11. Interview on 26 May 2004.
12. Sudhir Vyas, 'Crowd caned after CM's yatra speech at Morbi', Times News Network, 29 October 2002, http://timesofindia. indiatimes.com/articleshow/26592365.cms
13. 'Gujarat is not yet ready for polls: EC team', Times News Network, 9 August 2002.
14. 'Head-hunter Modi showcases Muslims', *Indian Express*, 16 September 2002,
15. Conversation in BJP office in Ahmedabad on 11 December 2002.
16. 'School kids told to roll out saffron carpet', *Indian Express*, 9 September 2002.
17. Darshan Desai, 'Dark Descent', *Outlook*, 23 September 2002.
18. 'A month later, Vajpayee admits: Gujarat a reason', *Indian Express*, 12 June 2004.
19. 'Modi's final pitch: Cong win Pak win', Express News Service, 10 December 2002.
20. Ibid.
21. Ibid.
22. Janyala Sreenivas, ' Modi returns to "G" word, says Cong will free Godhra accused,' *Indian Express*, 3 December, 2002.
23. 'PM listening, Modi to voters: What if your son doesn't return alive?' Express News Service, 10 December 2002.
24. Tanushree Chakraborty, 'Dangs' Tribals get a dose of Modi's Hindutva', *Indian Express*, 23 October 2002.
25. Darshan Desai, 'Dark descent', *Outlook*, 23 September 2002.
26. *Asian Age*, 11 November 2002.

27. Ibid.
28. *Sunday Express*, 19 October 2002.
29. Sujan Dutta, '*Beti* or *behn*, Modi sells a one-point message', *The Telegraph*, 11 December 2002, Modera, Patan district.
30. Anil Rana, 'Modi uses yatra to attack Sonia', *The Statesman*, 9 September 2002.
31. Deepal Trivedie, *The Asian Age*, 22 August 2002.
32. Interview on 12 December 2002—polling day.
33. Ibid.
34. Ibid.
35. Interview on 24 November 2002.
36. Interview on 25 November 2002.
37. Interview on 23 November 2002.
38. Ibid.
39. Ibid.
40. Interview with EC officials on 22 November 2002.
41. Interview on 23 November 2002.
42. Tanvir Siddiqui, 'The "Fatwa" that wasn't', *Indian Express*, 11 December 2002.
43. Interview on 24 November 2002.

'Truth is by nature self-evident. As soon as you remove
the cobwebs of ignorance that surround it,
it shines clear.'

—Mahatma Gandhi

7

Instigators or Informers: The Media

'It's also your fault,' a doctor in Ahmedabad told me. It was a year after the riots, but feelings were still strong. 'The media created the perception that riots were still on. That's why things didn't get back to normal soon.'

This was the icing on the cake—it wasn't the hero Narendra Modi, nor the angels from the Bajrang Dal, not even the police (what could they do?) who were blamed for the riots—no, it was the English press. They were the demons giving Gujarat a bad name. What would people abroad think? After all, they don't read the Gujarati papers, which tell us what we want to hear. Abroad, they read the English press, which said that Muslims were targeted.

I agree with my doctor friend. Some newspapers did fuel the riots in Gujarat. But he's blaming the wrong people. It wasn't the English media, but sections of the Gujarati press that sparked violence. Gujarat's largest selling newspapers—*Sandesh* and *Gujarat Samachar*—published false reports, rumours and biased reports that fanned the flames. Of the two, *Sandesh* was far more venomous.

On the day after the Godhra carnage itself, both newspapers reported that 'religious fanatics' pulled ten to fifteen girls off the train, kidnapped them and chopped off the breasts of two women. There was no basis to this report. When *Sandesh* staff contacted the district police superintendent, he told them that he had no knowledge of it. Still, they decided to publish it, based purely on rumours.[1]

The report stirred a lot of anger. Many riot victims blame this article for instigating trouble. Bajrang Dal activists used this story to round up people to join the mob. Later, Narendra Modi denied that the incident had occurred, but neither newspaper published a retraction. *Gujarat Samachar* printed a report saying that the article which appeared in *Sandesh* about the kidnapping of the women was false, but made no mention of their own blunder.[2]

Who cared as long as circulation rose? While Gujarat was burning, its leading newspapers were locked in a peculiar battle. It wasn't about who gets the news first, it was a race to be more provocative and communal. Both *Gujarat Samachar* and *Sandesh* raised the anti-Muslim pitch considerably. In many ways, they aided the VHP's propaganda machinery, stoking the fires and fuelling hatred. It was as if *Sandesh* had become the VHP's mouthpiece.

The day after the Sabarmati Express massacre, *Sandesh*'s front page headline screamed, '*Khoon ka Badla Khoon*' (Avenge Blood with Blood).[3] The article that followed was a VHP press statement. (The same slogan was shouted by a mob mourning the death of Indira Gandhi in Delhi in 1984, and was broadcast by Doordarshan.)[4]

On 1 March 2002, the day after the VHP's Bharat Bandh, a news item in *Sandesh* reprimanded Bhavnagar's leaders for maintaining peace. 'Hindus were burnt alive in Godhra. Leaders of Bhavnagar did not even throw a stone in the name of bandh. Ahmedabad, Vadodara, Rajkot had partly avenged the killing of Hindus in Godhra. In the case of Bhavnagar, the gutless leaders are hiding their faces under the guise of non-violence,' the report stated. Another headline in *Sandesh* on 2 March read, 'Bapunagar reels under blind private firing all day. If you do not kill the enemy they will kill you.'[5]

To increase circulation, you have to please the majority. The Hindu sentiment was paramount. Feeding communal stereotypes, they described Muslims as 'terrorists' and 'religious fanatics', while glorifying Hindus as 'devotees'. Areas with large Muslim populations were called 'dangerous mini-Pakistans'. Even when Muslims were killed, it was their fault. In fact, the residents of Tandalja in Vadodara were so upset by the malicious campaign against their neighbourhood (which is predominantly Muslim but also houses 7000 Hindus) that they filed several complaints against *Sandesh*.[6]

In several instances, *Sandesh* misreported events or selectively described them portraying Muslim victims as the perpetrators of violence. It published a false report about firing in Tandalja, although no such incident had occurred. *Sandesh* later printed a clarification after residents complained. But the damage was already done. A sub-heading in *Sandesh* on 4 March 2004 wrongly reported that the collector had proposed that the neighbourhood should be declared a 'disturbed area'. As a result, people were scared to go there. Milk vans and auto-rickshaws refused to enter, although there was no curfew or violent incident in the area.

They didn't even spare the relief camps. A banner headline in *Sandesh* on 15 March warned, 'In the name of shelter, migrants from other states enter city'. The article alleged that Muslim leaders were using relief camps as an excuse to set up illegal colonies.[7] If only the reporter had met one of the thousands of Muslim refugees, he would have realized they were longing to go back home. Hounded out, they had nowhere to go but the miserable camps.

The two giants of the Gujarati press have a record of notoriety. Judicial commissions of inquiry probing into the riots of 1969, 1981 and 1985 have blamed them for inciting violence. During the 2002 carnage, R.B. Sreekumar, additional DGP (intelligence), wrote to Ashok Narayan, additional chief secretary (home), two months after the pogrom, recommending that publications which provoked violence should be punished. But no action has been taken against them, because they are too powerful. Their role is similar to that of the Shiv Sena's mouthpiece *Saamna* during the Bombay riots in 1992–93. Shiv Sena chief Bal Thackeray had published provocative articles against Muslims. Under pressure from human rights activists, cases were filed against him, but no action was taken for several years. In July 2000 his old rival Chaggan Bhujbal initiated action against him when he became home minister in Maharashtra's Congress–NCP alliance government, but it was merely a political drama—Thackeray was arrested and immediately released on bail for only one such case.

In the 1985 riots, *Gujarat Samachar* supported the anti-reservation agitation against then CM Madhavsinh Solanki. Its circulation rose enormously then. Its coverage was so biased that two new publications, *Gujarat Today* and *Sambhav*, were born as a response. *Gujarat Today* reflects the voice of the minorities. Bhupat Vadodaria, a close friend of Solanki's, started *Sambhav*.

This time, compared to *Sandesh*, *Gujarat Samachar* was more restrained and even published positive stories of people helping each other. Probably this time, *Sandesh* didn't want to be left behind like in 1985, so it went all out to play on the popular mood.

Both newspapers are family-run businesses owned by conservative, upper-caste Hindus. The owners of *Sandesh* are Patels, a powerful business community. The owners of *Gujarat Samachar*, the Shahs, are Banias. Both communities form the core of the Sangh's support base. In an interview with the Editors' Guild Fact Finding Mission Report, the chief managing director and editor of *Sandesh*, Falgun Patel, described Gujarati newspapers as 'pro-Hindu', and criticized the English media for siding with the minority community.[8]

He described the Godhra incident as 'unforgettable', and

the reaction to it as 'justified'. Mr Patel admitted that his reporters did lose balance and were communalized all down the line. *Sandesh*, he said, 'editorializes the news' by 'balancing the news with its own version'. Patel also said that it was their editorial policy not to carry corrections and clarifications.[9]

It was a policy that had its rewards. Narendra Modi sent *Sandesh*'s editor a letter expressing appreciation for the newspaper's 'restrained' coverage of recent events in the best traditions of journalism.

Gujarat Samachar has a circulation of 8.1 lakh. *Sandesh* sells 7.05 lakh copies, Mr Patel told the Editors' Guild team. He claimed that *Sandesh*'s circulation had increased by 1.5 lakh copies since the violence began because of its 'pro-Hindu' stand. *Gujarat Samachar*'s owner-editor Shreyans Shah told the Guild team that circulation of his daily had increased by around 50,000 during the carnage. Sensationalism sells.

Gujarat 2002 was also the first widely televised riot. You could see the carnage 'live' in your drawing room. While people were being killed, the police did nothing to stop the violence.

As long as the channels kept televising footage of the burning train, the government didn't mind at all. The Sangh hoped that it would help incite people to come out on the streets during the VHP bandh the next day. But when the reports of the following days showed mobs in saffron bands armed and on the rampage, Modi was red in the face, and wanted to ban *Star News* for its critical reportage of the violence.

Many urban, middle-class Gujaratis like my doctor friend felt that the national English media—*Star News*, *The Times of India*—were 'biased against Hindus'. 'They only show Muslims who were attacked, and only Muslims in the camps. What about the Hindus who were killed?' he asked. What could the media do if the large majority of those killed were

Muslims? Yes, Hindus were killed, but the large majority of victims were Muslims and it was this community that was targeted. In the few incidents where Hindus were attacked, the press did report them, but the bulk of the coverage reflected the horror of the Muslims, because that was the truth.

Unlike national channels *Aaj Tak* and *Star News*, a few local television channels aired VHP propaganda. *JTV*, one of Vadodara's local channels, was the most vitriolic. 'It regularly broadcast provocative speeches by VHP leaders. It kept repeating gory footage of the Godhra massacre,' says Rohit Prajapati, a human rights activist. Many cable channels also broadcast jingoistic films like *Gadar*.

When the VHP insisted on holding a Ram Dhun rally[10] on 15 March 2002, the channel showed scenes of jubilation by the participants, but no scenes of the havoc they wreaked on Muslim localities along the way; it was almost as if the rally was a huge celebration. There was no reference to the tension in Vadodara—the rally was prohibited and many parts of the city were under curfew. Yet, Narendra Modi wanted to censor *Star News*, which was highlighting the police and state complicity in the crimes.

JTV remained unpunished. But the Vadodara police registered FIRs against local channels *News Plus* and *VNM*. They also suspended the licences of two cable operators. The commissioner felt that the cable networks had 'played havoc' by showing footage of rioting in Macchipith on 15 March 2002, and for repeating the footage the next day.

While images of the burning train were telecast so often that they were indelibly imprinted in public memory, why was there no mention of what happened before Godhra? Why were there no media reports about the trouble that kar sevaks created when the train stopped at Rudauli station in Uttar Pradesh on 24 February 2002, three days before the Godhra incident? They beat up people entering the train, jumped on their chests, stabbed them with knives and tridents, asking them to say 'Jai Shri Ram'. If this had been widely reported when it happened, would it have helped prevent the Godhra tragedy? Even after the burning of the train, when this incident came to light, no one from the media ever questioned the BJP or the VHP about it. It was never used to raise doubts about the government's claim that Godhra was a pre-planned terrorist attack.

For the first three or four months there were follow-ups in the English press, which put a lot of pressure on Narendra Modi, embarrassing him outside Gujarat. But eventually, the media tired of the story; they lost track of the trauma of the witnesses, of relief camps that were running more than a year after the violence. The media found it more convenient to focus on cases in cities like Ahmedabad and Vadodara. Only a few star witnesses like Zaheera, and later Bilkis, were tracked.

Zaheera's case became more controversial because she turned hostile in court and then disappeared from Vadodara. No doubt, Zaheera's turnaround, denying that she saw anything was very damaging to herself and to the process of justice for the victims. In fact, Zaheera and her family may not have even been fully aware of the legal problems and social isolation that it could bring. But here too, the media built her up as a heroine when she announced that BJP politicians forced her to turn hostile, and then just as quickly damned her as a villain when she turned to the other extreme denying her Supreme Court testimony. There was no nuanced understanding of what drove Zaheera to such extremes, the pressures that such high-profile witnesses face, how vulnerable they are and the trauma they have already undergone. Labels are far easier.

When Zaheera went back on her testimony before the Supreme Court, saying that she had been forced into making a statement by social activist Teesta Setalvad, *Tehelka* magazine did a sting operation showing that she had been paid to turn hostile in the Vadodara sessions court. But there were no answers as to why she turned hostile the second time round. *Tehelka* called her the 'Shame of Gujarat'. Why was Zaheera the chosen villain when not only in riot cases, but also in cases all over the country, witnesses are coerced with money into turning hostile? Any criminal lawyer will confirm that it happens, so why are riot victims expected to be angels upholding justice? Aren't they supposed to look out for their own safety, rather than rely on a police that allowed the attacks on them to begin with? There are many other riot cases in which the witnesses turned hostile, but the media didn't even report them. They were too far away from the cities.

There was little analysis or reflection on the lasting effects of the violence, on the continuing divide within Gujarat society, on why all this happened in the first place. There was no investigation on how the VHP had planned such large-scale attacks in different parts of the state, no reportage about the ways in which they had established such a vast network within the state.

During elections too, biases crept into the coverage. *India Today* distributed a lavish promotional CD about Narendra Modi just before the Gujarat state elections as part of a paid advertorial.

Despite a few flaws, the national media was excellent in their reportage of the violence, and let the rest of the world know what was happening in the first few days while Gujarat burned. Several journalists were attacked while on the job; were stopped by mobs on the road. A *Gujarat Today* office in Ahmedabad was ransacked. A VHP mob even pounced on the Editors' Guild team while they were at a meeting in Ahmedabad's Circuit House on 1 April 2002. The protesters pushed their way into the room and accused the editors of being one-sided and biased in their coverage.

Others paid a heavy price for insisting on reporting the truth. Sanjay, a crime reporter with *Sandesh*, wrote an article on a minor incident in the chawl next to the Jagannath temple in Ahmedabad. The temple is a spark plug in the city's communal history; several riots have started and spread from here. Sanjay's editor insisted that the temple was attacked and asked him to change his story. He refused. Sanjay picked up the phone and made his sub-editor check with the police commissioner and a temple trustee. Both confirmed that Sanjay's story was correct, but still the sub-editor insisted. The compromise was that the headline read: 'Attack on Jagannath temple foiled'. Sanjay paid for his honesty. The next morning, he got a call from the office asking him to hand in his resignation letter.

Sanjay was just a cog in a big machine. What actually happened didn't matter to those in power. It was more important to shape what people chose to believe was reality, to feed preconceived prejudices.

Between them, *Sandesh* and *Gujarat Samachar* have had a monopoly over the market. 'This has not only concentrated and centralized the power of the print media in Ahmedabad, but it has brought about a much greater uniformity of opinions and attitudes among literate Gujaratis. Both the print and the visual media have created over time a vertically and closely linked system of cultural and political communications which is overly marked by a majoritarian Hindu ethos,' says D.L. Sheth, a political analyst.[11] That monopoly was broken after the communal violence with the entry of a new newspaper, *Divya Bhaskar*. In a matter of months, *Divya Bhaskar*'s circulation had overtaken both giants, leaving them gaping. However, *Divya Bhaskar*'s stand is not very different from *Sandesh* or *Gujarat Samachar*'s, its entry into Gujarat was heralded by none other than Narendra Modi.

With the concentration of media ownership in the hands of a few, the variety of sources are diminishing, and the more powerful media houses are dictating the rules of the game. So while it may seem like there is a proliferation of media, the content doesn't vary much. Even with new newspapers

being launched, the reader doesn't have much of a choice.
    Eventually, even Sanjay had to shift to *Gujarat Samachar*.
Hobson's choice?

Notes

1. Interview with a *Sandesh* journalist who was present on the day
    when the story was being discussed.
2. Aakar Patel, Dileep Padgaonkar, B.G. Verghese, Rights and
    Wrongs, Ordeal by Fire in the Killing Fields of Gujarat, Editors'
    Guild Fact Finding Mission Report, New Delhi, 3 May 2002.
3. People's Union for Civil Liberties (PUCL) Vadodara, and Vadodara
    Shanti Abhiyan, *Violence in Vadodara: A Report*, 31 May 2002.
4. People's Union for Democratic Rights, People's Union for Civil
    Liberties, Report of a Joint Inquiry into the Causes and Impact of
    the Riots in Delhi from 31 October to 10 November 1984, p. 13.
5. People's Union for Civil Liberties (PUCL) Vadodara, and Vadodara
    Shanti Abhiyan, *Violence in Vadodara: A Report*, 31 May 2002.
6. One such complaint is with the Editors' Guild of India. See Aakar
    Patel, Dileep Padgaonkar, B.G. Verghese, Rights and Wrongs,
    Ordeal by Fire in the Killing Fields of Gujarat, Editors' Guild Fact
    Finding Mission Report, New Delhi, 3 May 2002.
7. People's Union for Civil Liberties (PUCL) Vadodara, and Vadodara
    Shanti Abhiyan, *Violence in Vadodara: A Report*, 31 May 2002.
8. Aakar Patel, Dileep Padgaonkar, B.G. Verghese, Rights and
    Wrongs, Ordeal by Fire in the Killing Fields of Gujarat, Editors'
    Guild Fact Finding Mission Report, New Delhi, 3 May 2002.
9. Ibid.
10. To lay the foundation stone for the construction of the Ram Temple
    in Ayodhya.
11. D.L.Sheth, 'Growth of Communal Polarization in Gujarat: The
    Making of a Hindutva Laboratory?', in Sandeep Pendse (ed.)
    Lessons from Gujarat, Vikas Adhyayan Kendra, Mumbai, 2003.

'No culture can live, if it attempts to be exclusive. There is no such thing as pure Aryan culture in existence today in India. Whether the Aryans were indigenous to India or were unwelcome intruders does not interest me much . . . my remote ancestors blended with one another with the utmost freedom and we of the present generation are a result of that blend.'

—Mahatma Gandhi

8

Looking Back:
Origins

'What's the big deal?' asked Rajat, a chartered accountant from Ahmedabad. 'It's not like we haven't had riots here before. We're used to it.'

'During festivals, some small riot breaks out in the walled city, especially during the rath yatra, Muharram and the kite-flying festival. The smallest little argument can spark trouble,' said Rajat.

Riots may not be a big deal for people like Rajat who live on the upmarket side of the Sabarmati river that flows through the city. They are rarely affected by the violence in the poorer parts of the city. But it's a question of life and death for those who live on the other side, where any fight can trigger riots.

Portraying Ahmedabad as a riot-prone city was a convenient way of justifying what happened after Godhra. The 2002 communal violence wasn't like any other small brawl in the walled city. There have been both minor and widespread conflicts in the past. The nature of these riots has changed over time, reflecting the politics of the period, since most major riots are politically instigated. However, in 2002 state collusion and lawlessness was of a kind never experienced before.

Riots in Gujarat before independence

The first record of a Hindu–Muslim riot in Gujarat can be traced back to 1714, when a rowdy bunch celebrating the spring festival of Holi accosted a Muslim on the street and threw gulal on him. Local leaders and priests entered the fray and the matter soon escalated into riots. The Muslim mob attacked the kazi's house because he was indifferent to their grievance, then they went on a loot and arson spree of shops and houses in the Hindu areas. The matter even reached the Mughal emperor in Delhi, who jailed people from both sides until they resolved their differences. Small incidents like these were reported in 1715, 1716, and during Maratha rule between 1732 and 1750.[1]

The conflicts then were different from the communal attacks of today. Many local fights took a communal turn. But these conflicts didn't lead to riots—the tussles were caused by clashes over business or personal rivalries. For instance, the riots in Surat in 1795 between Bania and Muslim traders happened because the Banias allied with the British.[2] Quarrels were within localities rather than between communities.[3]

Earlier conflicts were not only between Hindus and Muslims, but also between different castes, clans, sects or local community groups.[4] Tagging these conflicts with distinct 'Hindu' and 'Muslim' identities was a more modern concept moulded in the time of the British Raj, a product of its divide and rule policy among the country's middle classes and elite, who competed for jobs and opportunities.

Many historians feel that the Hindu–Muslim 'tension' was played up and written into our history by colonial historians. As India's history had a series of invaders and 'outsiders' becoming rulers, many of them Muslim, historical events were easily repainted with a communal brush. This has tainted our perception of history.

'For the first time, we taught them a lesson,' is a common

boast by many middle-class Hindus like Rajat after communal violence. They feel they are avenging centuries of 'Muslim tyranny' right from the time of Mahmud of Ghazni to the present-day terrorists in Kashmir.

Medieval times are portrayed as a period of 'Muslim rule' in which barbaric 'invaders' like Mahmud of Ghazni and Babur destroyed our civilization. These attacks were more about conquest and plunder than religion. 'There were alliances as well as wars between Hindu and Muslim rulers. Communal forces try to portray only the conflict,' says Asghar Ali Engineer, a Muslim reformist.[5]

In fact, Muslim rulers even persecuted other Muslim sects. Many Hindu rulers joined hands with Muslim kings. Rana Sanga collaborated with Babur against Ibrahim Lodi. Anandpal of Thanesar helped Mahmud of Ghazni, who had several Hindu generals helping him to raid the Somnath temple. Before attacking Somnath, Mahmud attacked the Muslim ruler of Multan. He also employed Hindus in high positions in his army and administration.[6] We hear a lot about the plunder by Muslim rulers, but we aren't told how Hindu kings demolished temples and Buddhist monuments. The Marathas ransacked the famous temple at Seringapattam when they attacked Tipu Sultan's kingdom. King Harsha of Kashmir (AD 1089–1101) systematically melted down all the metal images in his kingdom. Moreover, Muslim rulers also ruined mosques. Aurangzeb destroyed a mosque within the territory of Tanasha of Golkunda to dig out wealth hidden below it which he had hoarded. He also gave jagirs to several temples.[7]

Mahmud of Ghazni's raid of the Somnath temple in 1026 is often used as an example of 'barbaric' Muslim rule. Both the British, and Hindu nationalists, projected the Somnath raid as a reason for a Hindu–Muslim divide. But the event has been interpreted differently through the ages. The British were the first to create the perception that it stirred communal tension, says historian Romila Thapar. The earliest mention of 'Hindu trauma' was in a House of Commons debate in 1843, on whether the gates of the temple should be restored.[8] Some believe the British used this debate to appease religious sentiments and stir a non-existent Hindu 'trauma'. This was the new, communal interpretation of Mahmud of Ghazni's Somnath raid, says Thapar. 'It is, to put it mildly, incomplete and therefore distorted.'

Some more early signs of communal tension in Gujarat could be seen during the latter part of British rule. The first examples of this modern form of violence, says historian David Hardiman, 'occurred in the 1890s, in Bombay and Saurashtra, followed by Surat and Godhra in the 1920s, and Ahmedabad in 1941 and 1946.'[9]

'Hindu nationalism became a strong force in Gujarat after around 1900,' he says. 'Although Gandhi kept such forces at bay to some extent, they emerge in the period 1923–28, alienating many Muslims, who then turned to the Muslim League.' By the 1930s the Muslim League had gained strength in Ahmedabad and Kheda. There were frequent attempts to create trouble in Ahmedabad and Surat during symbolically important events—the civil disobedience movement, the Pakistan Resolution of 1940, the Quit India movement of 1942, the provincial elections of 1946, and most importantly during the partition of India in 1947.[10]

The Jagannath Rath Yatra sparked off violence in Ahmedabad in 1941 and 1946.[11] The violence remained confined to the walled city, which was a middle-class area then; working class areas were not affected. Both riots were contained relatively quickly.

Gujarat remained relatively untouched by violence during Partition. Only a few cities—Ahmedabad, Veraval in Saurashtra (site of the Somnath temple) and Godhra—had riots. 'What took place was episodic communal violence, but that did not ever appear as based on any sense of a deep-seated divide between Hindus and Muslims,' says D.L. Sheth.[12] 'It is not accidental that communities like the Piranas (part Hindu and part Muslim in their faith and practice) could survive till the recent onslaught by the Tableeq Jamaat and Hindutva movement.'

The communalism that resulted in Partition was the result of a conflict of interests between sections of the Hindu and Muslim elite. During Partition, more Muslims chose to live in India than shift to Pakistan.

Yet, Partition left its mark. It brought to India several Sindhi refugees, hostile to Muslims after their traumatic experiences during the violent separation of India and Pakistan. During Partition the Nawab of Junagadh in Saurashtra acceded to Pakistan, and it was only after a military operation that India regained the land.

A striking feature of the British period was the conceptualization of local conflicts as an undying, eternal communal divide. Historical 'memories' and myths were created in the span of a decade.

Post-Independence

Congress rule faced its first major threat from the right-wing Swatantra Party, which surfaced in the 1960s. It paved the way for the emergence of the Jan Sangh (later called the BJP). Its rise was essentially due to the coming together of feudal elements opposed to Nehru's policies, which they saw as socialist.

In the Swatantra Party, Patel businessmen and landowners joined hands with the former princes of small feudal states, the Darbars, to prevent any further land reform such as land ceiling legislation. This was Gujarat's first caste alliance— PAKSH (Patel and Kshatriya). Numerically, it was strong. It gave the Congress a tough fight in the 1965 assembly elections;

however, after losing, it disintegrated. There was a vacuum within the opposition. Gradually, the Janata Party took its place, which was an alliance between Congress rebels and the Jan Sangh in 1977–79. The inclusion of the Jan Sangh in this coalition gave it the legitimacy that it had lacked before.

Throughout Gujarat's history, the upper castes have fought to retain their dominance, whether it is through communal/caste riots, or through political organization and agitations like the anti-reservation movement. Leftist or trade union movements could not develop here. The Gandhian movement was strong, and they controlled the Majdoor Mahajan Sangh, the Ahmedabad mill workers' union. Gandhians were mainly involved in work like running ashrams, etc. Their social justice campaigns abated as they received patronage from the government after Independence.

1969: The nosedive

Two decades and a whole new generation later, Nehru's post-Independence push for rapid industrial expansion propelled the need for a larger unskilled workforce, and migrant labour moved to industrial towns like Ahmedabad. Like the rest of India, Ahmedabad was changing under the pressures of urbanization. As the city grew beyond the pols, traditional community ties weakened. Congress leaders, who ran the mill unions and had strong support from mill owners, could not keep workers united. The shifting dynamics within the Congress also led to a split within the party, with many rebelling against Indira Gandhi. The party was at its weakest point since it gained power.

Gujarat's first major communal outburst was in 1969. This time, cows started the riot. A Muslim Urs procession was passing the Jagannath temple in Ahmedabad on 18

September 1969. A herd of cattle returning to the temple premises ran into the procession. As usual, a minor quarrel started, but did not spark any more trouble on that day.

The next day, the Hindu Dharma Raksha Samiti (Committee to Protect the Hindu Religion), which consisted of religious leaders and Jan Sangh leaders, held meetings in Ahmedabad and Baroda. Soon after, mobs went on a rampage, targeting Muslims. There appeared to be an element of pre-planning to the violence. Handbills were distributed, spreading false rumours that Muslims had attacked the temple idol. Mobs roamed around with voters lists in order to identify Muslim homes and shops. The Gujarati press published false reports that Hindu women had been attacked in Gomtipur. This set off more clashes, which soon spread to Vadodara and some villages outside Ahmedabad.[14] The violence also reached north and central Gujarat.

With sentiments against Indira Gandhi running high, the Jan Sangh tried to use the violence to gain political mileage. It manipulated anti-Muslim resentment after the Indo-Pakistan war. Along with the RSS, the Jan Sangh played an active part in the riots by leading mobs, provoking people, funding the rioters and publishing hate pamphlets.[15] Congress leaders Morarji Desai and Indulal Yagnik went on fasts for peace. But some Congressmen, allied with local criminals and the police, instigated trouble or condoned the violence. The Justice Reddy commission, appointed to probe into the riots, criticized the role of the police, the Gujarati press and political organizations like the RSS and Jan Sangh.

1981: The birth of reservation politics

The next storm to hit Gujarat was in the form of the 1981 anti-reservation riots. These weren't communal, but caste riots. The agitation was mainly led by the Patels against reserved quotas for SCs (7 per cent) and STs (15 per cent) in educational institutions and government jobs proportionate to their share of the population. This was India's first anti-reservation agitation. The Jan Sangh and the Congress(O) supported it.

The upper castes felt threatened, but the insecurity was more perceived than real. Even today, Dalits in Gujarat are treated as Untouchables, not allowed to draw water from village wells and made to work in menial jobs.

Students in medical colleges across Gujarat started protests, and later, university teachers and government employees joined in and went on strike. Trouble started in Jetalpur village near Ahmedabad, where a Dalit boy was killed for participating in an upper-caste Navratri festival. The violence targeting Dalits spread mainly across four districts of central Gujarat—Ahmedabad, Mehsana, Kheda and Baroda—where there was a larger concentration of upwardly mobile Dalits.[16]

The violence was an upper and middle caste backlash to what they felt was an erosion of their dominant position in society. Upper castes, comprising mainly Brahmins and Banias, had controlled Gujarat politics until the mid-1970s. The Swatantra Party, an alliance of middle castes like Patels and Kshatriyas, had tried to challenge their authority.

The upper castes felt further threatened when the Congress, clutching at straws for a new strategy, decided to portray itself as the party for the downtrodden. In 1975, it launched its KHAM formula. It concentrated on winning over these vote banks, which when combined formed more than 60 per cent of the population. Until then, upper castes and Patels[17] had controlled Gujarat politics, but they were virtually eliminated from all the core positions within the ruling Congress party from 1980 onwards.[18] The upper and middle castes, the Brahmins, Banias and Patidars (called Savarnas), thus united to defend their domain.

1985: From caste to communal carnage

In 1985, the then chief minister Madhavsinh Solanki increased the OBC quota of reserved seats from 10 per cent to 28 per cent. This made 49 per cent of seats reserved (OBC plus SC and ST).[19] The anti-reservation agitation started once again. On 18 March 1985, the ABVP called for a Gujarat bandh. People were asked to ring bells from their rooftops to sound the death knell of reservations. On that day the bandh took a communal turn.[20] Hindu–Muslim communal riots broke out first in Ahmedabad and later in Surat, Baroda, Rajkot, Mehsana, Sabarkantha and Kheda,[21] going on for four months.[22]

The Justice Dave commission that inquired into the violence found that the Sangh Parivar colluded with local criminals and Congress dissidents to instigate the violence.

'Motives of the agitation . . . was opposing the anti-reservation policy but courses of events show that once the planning came in the hands of AVBP supported by BJP and VHP, further joined by Congress dissidents, and some other persons . . . the motive for continuance of the agitation and spreading the communal disturbances became the ouster of Madhavsingh Solanki.'[23]

The violence in 1985 accentuated divisions within Ahmedabad. There was an exodus from within the city. People who had lived together for decades felt unsafe with each other. Seeking safety in numbers, Muslims fled to Juhapura, a settlement that was originally a rehabilitation site for flood-affected refugees. With every riot, more Muslims have shifted here. As the city grew, many Hindus moved out of the narrow lanes of the walled city and bought bigger houses in the new suburbs across the Sabarmati river. With Muslims feeling under siege and huddling together in ghettos, many orthodox Muslim sects also gained ground. The Congress also nurtured religious leaders, especially within the conservative Jamiyat Ulema, an organization of Muslim clerics associated with the famous orthodox Islamic university at Deoband in western Uttar Pradesh.

For the first time, Dalits turned against Muslims in Ahmedabad's industrial areas during the 1985 violence. Until then, both had lived in solidarity—the mill workers' union, run by the Congress, had kept them united. Muslims sheltered their Dalit neighbours when they were attacked during the 1981 caste riots, but the mid-1980s was the time when the mills started closing. With the economy on the downturn, insecurity grew. Things started falling apart.

Unemployed youth, both Hindu and Muslim, turned to the underworld for work. In the mid-1980s, Ahmedabad's best-known don, Abdul Latif Sheikh, had a monopoly in the city's bootlegging business. He later diversified into smuggling. From his headquarters in Daryapur in Ahmedabad's walled city, Latif had a powerful fiefdom, established with the help of supportive policemen and politicians. Latif shared the spoils with the people within his locality by doing a lot of community work, which gained him popularity and further immunity from the law. He even won municipal elections from five wards in Ahmedabad. Latif was later killed in a police encounter, but his legend lingers on.

Though the underworld comprised both Hindus and Muslims, Latif emerged as the most powerful and brazen of these criminals. This added to a growing perception that Muslims were antisocial. People resented the government's complicity with the don. Political parties have often colluded with criminals, both Hindu and Muslim; it just so happened that the Latif gang was more powerful than others. This conveniently fed into RSS–BJP stereotypes about Muslims being criminals, stereotypes that ignored the many Hindu politicians and policemen who were his backers. It also fed into Sangh Parivar propaganda that that the minorities were being pandered to by the state, and nothing was being done to curb these 'elements'. The many holes in these claims of 'appeasement' were obvious, but ignored.

Jai Shri Ram: Yatra politics

After the 1985 agitation, the BJP sensed that it couldn't afford to alienate lower-caste voters. It started to woo Dalit and OBC vote banks to create a unified 'Hindu' force, and savarna was abandoned—the new rallying point was Hindutva. The party changed its anti-reservation stand. Ironically, the party's student wing, the ABVP, which had led the 1981/85 anti-reservation protests, also started talking about the need for SC/ST reservations.[24] Using Hindutva, the Sangh Parivar was able to create a rift between Dalits and Muslim workers in Ahmedabad's industrial areas.

The recession and closure of textile mills made their work easier. Rising unemployment and frustration eroded the bonds between workers. Several jobless workers joined the ranks of the underworld, which was thriving thanks to political patronage. Prohibition only helped their businesses grow. The BJP began to co-opt lower-caste youth into its structures, though rarely at leadership levels. There was little room for them in the Congress, with much older leaders occupying the space.

To 'unite' Hindus, the Sangh organized seven major yatras between 1983 and 1990. 'An attempt was made to associate virtually all non-Hindu communities with the yatras and to isolate the Muslims,' says sociologist Achyut Yagnik.[25] It was during this phase that the BJP's vote bank grew steadily. The yatras left a trail of destruction. In 1987, riots accompanied the BJP's Ram Janaki Dharma Yatra in parts of Rajkot, Kheda and Sabarkantha districts. For the first time, adivasis participated in communal violence, rushing from nearby villages to attack Muslim shops and houses.[26]

Later, the BJP's Ramshila Poojan Yatra in 1989 attracted tremendous support cutting across caste lines. Sangh activists led a door-to-door campaign to garner support for the construction of the VHP's dream of a Ram temple in Ayodhya. They used slogans, bhajans, legends, rituals and films to build religious nationalist fervour. The BJP broadened its base by recruiting volunteers for kar seva in Ayodhya. Building the temple was a matter of national pride; a re-building of India's glorious past after its destruction by the 'invader' Babur.

The yatra's chest-thumping slogan was *'Garv se kaho— Hum Hindu hain'* (Say it with pride, We are Hindu). The other was *'Muslim Babur ki aulad hain'* (Muslims are children of Babur). Bajrang Dal workers asked people, 'If you are Hindu, prove it by contributing Rs 1.25 for the Ramshila Poojan. If you don't, you prove that you are from a Muslim womb.'[27] From Ahmedabad's Dalit slums to remote adivasi villages, people gave bricks and money towards the project. That wasn't all they contributed; along the way they also created mayhem in 180 towns and villages in north and central Gujarat,[28] even after the state government banned the processions.

Yatra violence escalated when L.K. Advani started his rath yatra on 25 September 1990 from Somnath. It sparked off communal violence in twenty-six places, killing ninety-nine persons between 1 September and 20 November 1990.[29] Most districts in Gujarat were affected.[30]

Ironically, Somnath, where the yatra started, remained untouched by violence. This was mainly because the police were on red alert. Muslims were so scared that many deserted their homes or sent off their families to safer villages nearby. The entire state machinery was used to promote the yatra.[31] The chief organizer of the yatra was none other than Narendra Modi, the then general secretary of the Gujarat BJP. It would later help propel him to the position of chief minister.

The BJP used the yatras to mobilize Dalits and OBCs, but upper and middle castes still control the party. In 1991, as many as 63 per cent of the state and district leaders were from upper or middle castes—Brahmin, Bania, Patidar or Rajput.[32] The OBCs and Dalits remain the foot-soldiers. During riots, upper caste leaders mobilize mobs from Dalit and OBC localities. The BJP also recruited kar sevaks from the OBCs for the December 1992 Babri Masjid demolition.

The 1992 Babri Masjid demolition: Hindutva in high gear

The 'Dharma Yudh' (Holy War) was scheduled for 6 December 1992. The object was the destruction of the Babri Masjid and the foundation of a Ram mandir at Ayodhya. After prominent BJP leaders like L.K. Advani, Murli Manohar Joshi and Uma Bharati led the yatra that demolished the historic Babri Masjid, widespread riots engulfed India—in Mumbai, Surat, Delhi, and across north India. The most intense riots in Gujarat were in Surat, where more than 200 lives were lost over several months of conflict. Trouble abated quicker in Ahmedabad, Baroda and Godhra. In Mumbai too, a pogrom by the Shiv Sena continued throughout January 1993, killing more than 900.[33]

The Ram Mandir agitation was a turning point for the BJP, coming at a time when voters were looking for alternatives to the Congress. Though it did not result in any immediate electoral victories for the BJP,[34] it helped the VHP to expand its network in a few states.

The first BJP government at the centre came to power in May 1996. L.K. Advani was appointed home minister and deputy prime minister. Eleven years later, a special court in Rae Bareilly held BJP ministers Murli Manohar Joshi and Uma Bharati, BJP leader Vinay Katiyar and VHP leaders Ashok Singhal, Vishnu Hari Dalmiya, Acharya Giriraj Kishore and Sadhvi Rithambara guilty of provoking the violence that led to the demolition of the Babri Masjid.[35] But L.K. Advani was let off the hook, even though he was named in the CBI's chargesheet as part of the group egging on the kar sevaks at the site on 6 December 2002. What ensured his immunity?

In Gujarat too, the saffron wave swept the 1995 state assembly elections.[36] People voted for the BJP, hoping it was a 'non-corrupt' and 'disciplined' alternative to the Congress. But it wasn't a smooth ride; there were defections and horse-trading within the BJP, engineered by top leader Shankarsinh Vaghela. During this chaotic period, Gujarat had four chief ministers in the span of three years. Things settled down in the 1998 elections, when the BJP's Keshubhai Patel swept the polls.

But political stability didn't buy peace. Emboldened by their party's victory, local VHP and Bajrang Dal units became more militant. They used various campaigns to spread their roots throughout the state. The Hindu Jagran Manch, whose leaders have links with the RSS, held an anti-Christian rally on Christmas Day 1998 in the Dangs district in south Gujarat, which has a largely adivasi population. Around ten churches and prayer halls were burned or damaged.[37]

Muslims continued to be targets. The VHP became crusaders against mixed marriages—the 'capture' of Hindu girls by Muslim boys. In July 1998, fifty Muslim families had to flee their home in Randhikpur, Dahod district, central Gujarat, when VHP activists attacked two Muslim boys who had eloped with Hindu girls.[38]

Over the decades there has been a gradual but pervasive build up of bigotry. It is engineered resentment unfounded in fact, and devoid of any historical basis. Political forces of all colours—the British, the Congress and later the BJP—have either covertly or overtly twisted history, myth and identity to engineer communal resentment and large-scale violence.

Politics has long fed on insecurity and prejudice. People like Rajesh are the prey; they are the ones who have now grown to accept hate as normal, religious segregation as routine and riots as a way of life—just like Hindutva.

As Rajat says, 'We are used to it.'

Notes

1. Report of the Dave Commission of Inquiry into the violence in Gujarat from February to 18 July 1985, p. 68.
2. Asghar Ali Engineer, *Surat Shames the Nation in Communalism in India—A Historical and Empirical Study*, Vikas Publishing House, p. 185, and Lakshmi Subramanian, 'Capital and crowd in a declining Asian port city: The Anglo-Bania order and the Surat riots of 1795', *Modern Asian Studies*, 19, 2 (1985), pp. 205–37, Cambridge University Press.
3. Ghanshyam Shah, 'Communal Riots in Gujarat: Report of a Preliminary Investigation', *Economic and Political Weekly*, January 1970, p. 188.
4. Godhra is portrayed as a 'hotbed' of communal riots. In nineteenth-century Godhra, Sunni and Shia Muslims are known to have attacked each other, says David Hardiman, professor of History, University of Warwick, UK.
5. Asghar Ali Engineer, *Medieval History and Communalism*, Centre for Study of Society and Secularism, p. 19.
6. Ibid.
7. Ibid.
8. Romila Thapar, 'Somnath and Mahmud', *Frontline*, 10–23 April 1999.
9. E-mail interview with David Hardiman.

232 Scarred: Experiments with Violence in Gujarat

10. Ashutosh Varshney, *Ethnic Conflict and Civic Life: Hindus and Muslims in India*, Oxford University Press, 2002, p. 235.

11. The Yatra triggered many other riots in later years. It continues to be a communal spark plug, especially with the increasing role of the Sangh Parivar in its organization.

12. D.L. Sheth, 'Growth of Communal Polarisation in Gujarat: The Making of a Hindutva Laboratory?', *Manushi*.

13. Asghar Ali Engineer, *Communalism in India—A Historical and Empirical Study*, Vikas Publishing House, pp. xiv, 33, 185.

14. Ghanshyam Shah, 'Communal Riots in Gujarat: Report of a Preliminary Investigation', *Economic and Political Weekly*, annual number January 1970.

15. Ibid., p. 199.

16. Pradip Kumar Bose, 'Social Mobility and Caste Violence, A Study of the Gujarat Riots', *Economic and Political Weekly*, 18 April 1981.

17. Gujarat politics was controlled by some powerful Patidar politicians who were in the Congress, most notably Vallabhbhai Patel, and other Patidars after his death in 1950, such as Babubhai Patel. Chimanbhai Patel first became chief minister in the Janata Party in the late 1970s.

18. Achyut Yagnik, 'Hindutva as a Savarna Purana', in Ashis Nandy, Shikha Trivedy, Shail Mayaram and Achyut Yagnik (eds.), *Creating a Nationality: The Ram Janmabhoomi Movement and Fear of the Self*, Oxford University Press, 1995.
After being elected in 1980, Madhavsinh Solanki initiated revolutionary changes in the caste composition of his government. For the first time in the history of Gujarat, there wasn't a single Patidar minister in Solanki's cabinet. Also an unprecedented move was when an adivasi was appointed cabinet minister, holding the important irrigation portfolio. Another first: a Dalit was sent to the union cabinet as minister of state for home. Solanki himself was a Kshatriya. The lower castes, adivasis and religious minorities held more than 100 of the 180 seats in the legislature. (The Congress had a majority of 140 seats.)

19. 'Middle Class Politics: Case of Anti-Reservation Agitations in Gujarat', *Economic and Political Weekly*, vol. XXII, nos 19, 20, 21, Annual Number May 1987 and Nagindas Sanghvi, Gujarat:

A Political Analysis, Centre for Social Studies, Surat, p. 227.

20. Ghanshyam Shah, Under-privileged and Communal Carnage: A Case of Gujarat, Prof. Wertheim memorial lecture.

21. Asghar Ali Engineer, 'Communal Fire Engulfs Ahmedabad Once Again', *Economic and Political Weekly*, 6 July 1985.

22. Ibid.

23. Report of the Dave Commission of Inquiry into the violence in Gujarat from February to 18 July 1985, p. 93.

24. Achyut Yagnik, 'Hindutva as a Savarna Purana', in Ashis Nandy, Shikha Trivedy, Shail Mayaram and Achyut Yagnik (eds.), *Creating a Nationality: The Ram Janmabhoomi Movement and Fear of the Self*, Oxford University Press, 1995, p. 102.

25. Ibid., p. 107.

26. Ibid., p. 108.

27. Ghanshyam Shah, 'The BJP's Riddle in Gujarat', Thomas Blom Hansen and Christophe Jaffrelot (eds), *The BJP and the Compulsions of Politics in India*, Oxford University Press, 1999.

28. Achyut Yagnik, 'Hindutva as a Savarna Purana', in Ashis Nandy, Shikha Trivedy, Shail Mayaram and Achyut Yagnik (eds.), *Creating a Nationality: The Ram Janmabhoomi Movement and Fear of the Self*, Oxford University Press, p. 108.

29. Ghanshyam Shah, 'The BJP's Riddle in Gujarat', Thomas Blom Hansen and Christophe Jaffrelot (eds.), *The BJP and the Compulsions of Politics in India*, Oxford University Press, 1999, p. 248.

30. Only Jamnagar, Dangs, Sabarkantha and Junagadh remained peaceful. The agitation stirred trouble in Maharashtra, Karnataka, Uttar Pradesh, Bihar, Delhi and Hyderabad as well (see Asghar Ali Engineer, *Communal Riots After Independence*, p. 113).

31. Achyut Yagnik, 'Hindutva as a Savarna Purana', in Ashis Nandy, Shikha Trivedy, Shail Mayaram and Achyut Yagnik (eds.), *Creating a Nationality: The Ram Janmabhoomi Movement and Fear of the Self*, Oxford University Press, p. 110. The BJP was part of the alliance Janata Front government in power at the state level. Almost half of chief minister Chimanbhai Patel's ministry was from the BJP.

32. Ghanshyam Shah, 'The BJP and Backward Castes in Gujarat', Thomas Blom Hansen and Christophe Jaffrelot (eds), *The BJP*

and the Compulsions of Politics in India, Oxford University Press, 1999, p. 309.

33. According to the Srikrishna commission, the death toll was 900. Unofficial estimates say 1500.

34. In fact, in elections in five states in November 1993, the BJP lost, even in Uttar Pradesh.

35. Sharat Pradhan, Ayodhya case: Nothing against Advani, but M.M. Joshi will face charges, rediff.com, 19 September 2003.

36. The BJP won 122 of 182 seats. The Congress was reduced to just forty-four seats.

37. Christophe Jaffrelot, 'The BJP at the Centre: A Central and Centrist Party?' in Thomas Blom Hansen and Christophe Jaffrelot (eds.), *The BJP and the Compulsions of Politics in India*, Oxford University Press, p. 358.

38. Ibid., p. 359.

'Are we so fallen than we should be afraid of our own shadows?'

—Mahatma Gandhi

9

Borders

*'Save our country by boycotting Muslims economically
and socially.*

*Those who talk of Hindu–Muslim unity are only
maligning their own religion. There can be no equality
between Hindus and Muslims.*

*What is your security even in the most decent and secure
locality in spite of having security guards? Traitors and
terrorists are coming by the truckloads. They will kill your
security guards and enter your bungalows. They will murder
you in your drawing rooms and bedrooms.*

*We must organize ourselves, join Hindu organizations
and make financial contributions . . . After Godhra, cases
against several VHP members and Hindus have been
registered and many of them are in prison now . . . It is our
duty to protect their families and keep them from starving . . .
You will only be following your dharma by doing so . . .
Contribute to the VHP and avail of 50 per cent tax saving.'*
—From a fund-raising pamphlet published by the VHP's
state treasurer, Chinubhai Patel, circulated in
April 2002.

'Why Gujarat?' That's a question I'm often asked. Is
there something different about Gujarat that such
horrific violence occurred there? My answer is, no and yes.

No, because there is nothing unusual about Gujarat. It's

not as if the state is crawling with criminals. It is not dramatically different from other states in this respect.

What is distinctive about Gujarat is the fact that the VHP and BJP are far more organized and well entrenched here. Since their government retained power, there was no one to stop them.

Why are the forces of Hindutva more deep-rooted in Gujarat? Well, in some ways, the links between commerce, religion and politics are more clearly etched here than in most places. Gujarat has a large trading community of Banias and Jains, who have a great influence on the religious-cultural sphere. Caste associations and religious cults also help traders gain access to business and credit networks. Members of these groups help each other in business, arranging finance, setting up contracts, etc. for 'their people'. Several cults and gurus also have their headquarters here, like the Swaminarayan sect, and the ISKCON and Swadhyaya movements. Gurus and sants like Morari Bapu attract huge crowds at their meetings. All in all, it is a fertile soil for the VHP's brand of 'Hindu consciousness'.

It also has to do with Gujarat's wealth. One of India's most prosperous states, Gujarat has a large middle class and NRI population, which is largely conservative. Many from this prosperous, 'educated' class nurture deep anti-Muslim, anti-Pakistan prejudices and are the BJP's natural allies. Caste and caste-based bodies have deep roots here. Hindutva forces have manipulated caste distinctions for their political gain. OBCs and Dalits are fighting to fit into the growing middle class and gain political representation. Many have joined the VHP and Bajrang Dal to prove their 'Hinduness', or to clamber for employment and power. This is a stepping stone up the ladder, to be 'one of them'.

Gujarat's rapid urbanization has brought a certain alienation and rootlessness. In the last decade, however, the economy has changed. Economic growth has not translated into better living conditions for the large majority. Investments have shifted from the employment-generating small-scale industries to more capital-intensive industries like petroleum and power, where jobs are few. Inequality has grown and the rich, propertied class, many of whom have the same Brahmanical biases as the Sangh Parivar, have become more powerful. The lower castes, once united under the KHAM formula, are now fragmented after they were let down by the Congress. The VHP has capitalized on this and tried to play one group against the other. In building 'Hindu consciousness' it has pitted OBCs and lower castes against Muslims. The outcome of their propaganda was evident during the violence of 2002, when adivasis in central Gujarat targeted Muslim traders, or in places like Bapunagar, Ahmedabad, where they instigated Dalit labourers against their poor Muslim neighbours.

In rural Gujarat too, there has been growing unrest. The state faces a severe water shortage. Over one-third (nearly 9500) of Gujarat's villages, four metros and seventy-nine towns face water scarcity.[1] In the past few years, water riots have broken out in Bhavnagar and other parts of Saurashtra. In north Gujarat, overdrilling of borewells has resulted in sharply dipping water-tables. Water from these wells too is contaminated with fluoride.[2] The industrial belt in south and central Gujarat, which covers around 20 per cent of the state's land mass, commands over 70 per cent of the state's water resources, most of which are polluted.[3] The agricultural economy is also in the doldrums. The year 2002 was the fourth successive year of drought, and agricultural growth has been erratic and uncertain. Gujarat is plagued by drought and water shortages. The anxiety in the countryside was later reflected in protests by the Bharatiya Kisan Sangh, the farmer's wing of the BJP, against its own party's government.

The new liberalized economy has created large numbers of unemployed or underemployed people[4] who are part of the Hindutva movement's growing base, says economist Jan Breman.[5] Skewed economic growth has led to the informalization of Ahmedabad's workforce after the closure of its textile mills and other industries[6] since the 1980s. Those who were once regular employees have been forced into casual work, which is more exploitative and offers no social security. These marginalized workers, mainly from the lower castes, are part of the Sangh Parivar's lumpen force.

'Gujarat could be understood as an experiment for trying out what will happen to state and society under a policy regime which does not attempt to harness the most brutal consequences of a market-led mode of capitalist production. The total eclipse of Gandhian values . . . has also led to the shrinking of social space needed for humanising economic growth. The disappearance of a climate leaning towards social democracy and tolerance has been accompanied by an increase in communal hate politics,' says Jan Breman.[7] He calls the state's growth pattern 'lumpen capitalism'. In such an economy, labour standards are poor and employment is more difficult to come by. Many youth dreamed that education would open several opportunities for them, but this hasn't happened. They are still casual workers, looking for daily work.

This is where fundamentalist groups step in. The VHP's network in Gujarat is its largest, with 10,000 branches all over the state.[8] It provides a nationalist Hindu identity for several urban youth. It gives them a feeling of belonging to a group; a false sense of power. For many from lower castes, it offers them a feeling of dignity, of being accepted by mainstream Hindu society. Moreover, lumpenism is justified in the name of nation and religion. What more could a young goonda ask for? The VHP is also the only organization that works actively and in a sustained way to build its network. With the slow death of the Gandhian movement, the field was left wide open for Hindutva to take over. They seized the chance.

Parallel to the rise of Hindu extremist groups was the marginalization of Muslims that started with their ghettoization in 1985. This led to the growth of orthodox Muslim groups like the Jamiyat Ulema and Tableeq Jamaat, which expanded in big cities due to the isolation of Muslims. Several started social and welfare facilities like schools and dispensaries in the ghettos, where none had previously existed.

Gujarat has historically been an economic hub. It has a long history of trade and commerce across the Indian Ocean. Trade links with Arabia can be traced back to the Indus civilization.[9] Northern and western India have had commercial ties with Arabs, Turks, Afghans and Persians stretching back to many centuries.[10] Gujarati traders, especially the Bania community, have been involved in trade and finance.

Known for their sharp business acumen, the Banias have used their guild-like community ties to gather large amounts of capital and create monopolies and/or oligopolies. They have funded military operations of the nawabs and maharajas and even British trade. 'Centuries before the modern banking system, *Vaisya* (Bania) *shroffs* or bankers were the conduits of a highly monetized Indian economy, remitting vast sums around India at short notice through a sophisticated trust system based on *hundi* (promissory notes),' says Hamish McDonald, author of a book on Dhirubhai Ambani, who built India's largest business empire, Reliance Industries.[11]

This contact with international trade down the centuries has given Gujarat its large trading community. But most business still operates in the old-fashioned way, relying on caste and trade networks. Elders decide who has access to credit, business contacts and deals. For example, a community of diamond merchants from Palanpur have a network stretching right from the chawls of Ahmedabad where the gems are polished to the international diamond bourse in Antwerp, Belgium. Their business dealings are notoriously secretive and tightly entwined within their own community.

The heart of the VHP/BJP's support comes from this large trading community. Their traditional ideology appeals to these castes. There is little room for dissent. That's one reason why the VHP has grown so expansively here, compared to any other. Because its natural constituency is larger here.

During the freedom struggle and after, the Gandhian movement was strong at the grassroots level in Gujarat. Most villages had active Gandhian institutions like the Seva Dal. In Ahmedabad, the Majdoor Mahajan Sangh, the mill workers' union started by Mahatma Gandhi, had wide support among workers and mill owners. The union worked not only at the factory gate but also in workers' chawls and with employers' patronage. But the decline of the Gandhian movement opened spaces for the RSS to step in.

Tracing the roots of ghettoization, the rise of the Sangh accelerated after the decline of the Majdoor Mahajan Sangh, which provided a forum for interaction between working class communities. During the 1969 riots the union worked with the police to prevent violence by keeping them informed of latest incidents. On the third day of the violence, the union gave a call for workers to report back on duty. Workers of different castes and communities were asked to work in the same shift and protect each other. 'The trade union movement which used to be the main platform for collective action has withered away. Neither have other kinds of social movements been able to stem the rising tide of communalism,' he says.

By segregating people, ghettoization has further fermented religious bigotry. Like other cities in India, Muslims in Ahmedabad, Vadodara, Surat and other Gujarati cities are ghettoized. This has sharpened communal polarization. It's a vicious cycle. Each riot causes further ghettoization, which further segregates communities and leads to lesser interaction, deeper divisions and prejudices, setting the ground for trouble-makers to create more violence. The rot is so deep that riot betting has become common in Gujarat. There have been stories in major national dailies like *The Times of India* on bookies taking bets on whether riots will break out during religious festivals or elections. Ahmedabad's Rath Yatra has such a history of tension that every year people gamble on whether riots will erupt during the procession. Some bookies even try to engineer the outcome by throwing a stone into the crowd during a procession or political meeting.

In most big cities, migration patterns evolve so that communities live in clusters. Different groups live in their own exclusive building societies. For example, Christians and Parsis have their own housing colonies. Jains have built their own 'vegetarian' buildings. But most of these are voluntary choices. Muslims, however, are being forced into ghettos.

After Mumbai's 1992–93 communal violence, many Muslims fled to new settlements on the outskirts of the city. They sought safety in numbers. Mumbra and Jogeshwari emerged as large Muslim ghettos. In what is considered India's most cosmopolitan city, it is almost impossible for even middle-class Muslims to find housing. Dalits face similar problems.

Although Ahmedabad's walled city had separate Hindu and Muslim pols, there was interaction between them. As the city grew and people moved out of the walled city, the newer parts of Ahmedabad became more segregated. Ghettoization accelerated after the 1985 riots when the Muslims fled to Juhapura, on the outskirts of the city. Since then each subsequent riot has seen a further influx into Juhapura. Here, judges and businessmen live alongside carpenters and hawkers. A common tag binds them all—their religion. Well-off Muslims who would like to live in elite areas of the city cannot. People will not sell or rent houses to them. If Muslims try to build their own housing societies within these areas, the VHP ransacks them.[12]

The underworld in most cities is a happy mix of both Hindu and Muslim. Dawood Ibrahim, India's best-known mafia don, had Chotta Rajan, a Hindu, as his right hand man. In Mumbai, the gangster Arun Gawli has even contested and won elections. Ahmedabad's notorious ganglord, Latif, had several Hindus, including politicians, on his payroll.

Prohibition laws in Gujarat make bootlegging the most prosperous business. In cities like Ahmedabad, the politician–police–mafia nexus has kept the underworld flourishing. Each needs the other to survive. Gangsters often do a lot of community work within their localities and are sometimes more popular than politicians. That's why politicians need them—for vote banks, for booth capturing, for extortion, to do their dirty work. Are the politicians and the police less criminal just because they are public figures? Is the Shiv Sena's extortion racket in Mumbai any less criminal than other mafia gangs, Hindu or Muslim?

Muslims are branded 'anti-national' terrorists trained by Pakistan. It is true that there are extremist groups like the Lashkar-e-Toiba, Jaish-e-Mohammed and the Students Islamic Movement of India (SIMI). There are also groups like the Liberation Tigers of Tamil Eelam (LTTE) and scores of others that are never referred to as Hindu terrorists. Nor is the VHP, despite its involvement in the killing of over 1000 human beings in Gujarat and hundreds more all over the country.

After the 9/11 attacks in New York City, the US government's 'War on Terror' has fuelled the demonization of not only Muslims, but also Asians all over the world. It has been the excuse for a major rise in illegal arrests and racial profiling. The number of Asians stopped and searched under anti-terrorism laws increased by 302 per cent in a year (at the end of 2002–03), the British Home Office revealed. The British government initiated an inquiry into the police's use of stop-and-search powers and warned that a generation of young

Muslims was being alienated by 'Islamophobic' policing.[13] After London's terrorist bombs in July 2005, this paranoia has grown further. The London police even shot dead an innocent, unarmed man in public view at Stockwell tube station. Two days later they admitted it was an error. The general and growing anti-Islam feeling in the West has also fed into and nourished Muslim-baiters in India.

While working in Gujarat, I met quite a few who actively brewed this bigotry. In VHP camps, I saw how misconceptions are taught and how cadres are prepared 'to defend their religion'. These are organized efforts at capturing young minds and foot-soldiers, ingredients for cooking up a climate of fear, intolerance and prejudice that keeps people afraid on either side of the 'border'.

Love in a time of intolerance

When childhood sweethearts Reema Sompura and Anthony Rebello eloped and fled from Ahmedabad to Mumbai, they hoped to fade into the sunset. But the Bajrang Dal in their neighbourhood, Naroda, did their best to thwart a happy ending.

'We had to run away,' Anthony told me.[14] 'Her parents, who are Brahmins, would never have agreed. They don't like Christians and Muslims—people who eat meat. Her uncle is with the VHP. If her family had known, they would have beaten me up.'

So, on 5 February 2003, Reema and Anthony got married in court and ran away to Mumbai after six weeks. A few weeks later, Reema's mother went to meet Anthony's parents. She wanted them to convince the couple to return. She said she had no objections to the marriage. 'But we didn't go back. So, with the help of the Bajrang Dal, she put out a search warrant for us. We were dragged back home to face a court summons,' Anthony explained.

That was the end of the honeymoon.

In court, the judge kept delaying the hearings and though both of them were present in the courtroom, he would not ask them anything. Outside, the couple had to face Bajrang Dal activists led by local leader Mangubhai Maharaj. His men gathered outside the court premises to intimidate the couple. 'Reema's mother knows a lot of people in the VHP, including Dr Jaideep Patel. She asked them to help her get her daughter back,' said Anthony. 'One day as we were leaving the court, the Bajrang Dal mob beat me until I was lying on the floor. Then they pushed Reema (who was pregnant) on the ground, grabbed her and put her into their car.'

Anthony rushed to the magistrate for help, but he refused to get involved. People heard him shouting for help and stopped the car. His father called the police and he was taken to the local police station. 'The Bajrang Dal thugs were already waiting there. Mangubhai Maharaj threatened me and told me, "Today we will burn you like we burned the Muslims,"' said Anthony. The police officer took down his FIR. Then, he convinced the couple to separate and let Reema stay with her mother for the night to ensure their safety. Reema's uncle assured them that Anthony could take her home the next morning. The couple fell for the trap.

That night, Reema's family packed her off to her uncle's house in Rajasthan.

From then on, her life was in their hands. Reema's family made her sign a statement saying that she was forced to marry Anthony. 'Then, her uncle took her to an abortion clinic in Himmatnagar, Gujarat. Reema was put up in a farmhouse in Pirana where many other girls abducted from their husbands by the Bajrang Dal were also kept in captivity,' Anthony remembers. When her kidnappers found out that she had sneaked a call to Anthony, they kept her in Mangubhai Maharaj's house in Naroda with his second wife (yes, Mangubhai, the upholder of public morality, has two wives).

She stayed there with other girls who had been kidnapped.

Next, Reema's family arranged to get her married. They forced her to call Anthony's house and tell his parents that she wanted a divorce, but Anthony refused to grant her one. That's when the death threats began. 'I fled to Mumbai,' says Anthony. 'Soon after, they arranged Reema's wedding in her uncle's factory in Naroda. Three other girls living with her were also married off at the same time.'

But Reema was determined. She explained the entire story to her new husband. She called Anthony secretly, sneaked out of the house, hitched a ride on the highway, met him in Vadodara and went back with him to Mumbai.

Today Reema and Anthony still live in exile, but at least they are together. Refugees from a culture of intolerance where separation is the only solution. On 26 November 2004, Anthony and Reema were blessed with a baby boy, Aaron.

The Hindu saviour

'Come and meet me. I'll give you a bomb,' said Mangubhai, while I was asking him for an appointment.

Mangubhai Maharaj is one of Ahmedabad's most infamous and flamboyant characters. A prime accused in the Naroda Patiya massacre, in which more than eighty-three[15] were murdered, this small local goon still happily goes about his shady deals. He prides himself on being the self-appointed 'rescuer' of Hindu girls.

'I have rescued 496 girls from the clutches of their Muslim husbands. There are thirty-eight police cases filed against me for doing this seva. But I am not afraid. Let there be any number of cases. I will continue my work,' he tells me and my journalist friend while flipping through a file with newspaper articles that chronicle his crimes.[16]

'My strategy is simple. First, we file a case and get the police to trace them,' explains this short, bald, 'dedicated' worker of the Bajrang Dal. 'Once we know where they are, we go to their homes at night. We beat up the boy and take the girl with us.' His driver interjects, 'You should see how we beat the hell out of these miyas.' My eyes fall on the two lathis kept under the car seats. 'Of course, the girls don't want to come. But we force them. Later, they realize their mistake and thank us for rescuing them.'

'I don't believe in love marriages. People should marry within their own community. Love is not important, society is. These young girls get carried away with being in love. Communities are different, they should live separately,' he tells me.

Explaining how Hindu girls get 'tricked', Mangubhai tells us, 'These Muslim boys are lukha (time wasters). They give these girls some attention, take them out, treat them to cold drinks and these girls think they are in love. They are able to marry these girls in less than Rs 5000. They always catch girls from good families. Many of our Patel girls have also run off with some Salim or Latif.'

He opens a drawer and shows us pictures of some girls. 'See these girls. Aren't they beautiful? Don't they look like heroines?' he leers. Then he calls in some girls to talk to us and makes them stand in a row, on display as it were. 'Tell them about your Salim. Do you want to go back to him?' he asks. The girl responds, 'No. Now I'll get married to someone else.'

'We have put them up with our volunteers' families here. Now, we are planning to get them married. One of them has even got engaged to a boy in the US,' he explains. 'First they thought I was a goonda, now they think I am a God.' Sometime during the conversation, his phone rang. 'Yes, we got an e-mail. He will send Rs 50,000.' Suspecting that he may have made a business of marrying off the girls, we asked him, 'Why aren't the girls living with their parents?'

'Some have gone back, others are in touch with their parents. But they don't want to face the rest of the community.

Society looks at them differently. It shouldn't be like that. They have made a mistake and want to put the past behind them,' Mangubhai says.

What about his past? How did he join the Bajrang Dal? 'I joined twelve years back. I owned a steel-rolling factory which was shut down for violating pollution control norms. I was out of work for a year. One of my friends took me for their Ram Dhun sessions. I had nothing to do, so I joined the Bajrang Dal,' he recounted.

Now, Mangubhai has a new avatar. Sporting a thick diamond-encrusted gold chain and bracelet, he runs a business called 'Tridevi Finance'. His is the only air-conditioned office in a row of small grocery or retail stores. I also met one of his clients; a builder. 'I help him if anyone creates a problem. Rivals, government officials, it could be anyone. I smooth the road for his work,' he smiles mischievously.

We ask Mangubhai about his other work in Naroda. What happened during the riots? 'I wasn't there, so I don't know. I had gone to Sabarkantha. Yet, mine is the first name in the FIR. I am well known here, so they put my name,' he grins.

'Even at the riot commission hearing, I told them that Muslims are like diabetes and the Bajrang Dal is the medicine,' he said, proudly showing me the news clippings as proof. 'Our country will be so good if we all united. If all Muslims said Ram's name. '*Jo Ram ka nahin, woh kissi ke kaam ka nahin*' (He who is not Ram's is of no use). '*Miya kato, desh bachao*' (Kill Muslims, save the country).'

What about his family? Will his son follow in his footsteps? 'My son!' he says proudly. 'He is twelve years but learns fast. Before I go for any dhamal (riot), he checks my revolver to see that it is loaded. His Papa shouldn't get killed while fighting.'

As we leave his office, we realize Mangubhai is a man of his word. He delivered on his promise. He gave us more than just a bomb.

A Day at camp

Patan, 21 May 2003: The gates to the empty school were wide open. But there was a bamboo barricade. Two rifle-toting workers in trademark khaki shorts patrolled the entrance.

The sound of gun shots greeted us as we drove inside. Rifle training was under way.

I asked if I could take some photographs. That got the instructors very excited. Suddenly, they stood up straighter and shouted instructions with more authority. But the 'seniors' intervened. 'Why do you want to take pictures?' asked one of the organizers, hair and moustache cropped close in military style. 'All you people from the English press want to give us a bad name. Next, you will publish these pictures and say we are running a terrorist camp.' My denials fell on deaf ears. 'It's girls like you from the English press who have made us notorious. Except others have short hair, very modern. They don't respect Bharatiya culture. Show me your visiting card. I want to know where you are coming from.'

He was a bit perplexed when he saw '*The Hindu*' written on my card.

'See, we are on the same side,' I joked. But he wasn't convinced.

'Who is your editor?' he demanded.

'His name is N. Ram. *Dekho, hum dono Ram ki seva karte hain*' (See, both of us are working in the name of Ram), I told him. Finally, he smiled.

'Come meet our leader.'

I was ushered to meet the 'leader' from Delhi, Mr Surendra Jain. 'So, you are from *The Hindu*? We have asked that newspaper to change its name. They always criticize us,' he said. Immediately, the others were on guard. 'Let them keep writing. It's good to know what our detractors think. The more they write, the more we grow,' he boasted. 'It's thanks to the media-bashing that Modi won the Gujarat elections. People felt that it wasn't correct. We reacted in such a small way. Yet, we got so many abuses.'

I changed the topic and tried to get some information about the camps. 'For the past thirteen years, we have been running these camps. The basic aim is to prepare workers who are "*deshbhakts*". To organize youth to protect the country and religion. This summer, such camps are running in thirty-five places across the country,' Mr Jain explained. 'It's not only the duty of the state to protect the country. It's also the duty of all citizens. No one looks at all the social work we do. We did rehabilitation work during the Kutch earthquake. We have opened cow shelters all over the country. We are not anti-Muslim. We are the enemy of any person who hates India.'

After that, Mr Jain spoke to the young trainees on 'The Uniqueness of the Hindu Religion'. 'No one knows when Hinduism was born. The first person on earth was born in the form of a Hindu. The history of Hinduism is as old as humanity itself,' Mr Jain revealed. Some of his insights would startle both historians and theologians; yet, they might well be in tomorrow's textbooks.

'Christians and Muslims have killed crores of people and destroyed cultures in the name of religion. The history of their religions is tainted with blood. Hinduism is the only tolerant religion. Both Christianity and Islam say that the non-believers have no right to live. They can launch jehad against them. Finish them off,' he said.

Then, Mr Jain launched his call for action. 'In Gujarat, you have shown the way forward to the rest of the world. You have shown us the path of how to deal with jehadis. It was a victory of our religion,' he said. 'The concept of 'ahimsa' has been wrongly interpreted. It doesn't mean cowardice. It doesn't mean we don't respond when attacked. To bear injustices is not written in the Hindu religion . . . We are the ones who believe in immortality of the soul. Yet, we are the ones most afraid of death. The jehadis have no fear of death. They learn this at an early age in madrasas. We must also end our fear of death.'

Mr Jain's speech reached a frenzied pitch. He got progressively shriller as he tried to mesmerize his audience. A lunch break followed his speech. No one was allowed to speak during lunch hour.

Finally we were allowed to break the silence, and I got a chance to speak to the participants. Who are these boys? Where do they come from? What draws them to this camp?

Prajapati Hargovandas, twenty, joined after a colleague introduced him to the Bajrang Dal. He is an engineering student, and works in a weighing scale manufacturing company in Gandhinagar. His father is a farmer and moneylender. 'After attending this camp, I feel all Hindus should sign up to protect our religion against Muslims. I will go back to my village and invite the Bajrang Dal to do a trishul distribution ceremony there.'

But what's the need for a trishul?

'We should have weapons to protect our religion and our country. Muslims should be removed. They are spreading terrorism, communal violence and antisocial activities.'

What did he learn in this camp?

'We learn yoga, judo, karate, obstacle courses. There are discussions on religion and national issues. We are taught how to protect our country. If there is a conflict between Hindus and Muslims, how to deal with it. How to respect elders. What to do in a mandir. What to do if an earthquake strikes.'

But what's the need to learn rifle shooting, judo?

'It is necessary for self-defence. If there is a riot, and if the Dal sends us to fight terrorists, we should know how to fight and use weapons.'

A few had joined the Bajrang Dal following a minor communal incident in their village. 'In our village, some

Muslim boys teased a Hindu boy while he was praying in school. A fight broke out. After that, I was told to join the Bajrang Dal. All Hindus should unite—whether they are Patels, Thakurs or any other caste,' said Manubhai Satvara, a twenty-six-year-old marginal farmer and casual labourer from Sami in Patan district.

There is little doubt that the feeling of belonging within the Sangh Parivar attracts many. 'I am handicapped. But after joining this camp, I don't feel so. Everyone works together. My self-confidence has increased,' said Bharatbhai Vadher, twenty-five, a farmer. 'When I was a young boy, I remember one of the girls in our village was taken away by a Muslim boy. No one spoke out against this. That memory still haunts me. I will unite all Hindus in my village to see that something similar doesn't happen again.'

Some of the camp trainers are full-time VHP members. They live in the local shakha and work without any pay. The Sangh looks after their basic food and shelter. 'I live in the shakha headquarters and travel in the surrounding villages to recruit new members,' says twenty-two-year-old Devraj Desai, a rifle-shooting instructor from Dhansura village in Sabarkantha district. 'I was in the army for one year. One of my uncles died while serving in the army and another lost his leg. After that, my family asked me to leave the army. I always wanted to work for the nation, so I joined the Bajrang Dal in 1999.'

For many, Hindutva is a family tradition. 'I was in the RSS since I was ten years old. My entire family is part of it,' says thirty-year-old Ashok Vaghela, a lathi instructor who is a small trader from Ahmedabad. 'The Bajrang Dal teaches you more about security work compared to the RSS. But both have the same goals—to create a Hindu Rashtra. The Islamic and Catholic movements are a threat to our country. Islam is spreading terrorism. Christians are converting poor Hindus.'

Both instructors and participants recited the same lines. Their education was complete. So was the military-like discipline. 'We can't talk to you until our senior gives us permission,' the instructors told me. I had to conduct every interview with the camp organizer looking over my shoulder and prompting participants when necessary. As soon as the whistle blew, a young boy whom I was interviewing jumped up and said he had to leave.

The boys had to sit through another 'knowledge' session. The organizers didn't allow me to attend. I tried to listen, to catch snatches of enlightenment. The speaker was telling the boys how to prepare for an emergency—a riot, an earthquake. Who should be contacted, what should be done. One of the organizers saw me listening. 'He is telling them what they should do in case there is any civil disturbance,' he said.

After that, the organizers told me they had changed their plans. Instead of the evening physical training session, there was going to be a march through the town to make people aware of their public demonstration and trishul distribution ceremony the next day. Soon, I was asked to leave. 'We have let you stay here for long enough. It is time that you left,' said the organizer who had initially interrogated me. After being treated to such a generous helping of VHP-style Bharatiya culture, I didn't persist. I left immediately with a lingering suspicion about what was going to follow.

As we drove out, the guards had put down their rifles and were napping near the gate. But for the young men inside the camp, it was a dangerous awakening.

Boys in the hood

'I've never worked a day in my life. I live by cheating,' Hiren boasted to me.

'I don't ask for money. People pay me to get their work done. I take haftas directly from the cops. If they refuse, I threaten to make a phone call and get them transferred,' he said, explaining his modus operandi. 'What's wrong with it?

Who doesn't cheat? From top to bottom, everyone is part of it,' the tall, lanky Hiren laughed mischievously.

He described his exploits during the recent violence. 'They (the Muslims) put up a good defence (when we attacked). But there were too many of us. We burned everything,' said Hiren. 'They had to be taught a lesson. Didn't innocent people die in Godhra? For our innocents, their innocents must also die.' How did he feel being part of so much destruction? 'When you go with stones, bombs and petrol, you have to expect trouble. I saw many dead and injured people. I didn't feel anything. I wasn't scared.'

Hiren is one of Ahmedabad's army of unemployed youth, hustling to get by. I met him and his friends in Gomtipur. This was once a busy working class locality which housed textile mill workers. The mills were the hub of industrial activity in Ahmedabad. In the mid-century, textile and allied industries employed around half the city's workforce, but in the 1980s the textile mills started closing. Around 1,00,000 people lost their jobs.[17]

That's when the neighbourhood started falling apart. Gomtipur houses some of the poorest workers, mainly Dalits and Muslims. While the mills were prospering, they lived together.

During the 1985 riots and the recent violence, it was one of the few areas where Dalits attacked Muslims. Frustration due to unemployment increased communal friction. Retrenched workers were pushed into informal work where wages are low and uncertain. In the new informal labour market, workers' living standards have fallen drastically. The scramble for opportunities has led several youth like Hiren into the arms of the Hindu right. The collapse of a democratic climate has given way to communal hate politics.

The downslide of the mills coincides with the rise of the underworld in Ahmedabad. Many unemployed youth were recruited by the famed gangster Latif in his bootlegging empire. The new generation like Hiren have been taken into the fold of the Hindu extremist organizations, which give them a sense of identity and power.

Hiren is a local BJP leader, but his father, a former mill worker, was a diehard Congress supporter. 'It's because of the BJP government that the police stood aside and let us attack. They fired at Muslims. Not just here, but everywhere—in Naroda Patiya, Gulbarg Society,' said Hiren when I asked him why he joined the party. 'Even during the 1992 riots, we (Dalits) supported the BJP. The BJP is kattar (hardline) Hindu,' he says. 'Ever since the BJP has come to power, Muslim dadagiri is less. Now, more Hindu bootleggers have started business.'

Being part of the BJP has given Hiren and his friends power in their neighbourhood and a way to make a quick buck. But not all are convinced. Hiren's friend, Mahesh, thirty-six, is part of the local BJP. But he is more sceptical. 'Initially, I believed strongly in Hindutva. But later, I started reading more and after being with them, I realized that the BJP is not for Dalits. They only use us to stir trouble with the Muslims. Have they helped us find work? I've been with the party for twelve years. I'm still without a job,' says this part-time rickshaw driver.

Hiren and his friends went boldly forward when the BJP mobilized for an attack on Muslims. The party has gained support amongst unemployed youth looking for opportunities to acquire power locally and hustle their way through. Some have realized that it has got them nowhere. Others have gained through extortion and cheating. Still others have allowed the Hindutva frenzy to divert their attention from the real, unresolved problems within their neighbourhood.

Licence to loot. Freedom to flex muscle. But even after years of loyalty, there's still no work.

At the Border

They tore down the gates and built walls instead. Towering brick walls topped with shards of glass. We are at a 'border' in Vejalpur, Ahmedabad. A road separates the Hindu ghetto from the Muslim one. Not just the road, but fear too keeps them apart. Last year's communal pogrom has polarized Ahmedabad even further, pushing more people into ghettos.

'During the riots they threw stones, bombs and cylinders across the gate. We abandoned our home for four months,' says Rita Sathara from Venugopal Society, the Hindu side of the border.[18] Rita's children didn't want to return home. 'My two-year-old son would scream at night. He would say, "Mummy, give me a gun and I'll kill Muslims."' Rita wants to move out. But there's no money to pay the rent. 'Now, we are too scared to even go across the road to shops in the Muslim basti. We've even put grills on our doors.'

On the other side of the wall, you can feel the anxiety. After his shop was destroyed during the violence, A.N. Ansari has made his home a fortress. A high wall topped with shards of glass hems his family in. 'We were friendly with some Hindus. We used to celebrate festivals and weddings together. There was 100 per cent faith between us,' says Ansari.[19] 'But RSS people from outside are creating trouble. They attacked us from the Hindu society. During any festival, people on both sides are scared that a riot will break out.'

In Ahmedabad, the divisions accelerated after the 1985 riots. They have become sharper after the 2002 communal violence. Many Muslims prefer to cling to the safety of ghettos like Juhapura on the outskirts of the city, or Shah Alam, closer to the heart of the city. Some Hindu families have moved to newer suburbs on the western side of the Sabarmati river like Naranpura and Satellite, or Maninagar in the eastern part of the city. After last year's communal carnage, Muslims—regardless of their social status—are being pushed further into ghettos. A survey[20] of families who have shifted to ghettos in Ahmedabad and Vadodara since 1969 found that the largest shift was during the 2002 riots. Of those who migrated to the ghettos since 1969, 43 per cent moved in 2002–2003.

Communal violence has also divided small towns like Modasa, Himmatnagar and Kalol. Refugees who fled their villages and couldn't go back have been rehabilitated at the outskirts of these towns (because land at the border is cheaper). This has sharpened their isolation.

Many Muslims and Dalits were denied housing in certain areas because they were non-vegetarians. As Ahmedabad expanded beyond the walled city, the communal divide became sharper in the suburbs. Hindus moved from the walled city into newly developed areas on the other side of the Sabarmati river like Naranpura, Satellite or Vejalpur. Muslims remained within the walled city. A few shifted to areas like Shah Alam or Juhapura.

'Communities have lived in groups. But they had friendly relations with each other. The idea of isolation didn't exist until 1985,' says Professor Abid Shamsi, a retired university professor. With each subsequent riot, more refugees started moving to ghettos. Last year's violence added new dimensions to the economic and educational marginalization of Muslims.

Finding work is far more difficult in the ghetto. 'Business is less here. I can't even get work for ten days in a month. We are still living off loans from friends and family. But at least we are safe. It's a totally Muslim area. No one will attack us,' says Nawab Ali Sayyed, a refugee who has been pushed into Juhapura.[21] 'Our old home in Rakhial (a mixed industrial area) was closer to the city. I was a car dealer, my business is totally destroyed. My old Hindu associates don't do business with me any longer. We are all Indians first. It's only political leaders who have made us "majority" and "minority".'

Muslim businesses and workers are being edged out. Many

small shops were burned. Owners had to shift their business from Hindu areas to Muslim localities. 'I used to earn Rs 1000 every day in my shop at Satellite. Now, I barely earn Rs 2000 a month in Juhapura,' says Ismailbhai Ajmeri, a mattress maker. His trauma has taken a toll on his health as well. He has had two heart attacks after his shop was burned. He has no money for medicines or a bypass surgery.

A survey in Juhapura and Rakhial by Samerth, an NGO,[22] found that the incomes of riot-affected people fell by more than a third, on average. More than 20 per cent had to change their occupation because they lost their equipment during the riots. 'Communities live separately in several cities, towns and villages. But the difference here is that it's not out of choice. People are forced to move,' says Bhabani Das from Samerth.[23] Six out of ten migrations to ghettos were after communal riots. Of those who shifted, 68 per cent were Muslim.

Segregation isn't confined only to the poor and middle class; even the elite areas of Ahmedabad are ghettoized. Muslims can't buy an apartment in most middle-class or elite buildings. 'There are only a few buildings in elite areas like Paldi or Navrangpura that will allow Muslims. But in most other middle-class localities like Satellite, C.G. Road, Drive In or Vastrapur, no one will sell an apartment or a shop to a Muslim,' says Professor Abid Shamsi.[24] Property prices in elite areas are also higher for Muslims. 'The price for my house is double that of a flat in a Hindu building just around the corner. Since space for Muslims is very limited, there is a premium on it,' he said.

Even that minuscule space is not secure. Aman had to sell his new flat in Paldi, Ahmedabad without living in it for a single day. The VHP's idea of a housewarming was to attack, explode bombs in the lift and burn cars in the parking lot. 'The building was just completed in 1999. As soon as a few Muslim families started living there, VHP activists attacked,' says Aman.[25] They got an order from the court, saying that

Muslims could not live there because it was a Hindu area. All flats were sealed. 'I had to sell my flat at a price less than what I paid for it. That's because when Muslims buy real estate, the rates are always higher.' Even while searching for another house Aman did not reveal his name. His flat is registered in the name of a trust he works for.

Just the presence of a Muslim is seen as a threat. 'If one Muslim buys a flat, then they capture the entire building,' Rajat, a chartered accountant, told me.[26] 'If one Muslim enters, then all the Hindus have to vacate because of non-vegetarian cooking. Even I would leave my flat if a Muslim enters the building. I am a Jain. I can't tolerate this. They have started capturing societies in Paldi. It is their mindset to stay together.' But all Hindus aren't vegetarian. How come Rajat doesn't object to them?

Every round of riots has sharpened the divisions. Pervin and Parul share a lot in common—they work in an NGO and live in the same area. But they refuse to visit each other's homes because it means crossing the border. 'We live on either side of the border. Parul in Vejalpur, and I in Juhapura. We take the same bus to work. But Parul won't come to my house. They call Juhapura mini-Pakistan. All the people living here are working people. Where are the terrorists?' asked Pervin.[27]

Parul's reason for not visiting her friend—the fear of a riot erupting at any point. 'You can't be sure. Nowadays, the smallest argument can spark a riot. Then, Pervin's family may not be able to save me. I will be the only Hindu there,' she explained.[28] Separation has heightened the fear of the unknown, Parul feels. 'All these years, I've never stepped into Juhapura. I've always been told it's filled with criminals. That's before I met Pervin.' Then she adds thoughtfully, 'If I feel unsafe being in a minority in Juhapura, can you imagine how Muslims feel? They are a minority everywhere. But they have no choice. They have to go out to work.'

Another common prejudice amongst Hindus—'Muslims have pushed Hindus out of the old, walled city and taken over their houses.' The VHP is fuelling this myth; the reality is that both Hindu and Muslim families have moved out of the old city. Many have shifted in search of larger houses in the suburbs. 'Recently, the VHP launched a protest against the sale of two Hindu shops to a Muslim in the walled city. The truth is, Hindu houses haven't been bought over by Muslims, but by Hindu traders for shops or warehouses,' says Hassan Pathan, a municipal corporator.[29] 'More Hindus may have moved out of the walled city because they can afford to. Muslims are poorer, so they can't shift out.'

A law meant to prevent land grab during riots has actually accentuated divisions. The Gujarat Prohibition of Transfer of Property in Disturbed Areas Act, 1991 was enforced to prevent the forcible sale of property in places designated as 'disturbed areas'. 'This act is being misused to prevent Muslims from buying flats in posh areas. A number of cases have been filed by third parties when Hindus sell a flat to Muslims. This is used as a form of harassment so that the transaction is delayed because of the court case,' says a civil lawyer.

The classroom has been split too. 'My children studied at a school in Paldi. We got a phone call from the school informing us that the admission of all Muslim students was cancelled,' said Sumaiya Mansoori, a resident of Juhapura.[30] Many fearful parents have shifted their children to schools within ghettos, where standards are not up to the mark. After the violence, children from riot-affected areas like Naroda Patiya simply dropped out because they were too scared to go back to school.

Exclusion is breeding prejudice on both sides. 'The youth have strange misconceptions about the "other" community. Right now, the older generation still has warm relations with their Muslim friends and clients. During the past three riots, my Hindu friends protected my family in their homes. But in ten years, that person-to-person contact may no longer exist,' said Professor Shamsi.

As the walls get higher, it's becoming increasingly difficult to see 'the other side'.

An entangled sufi

Pir Imam Shah Bawa's devotees are chained at the feet. They close their eyes and pray fervently while walking towards the Sufi saint's tomb, the Hazrat Pir Imam Shah Bawa Roza in Pirana village, outside Ahmedabad. If the chain disentangles in the first few steps, they say that your prayer will be granted soon. If not, it's a sign that it will take some time.

Today, the pir's followers are entangled in a dispute that could threaten the existence of their faith. Pirana's residents still follow Imam Shah Bawa's teachings of love and harmony, a Sufi-inspired amalgam of both Islam and Hinduism. But powerful religious heads close to the Sangh Parivar are trying to communalize their belief, reducing it to little more than a sect of Hinduism. In the heat of the conflict, the Quran hand-written by the pir, which used to lie near his tomb, mysteriously disappeared. It's called 'mini-Ayodhya'.

Pir Imam Shah Bawa founded the Satpanth ('true path') faith around 600 years back. He taught tolerance and the universality of all religions. The sect is an offshoot of Ismaili teachings, a liberal branch of Shiite Islam followed by the Khoja followers of the Aga Khan.

All eighteen communities living in Pirana, from different castes and religions, are devotees of Imam Shah Bawa. The shrine also attracts followers from different parts of India. Hindu followers, called Satpanthis, comprise 85 per cent of the sect. Many are not from Pirana village. Several are from the Kutchi Patel community. Muslim followers called Saiyads, are considered to be the saint's direct descendants. Devotees did not define themselves as Hindu or Muslim until they were forced to do so by the British census in the mid-nineteenth century. The pressure of Islamic reforms and the rise of Hindu revivalist groups also made them adopt clearly defined religious identities.

After the death of the saint, a shrine was built over Imam Shah Bawa's tomb in Pirana. Within the complex, they also built a *dholia* where he used to sleep, a mosque and a graveyard. Till 1931, the dargah complex was private property belonging to the Saiyads, and was administrated by the head of the Satpanthis called a 'Kaka'. Some Satpanthis filed a case against the then Kaka Ramji Laxman (also a Patel) for misusing funds, according to an article by researcher Dominique Sila-Khan.[31] The court ordered that a public trust should be set up to manage the property. The committee was to consist of seven Satpanthi and three Saiyad representatives elected every five years. But elections haven't been held for the last fifteen years.

A conflict between the Satpanthis and the Saiyads emerged when the last religious leader, Karsan Das Kaka, tried to 'hinduize' the belief. The dispute has resulted in a spate of legal battles. In the late 1980s the Kaka made several changes to the literature, rituals and prayers, removing any hint of Islamic influence. When I visited the shrine, the guide appointed by the trust made it a point to keep telling me, 'This is a Hindu samadhi mandir (memorial temple). It has no connection with Islam.'

'Our prayers had words like 'Om' as well as 'Rehman' and 'Rahim'. The shrine administration have taken out the Islamic words. They are destroying the meaning of the philosophy,' said Bharat Patel, a carpenter who lives in Pirana.[32] He is also a Satpanthi, but resents the hijacking of the sect by a few powerful Kutchi Patels. 'They are like a gang. It's become very political. The VHP, Bajrang Dal and the police are with them. Anyone who questions them is taken to the police station. There is no meaning to the Satpanth any more. It has become very casteist. In the gurukul, they only look after the children of Kutchi Patels, not others. I used to go to the shrine every day, but since they have destroyed it all, I don't go there. We don't get any respect.'

In the post-Babri Masjid demolition fervour, the VHP allied with Karsan Kaka and shrine trustees to arrange a huge Sadhu Sammelan (meeting of religious leaders) inside the dargah complex in 1993. They pledged to 'reconvert' to Hinduism and change the shrine into a temple.

The dargah was renamed Prerna Pith or 'Samadhi Mandir'. The Kaka discarded his old title and re-appointed himself 'Maharaj' and 'Acharya'. The trust cut off water and electricity supply to the masjid, saying that it was not part of the dargah complex. The 'Om' symbol was painted all over the shrine. The *dholia* where Imam Shah Bawa used to sleep was renovated with pictures of Hindu gods.

The 2002 communal violence further emboldened the VHP. Led by Bajrang Dal leader Mangubhai Maharaj, they stopped the traditional Tazia procession from the masjid to the dargah on Muharram in January 2003. Both Hindu and Muslim devotees participate in this procession. A barbed wire fence was built separating the masjid from the dargah and two entrances to the dargah were sealed off.

'In our village, there is no discrimination. Only they are creating it within the shrine,' said Chandrakant Patel, a Pirana resident from the Kutchi Patel community.[33] 'We used to pray at both the masjid and the dargah. After they put up the fence, it has become difficult to walk across and pray in both. They blocked the route of the Tazia procession. Both Hindus and Muslims haven't done Tazia for two years. They are doing this to harass us. They want to cut off the Saiyads totally and gain full control.'

Two Qurans placed near the pir's tomb mysteriously disappeared. One of them was hand written by Imam Shah Bawa. Other Islamic books lying near the tomb were also removed. A wooden box with silver used during the Muharram procession also disappeared. Framed copies of a farman, a document from the emperor Aurangzeb donating forty-five acres of land and money to the trust, also vanished. The original copy of this document is written on a silver plate, which is in the trust's possession. The fifty-year-old tomb of Saiyad Taskdukhusain, a trustee, located just twenty feet from the dargah, was demolished. There is no sign of its existence.

Ironically, Saiyads in Pirana who filed a case against the disappearance of these historic treasures were arrested for looting and sent to Sabarmati Central Jail. What did they supposedly loot? Prasad from the temple—jaggery, sugar, coconuts. Every day, prasad from the dargah is supposed to be given to the Saiyads. It is an old custom. But in 1998 the administration stopped the practice in a move to further isolate the Saiyads. After an argument, they got the Saiyads arrested for armed robbery.

When I visited the dargah, I met the present religious head, Nanakdas Kaka, who calls himself Guru Maharaj Jagatguru Satpant Acharya. His followers directed me to the first floor of the building where this forbidding, bearded man was seated on a throne, blessing all the devotees who fell at his feet. When I told him I wanted to interview him, he immediately took me into his room, a dark, wood-panelled space where huge frames of himself and previous religious heads were put up alongside his collection of guns. It was decorated with gaudy rugs and velvet bedcovers. When I started to take his picture, he asked me to wait. He quickly went to get his saffron turban, wore it and then posed, looking formidably at the camera.

The guru denied that the missing documents or monuments ever existed. He said that the Satpanthi faith was a 'Vedic religion' which had followers from various communities. When I asked him whether the shrine was a dargah or a mandir, he said, 'Muslim followers call it dargah.

It's a difference in language. But all donations are given by Hindus, not Muslims.'[34]

The dargah administration is doing everything to erase its 600-year-old history. But many devotees won't let them forget the past.

Only a miracle can free the chains now binding Imam Shah Bawa's followers. And the signs are that it may take some time.

Twisted textbooks

'*Join the following sentences to make them one:*
There are two solutions. One of them is the Nazi solution. If you don't like people, kill them, segregate them. Then strut up and down. Proclaim that you are the salt of the earth.'
—A question in the English examination paper of the senior secondary and higher secondary school examinations held by the Gujarat government on 21 April 2002.[35]

'*What is the basic difference between Miyans and Others?*'
—Examination papers in classes V and VI in Gujarat government schools.[36]

For the Hindutva laboratory to be effective, indoctrination has to start early. Over the years, a mixture of bad pedagogy and communal or casteist history has influenced young minds.

If our textbooks are to be believed,

- Hitler should be admired[37]
- Muslims, Christians and Parsis are 'foreigners'
- The people of the Harappa and Vedic civilizations were the same,[38] and
- 'The first man was born in India.'[39]

These are just a few of the misconceptions that have been

recently introduced into government school learning.

Soon after the BJP came to power in the centre in 1999, it started rewriting textbooks. Ideology took precedence over information and accuracy. Schools like Vidya Bharati run by the RSS and its affiliated organizations were given state funding. The government changed school syllabi. It reconstituted committees like the National Council for Educational Research and Training (NCERT), which frame school curricula.

The changed syllabus does more than depict a communal view of history. The content of the books shows no respect for facts or veracity; Muslims and Christians become 'foreigners'—even 'immoral'. For example, the social science textbook of class nine in Gujarat talks about the 'Problems Of The Country And Their Solution'. It says, 'Apart from Muslims, even Christians, Parsis *and other foreigners* (italics author's) are recognised as minority communities.'[40] Later, it adds, 'The priests of Catholic Churches have accumulated plenty of wealth through unjust taxes and illegal fees. And they spend the money on worldly pleasures and immoral behaviour.'

In middle school textbooks,[41] nine out of thirty-five chapters in the history textbook are devoted to mythology. The history of the freedom struggle is written as biographies of various freedom fighters, ignoring the mass struggles during that period. Ambedkar has been excluded from this book.

Gujarat's textbooks glorify Europe's fascist dictators— Hitler and Mussolini. This closely reflects the RSS ideology, which was inspired by European fascism. The social science textbook for class ten praises the Nazi chief in a section titled 'Internal Achievements of Nazism'. Here, the Holocaust is not mentioned. The only hint at the persecution of Jews is in one sentence—'Hitler adopted a policy of opposition towards the Jews and advocated the supremacy of the German race.'[42] The rest of the text speaks only of his 'achievements':

> '*Hitler lent dignity and prestige to the German government within a short time by establishing a strong administrative set-up. . . . Hitler adopted a new economic policy—brought prosperity to Germany—began efforts for eradication of unemployment. Made untiring efforts to make Germany self-reliant within one decade. Instilled a spirit of adventure into the common people. But in doing so, led to extreme nationalism and caused the Second World War.*'[43]

In the same textbook, Mussolini is also praised uncritically, with no mention of any repression during his regime.

> '*He established a strong, stable government in Italy. He made Italy prosperous and powerful. All the institutions of the state functioned according to the tenets of fascism.*'[44]

There was official sanction and backing for efforts to spread the RSS ideology in government schools. In January 2001, the Gujarat government's education department issued a circular directing all schools in the state to subscribe to the RSS mouthpiece, *Saamna*. But it wasn't implemented due to widespread protest. The government also tried to impose its ideology by restructuring the grants made to tribal welfare institutions. A part of the grant amount would be paid to them in kind—with copies of Hindu scriptures. Gujarat was one of the first states to request UGC funding for courses in 'Vedic Astrology'. The Baroda Sanskrit Mahavidyalaya of the Maharaja Sayajirao University of Vadodara was reportedly one of the major recipients on this score. When the BJP came to power at the centre, it launched courses in 'Vedic Astrology'.

In January 2002 the education department ordered that all grant-in-aid schools must perform *dharti poojan* on January 26, the day on which a killer earthquake had devastated Gujarat in 2000. India is a secular state. Religion is not supposed to enter public life. On the other hand, the

Gujarat government has deliberately disregarded minority rights. Muslim children have had to sit for exams on Id. The government removed Good Friday from its list of public holidays in 2004.[45]

This isn't the first time that the Sangh Parivar has meddled with education. When the Jan Sangh was one of the allies in the Janata government that came to power in 1977, it tried to ban school textbooks written for the NCERT by some of the country's finest historians. The attempt failed not just because the NCERT resisted it but also due to a countrywide protest.[46]

In 2004, immediately after the Congress-led UPA government came to power, one of the first policy measures it announced was to remove communal bias in the school syllabus that the BJP-led coalition had introduced.

The main themes underlying the communal view of history are:

- The glorification of India's past by falsely attributing several discoveries and conquests to our subcontinent. For example, 'The first man belonged to this land.'[47] 'Jesus Christ roamed the Himalayas and drew his ideas from Hinduism.'[48]

- It portrays Vedic society as supreme and claims that Aryans did not enter from foreign lands, but were an indigenous race. 'But about the Aryans who were the builders of Bharatiya Sanskriti in Bharat and creators of the Vedas, this view is gaining strength among the scholars in the country that India itself was the original home of the Aryans.' (Archaeological and historical evidence does not support this theory.)[49] 'With the finds of bones of horses, their toys and yajna altars, scholars are beginning to believe that the people of the Harappa and Vedic civilisation were the same.'[50]

- The description of all Muslim rulers is as 'barbarous outsiders' who persecuted Hindus alone. 'The followers of Islam in this country whether they came as traders or as invaders—but with this country they could never establish full cultural harmony. One basic reason for their separateness was the basic principle of their religion, which is monotheism. There was continuous mutual struggle between the two cultures.[51]

'The advent of Islam might have been a boon to the Arabs who got united under its banner . . . but it has been a curse for the people outside Arab world because wherever the Islamic hordes went, they not only conquered the countries, but killed millions of people and plundered their homes and places of worship and destroyed their homes, places of worship and above all their artworks . . . Why these atrocities? Because Islam teaches only atrocities.'[52]

- There has been a conversion of mythology and religious belief into fact. 'Rama and Krishna took birth here to destroy evil and defend justice, religion and Sarasvati, and God took birth here many times to make this land pure.'[53]
- There is a glorification of RSS and other Sangh Parivar icons as freedom fighters, although they were not part of the Independence struggle. There is also a convenient omission of Mahatma Gandhi's assassin, Nathuram Godse's affiliation with the Hindu Mahasabha.

The communal interpretation of history goes back to colonial times when the British historian James Mill divided Indian history into the Hindu, Muslim and British periods. As historian K.N. Panikkar points out, 'this view has had an abiding influence on Indian historiography'. Many Indian historians of vastly different ideologies have rather uncritically accepted this notion. As Dr Panikkar puts it, 'The history of India is seen through a series of stereotypes rooted in religious identity.'[54]

Hindutva's proponents take Mill's view one step further.

They impose the theory that Indian society merely consisted of two hostile, monolithic communities, Hindu and Muslim. All evidence to the contrary is simply ignored.[55]

After Partition, communal historians emerged on both sides of the border. In Pakistan, says leading medieval historian Irfan Habib, 'the history of "Muslims in India" is now projected as a struggle for a separate nation right from AD 712. (That is) from when Muhammed bin Qasim entered Sindh at the head of an Arab army.'[56] In India, points out Habib, 'historians like R.C. Majumdar projected the entire period from AD 1200 onwards as one of foreign rule'. In this view, 'Muslims were alien to Indian (Hindu) culture; the Hindus, oppressed and humiliated, wished nothing better than to slaughter the *Mlechhas* (Muslims); the British regime was a successor more civilised than "Muslim rule"; yet real opposition to the British came from Hindus, not Muslims, even in 1857.' Sadly, these 'have all become firm truths for a very large number of educated people in India,' says Habib.[57]

Muslim conquerers who entered India during medieval times are portrayed as barbaric invaders whose *jehadi* zeal destroyed a golden period of India's history. 'They forget that there were wars between various local rulers and they tried to seize each others' territories and even invited outsiders to humble their rivals. They also minimize the caste conflict and oppression of tribals and the destruction of their way of life,' says Asghar Ali Engineer.[58]

The Sangh's view of history projects all Muslim kings as 'the enemy' who plundered and destroyed temples. In fact, the conflicts were not religious but often political battles between rulers fighting over kingdoms. Moreover, wars and truces were both for political ends. For example, Rana Pratap collaborated with Babur against Ibrahim Lodi. When Shivaji fought against Aurangzeb, the Pathans joined him. Maulvi Haider Ali Khan was his personal secretary. Aurangzeb demolished temples in rival territory, but protected those in areas of his allies and even gave jagirs to some temples.[59]

The very idea that every Muslim 'entered' this country as an 'invader' has no basis in fact. 'Those associated with Islam had come through various avenues, as traders, as Sufis and as attachments to conquerors,' says Romila Thapar. 'The Arabs, Turks, Afghans and Persians were familiar with northern and western India, since they were not only contiguous people but linked by trade, settlement and conquest, links which went back virtually unbroken to many centuries,' says Thapar.

It is simplistic and misleading to view communities merely as Hindu or Muslim. They had diverse, multiple identities like caste, class, language, and viewing them through a purely religious lens goes against historic evidence. Within both religions, various communities and castes with separate cultures exist.

The 'history' taught to children across the country views 'the outsider' as the 'enemy' who brought about the decline of 'Hindu rule'. But then, who can we call the 'outsider'? What was 'Hindu rule'? India's history is rich with the intermingling of different people and societies who entered the subcontinent at different points in time. We now have 4635 identifiable communities of mixed ancestry and it is virtually impossible to trace their roots.[60] Our culture is diverse due to the amalgam of these various influences.

Muslims from Iran, Central Asia and Arabia who settled down in the subcontinent at different points in time formed distinct communities and were known by different names. The followers of Hinduism are also very diverse. The religion is practised differently in varied regions and cultures.

Research and textbook writing was brought to heel under the BJP government. Sixty positions of professor and reader in the NCERT were given to people close to the Sangh Parivar. They were chosen by a former RSS pracharak, Dr K.G. Rastogi, who has boasted that he killed a Muslim woman during the

Partition riots in 1947 to save her from being raped by a mob, and claims it as a 'qualification' in his memoirs.[61]

Other Sangh 'historians' like P.N. Oak had approached the Supreme Court to declare the Taj Mahal a 'Hindu Temple-Palace', which he claims was named 'The Tejo Mahalaya'.[62] The court dismissed his petition. But that has not stopped Mr Oak and the Sangh from trying to look for a temple under other medieval structures. It has formed around 400 branches of the RSS-inspired Bharatiya Itihas Sankalan Samiti (Indian History Committee), whose aim is to prepare the history of all districts keeping as the ideal the history written by P.N. Oak.[63]

Under the BJP, the NCERT's new National Curriculum Framework planned to take history out of school textbooks until class ten, claiming that it would lighten the load of the current heavy schoolbag. Only certain 'themes' from history were to be integrated with Civics and Geography and taught as one subject.[64] Incidentally, the Pakistani government had attempted the same kind of distortion of history in the 1970s. History was introduced only in high school, and that too, a twisted version of it. The Sangh Parivar's history writing was a mirror image of what was being doled out by its enemies across the border.

RSS schools like Vidya Bharati and Saraswati Shishu Mandir have been teaching these myths for years. The National Steering Committee on Textbook Evaluation (1993–94) appointed by the NCERT itself, concluded that the main purpose these books serve is to gradually transform young children into 'bigoted morons in the garb of instilling patriotism in them'.[65]

The Sangh's reach into young minds goes far beyond textbooks. Its network of volunteers includes a large number of schoolteachers. They inculcate the Sangh's values in their students.

'When I was in Standard Eight, I had a teacher who used

to tell us to join the Bajrang Dal . . . that we should unite against Muslims. I objected. But she said that she was not talking against me, but against Pakistan,' remembers Mohammed Maleikh, a peace volunteer in Naroda Gaam, Ahmedabad.[66] 'She kept telling us to join the shakha. I also went for two days. But they don't allow Muslims. They teach people to be against us.'

With even teachers feeding children with misconceptions, is there any wonder why prejudices are so pervasive?

Saffron sympathy: Wired across the globe

Lord Adam Patel was one of the many overseas Indians moved by the tragedy of the Kutch earthquake in 2001. A Labour Party MP in the UK, Lord Patel, along with other public figures in the Indian diaspora, used their clout to help gather funds to send back home. He was a patron of Sewa International's Earthquake Relief Fund. But Lord Patel was in for a jolt.

He found out that Sewa International's mission was not purely 'sewa' (social service). The money was being given to RSS-affiliated organizations that propagate hatred against Muslims and Christians. The Sangh Parivar was involved in the communal violence that crippled Gujarat in 2002. Once he was aware of Sewa International's links, Lord Patel resigned as a patron.

'I very much regret ever having been part of this racist organization . . . Sewa International is a front for militant Hindu organizations . . . I am sure a lot of the donors don't realise the money is being sent to help terror groups like the Rashtriya Swayamsevak Sangh,' he said in an interview with a British newspaper.[67]

A British group called Awaaz exposed the RSS's charitable facade. It published a report which traces how, in the guise of earthquake relief, millions of pounds raised by Sewa

International have gone to RSS fronts. They found that all the £2 million collected for quake reconstruction and rehabilitation were given to Sewa Bharati, an RSS affiliate. The report provides insights into how Hindutva groups operate at the international level through different front organizations and charities.

'Sewa Bharati's activities around both the Gujarat Earthquake and the Orissa cyclone in 1999 demonstrate a pattern in which a natural, human tragedy is used to enable the dramatic expansion of RSS institutions through the use of overseas funds,' said the report.[68] In 2002, a similar report called *A Foreign Exchange of Hate* exposed how a fund-raising charity in the US called the India Development and Relief Fund (IDRF) was funding Sangh Parivar activities in India.

Sewa Bharati started RSS shakhas during the rehabilitation of Badanpur village. Reports allege that the RSS was distributing relief selectively to upper-caste victims and neglecting Dalits and Muslims. The RSS was also organizing shakhas in relief camps. At Adhoi village, VHP preachers gave lectures every night on the need to be vigilant against Christians and Muslims. RSS volunteers allegedly threatened other relief workers to leave Kutch. They accused them of receiving foreign funds to convert people to Christianity.

Almost a quarter of Sewa International's earthquake relief funds went to RSS schools. The National Steering Committee on Textbook Evaluation (1993–94) appointed by the NCERT criticized the teaching material in these schools for being 'blatantly communal'. The Madhya Pradesh government revoked Sewa Bharati's registration after reported attacks on Christians.

While appealing for funds, Sewa International did not disclose its associations with the Hindu Swayamsevak Sangh (HSS), the RSS's UK branch or with Sewa Bharati. 'Sewa International funded Sewa Bharati for rebuilding work, but it was the RSS that conducted ceremonies for the start of rebuilding work or handed over the completed villages to residents,' the report said.

Sewa International refuted accusations that it was funding hate campaigns in India. It confirmed that its earthquake relief funds went to Sewa Bharati and that it was not a part of HSS. 'Sewa International is a non-religious, non-political and non-sectarian organization, which believes in equality. At all times, Sewa International encourages social integration and not social division,' said Shantibhai Mistry, Sewa International's representative, in a letter to the newspaper that had published Lord Adam's interview.

'The view expressed in the newspaper, in which Lord Adam implies that Sewa International is a front for militant activity, which incites racial hatred, is both outrageous and offending. Sewa International has always openly condemned violence, terrorism and racial discrimination in the past and will continue to do so in the future,' said Mistry.

He maintained that Sewa International's dealings were transparent. 'Many individuals such as the Lord Mayor of Coventry and the former mayor of Derby together with several Labour MP's and representatives from the media have visited the earthquake-affected areas of Gujarat and have personally approved, endorsed and commended the rehabilitation work carried out by Sewa,' he said. Refuting allegations, Sewa International said it encourages donors to visit the projects that their money has funded and provides assistance to those who wish to do so.

However, the Awaaz exposé has seriously dented their claims and credibility. Besides earthquake relief, many questions have also been raised about Sewa International's other projects. Most of the £260,000 raised by Sewa International UK for the Orissa cyclone relief after 1999 went to a key front of the RSS, the Utkal Bipanna Sahayata Samiti (UBSS). 'The Hindu Swayamsevak Sangh UK said the funds would be channelled through RSS volunteers. It also said it funds organizations that get their workforce from the RSS,' said the Awaaz report.

Lord Adam and others are appealing to the UK government to get Sewa's status as a charity revoked. In India, such funding is a violation of FCRA (Foreign Contribution Regulation Act) regulations, since the money is being used to fund political ends under different guises.

In the US too, the 'Saffron Dollar' campaign against the IDRF hurt its image. Although the IDRF insists it has nothing to do with the VHP or RSS, evidence in *A Foreign Exchange of Hate* shows its close links with them. A fund-raising charity set up in the US to collect funds for Indian NGOs 'assisting in rural development, tribal welfare and urban poor', 80 per cent of the IDRF's money goes to Sangh Parivar-affiliated organizations. In documents submitted to the US government's Internal Revenue Service (IRS), the IDRF lists nine organizations as a representative sample of those it funds. All are part of the Sangh. Many of the IDRF's founders are closely connected with the RSS and its many wings. In fact, VHP America and other Sangh websites list IDRF as a 'Hindu charity'.

A large chunk of the money went to organizations that promote the Sangh's version of Hindu culture and for schools in tribal areas. Organizations like the Vanvasi Kalyan Parishad have been fuelling anti-minority sentiments among adivasis and conducting 'reconversion' ceremonies. Most adivasis have their own culture and beliefs. The Sangh wants them to switch to its brand of Hinduism. In many places like the Dangs, Vanvasi Kalyan Parishad leaders have been involved in violence against Christians in 1999.

The IDRF and Sewa International are only one part of the Sangh Parivar overseas. The VHP and HSS have support from Indians settled abroad. They organize religious meetings and discussions. They arrange visits for young people to attend RSS camps in India where they are taught about 'Indian culture'. In the last decade, the Sangh's support base has grown in parts of the US with larger concentrations of professional Hindu migrants—largely the west coast, the north-east and the southern states of Florida and Texas, says the report on the IDRF.

Indians abroad are far more attracted to the Sangh's simplistic Hindutva ideology. While trying to hold on to their roots, many are attracted to the most conservative and traditional views on Hinduism and Indian culture. Says Romila Thapar, 'This ideology provides them with a compensation for being a minority in the country of their adoption. Indians settled in the white world, however wealthy and established they may be professionally, do not command the social, cultural and political resources of the white elites among whom they live. This has led some to adopt a ghetto mentality and attempt to package Hindu religion and culture in a marketable form as provided by agencies such as the VHP, which encourages them also in the fond belief that Hindu culture has a superiority far exceeding all other cultures in age, in quality and in unbroken continuity.'[69] That clinging to an image of their original home and roots—a vision strongly challenged within India itself—is not unique. Other diasporic peoples too buy into such ideas. For example, Zionist groups in the US are important funders and supporters of extreme right parties in Israel.

In the US, a large part of the IDRF's fund raising is through electronic means such as money transfer portals, charity portals or company foundation portals. Many large corporations match employee donations to charities and end up giving a lot of money to the IDRF. From 1993–95, the VHP in America had signed up with AT&T, for a programme in which a fixed percentage of any subscriber's total telephone bill could be directed to a non-profit organization of his or her choice if the organization was registered under the AT&T programme. But AT&T withdrew support after it was under pressure from people who were appalled by the VHP's misuse of charity.

Just as the Sangh's network has attracted several overseas Indians into its fold, many other NRIs like those from Awaaz and the Saffron Dollar campaign are also working to make people more aware about the covert and divisive nature of Hindutva groups. Their reports from the US and UK are eye-openers for many who are misled by charities and donate without knowing what their money is being used for and by whom. Charity is not always harmless and benevolent.

No entry, Mr Modi

In his state, Narendra Modi is considered 'Gujarat no Sher' (The Lion of Gujarat), but outside, he's an outcast. The first time Modi paid a price for the Gujarat pogrom was three years later, when the US denied him a diplomatic visa and revoked his tourist/business visa on 18 March 2005 because he was 'responsible for, or directly carried out, at any time, particularly severe violations of religious freedom'.[70] Although he had a valid business visa, Modi applied for a diplomatic visa. Not only was he denied the diplomatic visa, but his current business/tourist visa was also cancelled.

The chief minister was to visit the US on a 'business trip'. He was invited to give a speech at the Asian-American Hotel Owners Association in Fort Lauderdale, Florida (the 'Patel Motels') and at a public meeting in New York. But effective campaigning by NRIs who formed the Coalition Against Genocide (CAG) stopped his entry into the US.[71] A Congressman from Pennsylvania, Joe Pitts, and twenty-one other Congressmen sent a letter to the secretary of state, Condoleeza Rice, requesting that Modi be denied permission to enter the US 'due to numerous reports of his involvement in horrific human rights violations in India'. In his letter, Pitts pointed out that the US Department of State reported that 'in

Gujarat, there continued to be credible evidence of prejudice in favour of Hindus and an unwritten policy of impunity against the perpetrators of the 2002 religious violence.'

A snubbed Modi immediately went on the offensive. He said that it was an insult to the nation, to which we must give a 'fitting reply'. 'By denying me a visa, the US government has not lived up to its claims that it respects democracies. America must not forget that my government was elected after the riots in a free and fair election,' he said. 'Tomorrow, if the American army chief seeks to visit India, should we look at the US track record in Iraq and deny him a visa?' Modi argued that no court has delivered any verdict on Godhra and the violence that followed. 'If the riots are the reason why I have been denied a visa, on what basis has this decision been taken?' he asked.[72] His supporters held protests where they burned the American flag and effigies of George W. Bush. The Congress and its allies publicly denounced the US decision, while secretly smirking to themselves. Finally, there was someone ready to shame Modi.

Soon after, Modi's visit to London to be part of the 'Vibrant Gujarat' show at the Royal Albert Hall was mysteriously 'cancelled'. While Modi's office said it was for 'security reasons', it is believed that his supporters in the UK Labour Party were asked to persuade him to stay away. The Labour Party was jittery about what effect his visit would have on the Hindu and Muslim votes for the upcoming election.[73]

Modi's visit was to campaign for his political representatives in the UK, both in the Labour Party and members of the HSS. It was part of 'Operation Hindu Vote', an attempt by the HSS to get the 'right kind' of Hindu MP into the British Parliament; someone with a saffron stamp. The attempt was to export Hindutva politics to the UK.

But then, Imran Khan, a UK-based human rights lawyer, announced publicly that he would secure a warrant to get Modi arrested on his arrival in the UK. Labour leaders got jittery, knowing that either way, they would lose. If Modi was arrested, it could upset their Hindu voters. If he wasn't, Muslims would have been angry. They discreetly got him to stay away, averting any embarrassment.

The snubs to Modi, especially from the West, where his middle-class admirers aspire to be, were effective. They brought back the spotlight to his complicity in Gujarat's violence and the continuing discrimination against riot victims and minorities in his state.

Nishrin Hussain, the daughter of Ahsan Jafri, who now lives in the US and was part of the CAG felt it was their first small step towards justice. 'Supporters of Modi have painted the US denial of visa as a slap not just in the face of Modi, but the whole country. I agree. This is indeed a slap in our face. It is because we as a democratic country with strong values and a competent constitution and judiciary have failed to slap him despite knowing fully well his guilt, his culpability and his crimes against humanity,' she said.[74]

'Someone else had to do it for us.'

Notes

1.   White Paper on Water in Gujarat, prepared for the Department of Narmada Water Resources and Water Supply, Government of Gujarat, 2000, p. 4.
2 .   2826 villages have wells contaminated by fluoride, according to the White Paper on Water in Gujarat, prepared for the Department of Narmada, Water Resources and Water Supply, Government of Gujarat, 2000.
3.   White Paper on Water in Gujarat, prepared for the Department of Narmada Water Resources and Water Supply, Government of Gujarat, 2000, p. 4.

4.   There was a 10.29 per cent deceleration in employment in the organized sector from 1998 to 2002, according to state government planning commission documents, says an article by Rajiv Shah, 'Gujarat's job growth at 15-year low', *The Times of India*, 15 April 2002. Also, the number of marginal workers (people with less than six months of work in a year) increased by 4.13 per cent in rural areas from 1991 to 2001. In urban areas, there were 40.9 lakh marginal workers in 2001 as compared to 25 lakh in 1991.

5.   Jan Breman, 'Communal Upheaval as Resurgence of Social Darwinism', *Economic and Political Weekly*, 20 April 2002.

6.   24 per cent of Gujarat's 2059 medium-and-large scale industries are closed, according to a census by the Gujarat Industries Commission. Rajiv Shah, '24 per cent of industrial units in state closed', *The Times of India*, 23 July 2002.

7.   Jan Breman, 'Communal Upheaval as Resurgence of Social Darwinism', *Economic and Political Weekly*, 20 April 2002.

8.   Statistics from Dr Jaideep Patel, general secretary, VHP Gujarat, interview on 29 January 2005.

9.   Romila Thapar, 'The Tyranny of Labels', in K.N. Panikkar (ed.), *The Concerned Indian's Guide to Communalism*, Viking, 1999, p. 5.

10.   Ibid., pp. 4–5.

11.   Hamish McDonald, *The Polyester Prince: The Rise of Dhirubhai Ambani*, Allen & Unwin Pty. Limited, 1999.

12.   Joydeep Ray, 'Muslim families forced out of Paldi homes', *Asian Age*, 6 February 2000.

13.   Islamophobic policing alienating young Muslims: UK government, Rediff.com from PTI, 3 July 2004. http://in.rediff.com/news/2004/jul/03brit.htm

14.   This story is based on an interview with Anthony in March 2004. Supplemented by news reports and talks with Mangubhai Maharaj.

15.   83 is the official figure stated by the police. Many more are thought to have been killed and their bodies never found.

16.   Interview on 10 September 2003.

17.   Jan Breman, *The Labouring Poor in India*, p. 322.

18.   Ibid.

19. Interview on 10 September 2003.
20. Impact of Communal Violence on the Livelihood of the Informal Sector: Case Study of the 2002 Riots in Ahmedabad and Vadodara, Samerth, Ahmedabad, August 2003.
21. Interview on 10 September 2003.
22. Impact of Communal Violence on the Livelihood of the Informal Sector: Case Study of the 2002 Riots in Ahmedabad and Vadodara, Samerth, Ahmedabad, August 2003.
23. Interview on 10 September 2003.
24. Interview on 12 September 2003.
25. Ibid.
26. Interview on 10 September 2004.
27. Interview on 28 February 2003.
28. Ibid.
29. Interview on 12 September 2003.
30. Interview on 10 September 2003.
31. Dominique-Sila Khan, 'Liminality and Legality: A Contemporary Debate among the Imamshahis of Gujarat', Imtiaz Ahmad and Helmut Reigeld (eds.), *Lived Islam in South Asia: Adaptation, Accomodation and Conflict*, Social Science Press, Delhi.
32. Interview on 8 August 2004.
33. Ibid.
34. Ibid.
35. English examination paper of the senior secondary and higher secondary school examinations held by the Gujarat government on 21 April 2002.
36. Monobina Gupta, 'In Gujarat, Adolf catches them in schools', *The Telegraph*, 29 April 2002.
    http://www.indowindow.com/akhbar/article.php?article=107&category=7&issue=17 Monobina Gupta, In Gujarat, Adolf Catches 'Em in Schools, the *Telegraph*, 29 April 2002. http://www.indowindow.com/akhbar/article.php?article=107&category=7&issue=17
37. Rathin Das, 'In Gujarat's textbooks minorities are foreigners', *The Hindustan Times*, 25 July 1999.
38. Taken from Nalini Taneja, 'In the name of History: Examples from Hindutva-inspired school textbooks'.
39. *Gaurav Gatha*, a textbook used in Shishu Mandirs and government

schools in BJP-ruled states. p. 8. Taken from Nalini Taneja, 'In the name of History: Examples from Hindutva-inspired school textbooks'.

40. Monobina Gupta, 'In Gujarat, Adolf catches them in schools', *The Telegraph*, 29 April 2002. http://www.indowindow.com/akhbar/article.php?article=107&category=7&issue=17

41. Survey of Gujarat middle school textbooks done by Dr Nandini Manjrekar, M.S. University of Baroda; Monobina Gupta, 'In Gujarat, Adolf Catches Them in Schools', *The Telegraph*, 29 April 2002. http://www.indowindow.com/akhbar/article.php?article=107&category=7&issue=17

42. Monobina Gupta, 'In Gujarat, Adolf catches them in schools, *The Telegraph*, 29 April 2002. http://www.indowindow.com/akhbar/article.php?article=107&category=7&issue=17

43. Ibid.

44. Ibid.

45. Concerned Citizens Tribunal report, vol. 2, p. 151.

46. Mridula Mukherjee and Aditya Mukherjee , 'Communalisation of Education: The History Textbook Controversy: An Overview'. (Revised version of an article in Mainstream, Annual Number, 22 December 2001.) http://www.sacw.net/HateEducation/MridulaAditya122001.html

47. Gaurav Gatha textbooks taught in government and Shishu Mandir schools, p. 8. Nalini Taneja, In the name of History.

48. Sanskrit Gyan textbooks taught in Vidya Bharati and Shishu Mandir schools, from Nalini Taneja, In the Name of History.

49. High School Itihaas Bhaag 1 (HSIB 1), p. 48, Nalini Taneja, In the name of History.

50. Ibid., p. 43. History textbook for secondary schools, Government of Uttar Pradesh revised in 1992 to suit the communal interpretations of Indian history. Nalini Taneja, In the name of History.

51. HSIB 1, p. 280, from Nalini Taneja, In the name of History.

52. A college-level history text in Maharashtra, from *Religious Bias in India's Textbooks*? United Press International, 21 August 2003.

53. Gaurav Gatha, p. 4, the textbook for Class 4, Sarasvati Shishu Mandir. Nalini Taneja, In the name of History.

54. K.N. Panikkar, 'Outsider as Enemy: Politics of Rewriting History

in India', *Akhbar*, July 2002, no. 3.

55. Romila Thapar, 'The Tyranny of Labels', in K.N. Panikkar (ed.), *The Concerned Indian's Guide to Communalism*, Viking, 1999.

56. Irfan Habib, History and Interpretation: Communalism and problems of Historiography in India. www.sacw.net/ India_History/IHabibCommunalHistory.html

57. Ibid.

58. Asghar Ali Engineer, *Medieval History and Communalism*, Centre for Study of Society and Secularism.

59. Ibid.

60. K.N. Panikkar, 'Outsider as Enemy: Politics of Rewriting History in India', *Akhbar*, July 2002, no. 3.

61. Nalini Taneja, *The BJP's Assault on Education and Educational Institutions*, published by Communist Party India (Marxist), New Delhi, September 1999.
     'Confessions of a Murderer who is BJP's top don in education', *Asian Age*, 25 October 1999.

62. www.geocities.com/Athens/Ithaca/3440/tajmahal.html, www.hindunet.org/hindu_history/modern/taj_oak.html, P.N. Oak, *Taj Mahal, The True Story*, A. Ghosh Publisher, Texas, USA.

63. K.N. Panikkar, 'Outsider as Enemy: Politics of Rewriting History in India', *Akhbar*, July 2002, no. 3.

64. Mridula Mukherjee and Aditya Mukherjee , 'Communalisation of Education: The History Textbook controversy: An Overview'. (Revised version of an article in *Mainstream*, Annual Number, 22 December 2001.) http://www.sacw.net/HateEducation/ MridulaAditya122001.html

65. Ibid.

66. Interview on 23 September 2002.

67. Amardeep Bassey, 'Peer quits charity linked to race riots militants', *Sunday Mercury*, 11 August 2002.

68. In Bad Faith: British Charity and Hindu Extremism, www. awaaz.org

69. Romila Thapar, 'The Tyranny of Labels', in K.N. Panikkar (ed.), *The Concerned Indian's Guide to Communalism*, Viking, 1999, p. 30.

70. Rediff.com, Modi denied visa to visit US, 18 March 2005, http:// in.rediff.com/news/2005/mar/18guj.htm

71.   www.coalitionagainstgenocide.org
72.   Rediff.com, Modi denied visa to visit US, 18 March 2005, http://
      in.rediff.com/news/2005/mar/18guj.htm
73.   Sanjay Suri, 'A still-born labour', *Outlook*, 11 April 2005. www.
      mail-archive.com/sacw@insaf.net/msg00304.html
74.   A letter from Nishrin Hussain, A slap in the face, www.mail-
      archive.com/sacw@insaf.net/msg00304.html

'A drop torn from the ocean perishes without doing any good. If it remains a part of the ocean, it shares the glory of carrying on its bosom a fleet of mighty ships.'

—Mahatma Gandhi

I finished this book in May 2005. As it neared completion, I was happy that certain positive changes were making the book more and more redundant.

The Supreme Court delivered unprecedented judgments to ensure justice. It shifted Zaheera's case outside Gujarat to Mumbai and ordered a reinvestigation. No such action had been taken in previous communal violence cases. But despite the Supreme Court's support, Zaheera and her family turned hostile during the retrial once again. One can only guess who the powerful forces behind her somersault are. If the Sheikh family wanted to return home to Vadodara, they had to keep shut.

In Bilkis's case, the court ordered a CBI investigation, which charge-sheeted several of those involved in the crime as well as the policemen involved in the cover-up. Her case was also transferred to Mumbai. Ten more cases are still to be heard by the Supreme Court. In these cases too, the victims are demanding a re-investigation and a trial outside Gujarat. The court has also ordered a police review of more than 2000 cases that were closed as 'true but undetected'.

The Supreme Court's criticism of the criminal justice system in Gujarat has forced the administration to prove itself. Sub-inspector R.J. Patil (from Kalol police station) was arrested in August 2004 for destroying evidence. He burned the bodies of the thirteen Ambica Society massacre victims, so that they could not be used as evidence. In response to the Supreme Court's criticism of Gujarat's judicial system, government prosecutors have been pushed to file appeals in the Pandharvada and Limbadia Chowkdi cases where the accused were acquitted by the district courts.

On the political front, the BJP-led alliance was voted out of power in the national Lok Sabha elections in May 2004. In Gujarat, the BJP lost seven seats. Many of its allies, and even former prime minister Atal Bihari Vajpayee said the Gujarat violence was one of the factors that led to its national defeat. How far that is true needs to be questioned. Many were looking for excuses to deflect the blame away from themselves. The BJP's loss was mainly because voters, especially the rural poor, were angry that the government failed to address their basic problems. The BJP's 'India Shining' campaign backfired. After its overthrow, the BJP decided to go back to its USP—Hindutva.

The new Congress-led UPA government immediately undid a lot of the damage caused by Vajpayee's government. For one, it asked for a review of all the communally tainted textbooks brought in by the previous regime. Railway minister Lalu Prasad Yadav appointed an independent inquiry into the Godhra incident.

Emboldened by the BJP's falling support, refugees from Pavagadh, who were not allowed to return home for more than two years, finally gathered the courage to stand up for their rights. They demanded that the collector resettle them back in their homes and provide them with proper security. VHP activists in the village had harassed any Muslim family that dared to return. Their shops en route to the famous pilgrimage site in the village were captured. Earlier, these refugees were too scared to return but now the defeat of the BJP government at the centre has given them some courage.

Both the POTA central review committee and the Bannerjee report appointed by the railway ministry ruled that Godhra was not a terrorist conspiracy. This was the first time there was an official government line that countered the conspiracy theory. Narendra Modi remains in power, though his position is rather precarious because he is very unpopular within his own party.

Things do seem to be looking up, but let's not forget that the minorities in Gujarat still feel under siege. There is still a lot of insecurity. People hesitate to stand up for their rights. Segregation exists right from homes to classrooms to hospitals.

The Sangh Parivar is still the dominant political force in Gujarat. Its extremist fringes are adamant on ushering in a Hindu Rashtra. The VHP has a list of monuments all over the country that it wants to demolish and capture. More youth are initiated into the fold every year at the VHP and Bajrang Dal camps. Not only in Gujarat, but also in Rajasthan, Orissa, Madhya Pradesh and other states, the VHP has sparked trouble between adivasis and Muslims.

To counter them, egalitarian political forces have to be as organized. The schooling of stereotypes must be curbed so that children are not fed false prejudices. Reactionary forces within the minorities also have to be countered. They too keep people trapped in closed mindsets. Many liberal Muslims have been attacked or excommunicated for speaking out against the orthodoxy.

Could such a tragedy happen again? No one knows.

Glossary

Adivasi: ('first dwellers') Refers to indigenous people from different tribes. They comprise 8–10 per cent of India's population.

Aga Khan: Religious head of the liberal Ismaili Khoja sect.

Akhil Bharatiya Vidyarthi Parishad (ABVP): Student wing of the BJP.

Babri Masjid: A masjid thought to have been constructed by a general of the Mughal emperor in the sixteenth century at a site where some Hindus believe Lord Ram was born. A platform sacred to Hindus remains beside the mosque.

Bajrang Dal: The youth wing of the VHP, trained as a fighting squad. Its cadres are mobilized for the VHP's various campaigns like the Babri Masjid demolition, anti-Christian attacks, anti-cow slaughter campaigns, etc.

Bania: Middle castes, mainly traders and moneylenders, known for their business acumen.

Bhil: A tribe in Gujarat.

Charge-sheet: Document prepared by the police after preliminary investigations are done, in which they list the accused and the charges against them as well as the witnesses' statements. Court proceedings are based on the charge-sheet.

Collector: A government official in charge of the administration of a district; the top bureaucrat of that district.

Dalit: (means 'ground down' or 'oppressed') Member of India's lowest caste. The Indian Constitution lists these oppressed castes as 'Scheduled Castes' who are entitled to affirmative action reservations in government jobs. Dalits constitute 7 per cent of Gujarat's population and 16.2 per cent of India's total population.

Darbars: Rajputs (a warrior caste) who were minor feudal rulers and landlords. They constitute 5 per cent of Gujarat's population. Darbars are part of the politically created Kshatriya community.

Fatwa: Interpretation by the ulema (high clergy) of the shariat (or Islamic law), of contentious issues and controversies.

Fidayeen: Suicide killers.

Harijan: Mahatma Gandhi's name for lower caste Dalits. They constitute 7 per cent of Gujarat's population.

Hawala: Illegal transfer of money between India and other countries.

Hindu Rashtra: The Hindu nation that is the final goal of the Sangh Parivar and Hindutva ideologues.

Hindutva: Hindu fundamentalist ideology that aims at the creation of a 'Hindu Rashtra'.

Inter Services Intelligence (ISI): Pakistan's intelligence wing, believed to be training and funding terrorist groups in Kashmir.

Jagannath Rath Yatra: A religious procession to the Jagannath temple during its annual festival in July.

Jai Shri Ram: Literally means 'Hail Lord Ram'. A slogan used during the Ram Mandir campaign.

Jains: Followers of Jainism, a religion that preceded Buddhism but whose teachings of non-violence, preached by Mahavir, are similar.

Jaish-e-Mohammed (JeM): (Army of the Prophet Mohammed) A relatively new terrorist outfit which has links with Pakistan. The outfit was launched on 31 January 2000 by Maulana Masood Azhar in Karachi following his release from an Indian jail after a swap with the hostages of the hijacked Indian Airlines flight IC 814 on 31 December 1999.

Jamiyat Ulema: An organization of Muslim clerics associated with the orthodox Islamic university at Deoband in western Uttar Pradesh.

Jehad: This has two meanings. The first is 'greater jehad', or the struggle for purity from within. The second is the fight for social justice, which motivated armies to defend their holy places and communities from attack. In modern times, extremist groups have interpreted jehad to mean a war for religion.

Judicial commissions: Appointed by the government under the Commissions of Inquiry Act to probe any matter of public interest to give recommendations on how to tackle such issues in the future. They do not have any power to punish; they can only recommend that the government take action.

Kar sevak or Ram sevak: A volunteer recruited by the VHP and other Sangh Parivar groups to attend religious ceremonies organized by the VHP near the Babri Masjid.

Kutchi Patel: Patel community from the Kutch region.

Lashkar-e-Toiba (LeT): Reportedly one of the largest terrorist outfits operating in Jammu and Kashmir. It is suspected of involvement in the 13 December

2001 attack on the Indian parliament in New Delhi.

Madrasa: Theological school which dispenses Islamic education.

Miya: Derogatory word for Muslims.

Muharram: Mourning period of 10–30 days observed by Muslims in memory of Hassan and Husain, the Prophet's grandsons, who were killed in Karbala.

Other Backward Caste (OBC): Socially and economically backward castes. There are eighty-two communities classified as OBCs in Gujarat, a few of which are Muslim and Christian.

'Panch' witnesses: Witnesses who are present when the police conduct a field investigation at the scene of a crime.

Panchayat: Local self-government at the village level.

Patidars or Patels: A middle-caste agricultural community. They constitute 15–20 per cent of Gujarat's population. Many of them have migrated abroad, but still retain a very strong influence over Gujarat politics.

Pols: Narrow, congested lanes in Ahmedabad's walled city, divided along community lines.

Pracharak: An RSS leader.

Ram Dhun: Chants to the name of Lord Ram.

Ram Janmabhoomi movement: A campaign organized by the Sangh Parivar since the late 1980s to construct a temple at Ayodhya. On 6 December 1992 their activists led a huge protest and broke down the historic Babri Masjid located at the site which they believe is Lord Ram's birthplace. Their claim to the land will now be decided by the Supreme Court. The Ram Janmabhoomi campaign has led to much communal strife over the years.

Rashtriya Swayamsevak Sangh (RSS): A Hindu chauvinist organization formed in 1925–26.

Sangh Parivar: A term used to describe the group of organizations closely tied to the Hindu nationalist RSS, like the VHP, BJP and Bajrang Dal.

Sarpanch: Village head.

Savarna: Upper, middle and some backward castes who fall within the caste system (called the 'varna' system), as opposed to 'avarna', the lower castes who are not part of the varna system and are considered Untouchables.

Seva Dal: Social service wing of the Congress Party, founded during the time of the freedom struggle.

Shakha: A local unit or branch of organizations like the Bajrang Dal or VHP. They organize meetings, discussions and recreational activities.

Shila Daan: The ceremony in which the Sangh Parivar organizations laid the foundation stone for the construction of the Ram temple in Ayodhya.

Tableeq Jamaat: An orthodox, purist movement of Islam which doesn't follow any rituals, but is very particular about behaviour, dress and practices.

Taluka: A district subdivision.

Tazia: A procession taken out on the tenth day of Muharram.

Urs: Annual festival to mark the birth or death anniversary of a Sufi saint.

Vaghari: A name, now considered derogatory, of a nomadic tribe of OBCs, once labelled as a 'criminal tribe' by the British. They are now called 'Devipujaks'. They remain very economically deprived.

Vanvasi Kalyan Kendra: (Tribal Welfare Centre) An RSS-affiliated organization working in adivasi areas to convert them to the Hindutva world-view.

Bibliography

Reports

People's Union for Civil Liberties, Vadodara and Vadodara Shanti Abhiyan, Violence in Vadodara: A Report, 31 May 2002.

Crime Against Humanity, An Inquiry into the Carnage in Gujarat, volumes 1 and 2, Concerned Citizens Tribunal—Gujarat 2002, published by Citizens for Justice and Peace.

Kavita Punjabi, Krishna Bandopadhyay and Bolan Gangopadhyay, The Next Generation: In the Wake of the Genocide, A Report on the Impact of the Gujarat Pogrom on Children and the Young, Kolkata, August 2002.

The Survivors Speak: How has the Gujarat Massacre Affected Minority Women?, Fact-finding by a Women's panel sponsored by Citizens Initiative, Ahmedabad, 16 April 2002.

Aakar Patel, Dileep Padgaonkar and B.G. Verghese, Rights and Wrongs, Ordeal by Fire in the Killing Fields of Gujarat, Editors' Guild Fact Finding Mission Report, New Delhi, 3 May 2002.

Carnage in Gujarat: A Public Health Crisis, Report of the Investigation by Medico Friends Circle, 13 May 2002.

Path of Humanity, Charkha—Development Education Network, Ahmedabad, 2003.

Communalism Combat, Genocide: Report on the Violence in Gujarat, Religious and Cultural Desecration, March–April 2002.

Human Rights Watch, 'We Have No Orders to Save You': State Participation and Complicity in Communal Violence in Gujarat.

An Enquiry into the Reasons for the Burning of Coach S6 of the Sabarmati Express by the Hazards Centre, New Delhi, January 2005, by A.K. Roy, Dinesh Mohan, Sunil Kale and S.N. Chakravarty.

Interim Report of the High Level Committee on Incident of Fire on 9166 Sabarmati Express at Godhra Station, 17 January 2005.

In Bad Faith: British Charity and Hindu Extremism, Awaaz—South Asia Watch, UK, 2004. www.awaazsaw.org

The Foreign Exchange of Hate: IDRF and the American Funding of Hindutva, Sabrang Communications and Publishing Pvt. Ltd, Mumbai and the South Asia Citizens Web, France, 2002. www.stopfundinghate.org

Impact of Communal Violence on the Livelihood of the Informal Sector: Case Study of the 2002 Riots in Ahmedabad and Vadodara, Samerth, Ahmedabad, August 2003.

The Terror of POTA and other Security Legislation: A Report on the Peoples' Tribunal, New Delhi, March 2004, ed. Preeti Verma, Combat Law Publication, 2004.

Nalini Taneja, The BJP's Assault on Education and Educational Institutions, published by Communist Party of India (Marxist), New Delhi, September 1999.

People's Union for Democratic Rights, People's Union for Civil Liberties, Report of a Joint Inquiry into the Causes and Impact of the Riots in Delhi from 31 October to 10 November 1984.

Twenty Years of Impunity: The November 1984 Pogrom of Sikhs in India, Ensaaf, www.ensaaf.org/20years/html

Report of the Dave Commission of Inquiry into the incidents of violence and disturbances which took place at various places in the state of Gujarat from February to 18 July 1985, by Hon. Mr Justice V.S. Dave, Judge, High Court of Rajasthan, Ahmedabad, April 1990.

Damning Verdict, Report of the Justice B.N. Srikrishna Commission appointed for inquiry into the riots at Mumbai during December 1992–January 1993 and the March 12, 1993 bomb blasts, published by Sabrang Communications and Publishing Pvt. Ltd, Mumbai.

Books

Ed. Siddharth Varadarajan, *Gujarat: The Making of a Tragedy*, Penguin Books, India, 2002.

Jan Breman, *The Labouring Poor in India: patterns of Exploitation, Subordination and Exclusion*, Oxford University Press, 2003.

Nagindas Sanghavi, *Gujarat: A Political Analysis*, Centre for Social Studies, Surat.

Mukul Kesavan, *Secular Common Sense*, Penguin Books, India, 2001.

Asghar Ali Engineer, *Communalism in India—A Historical and Empirical Study*, Vikas Publishing House.

Asghar Ali Engineer, *Communal Riots After Independence: A Comprehensive Account*, Shipra Publications, Mumbai, 2004.

Ashutosh Varshney, *Ethnic Conflict and Civic Life: Hindus and Muslims in India*, Oxford University Press, 2002.

Rafiq Zakaria, *Communal Rage in Secular India*, Popular Prakashan, 2002.

Ed. Thomas Blom Hansen and Christophe Jaffrelot, *The BJP and the Compulsions of Politics in India*, Oxford University Press, 1999.

Ed. Ghanshyam Shah, *Caste and Democratic Politics in India*, Permanent Black, Delhi, 2002.

Ram Puniyani, *Communal Politics: An Illustrated Primer*, EKTA—Committee for Communal Amity.

Ed. K.N. Panikkar, *The Concerned Indian's Guide to Communalism*, Viking, 1999.

Vibhuti Narain Rai, *Combating Communal Conflicts: Perception of Police Neutrality during Hindu–Muslim Riots in India*, Anamika Prakashan, Allahabad, 1998.

Pravin Sheth and Ramesh Menon, *Caste and Communal Timebomb*, Golwala Publications, Ahmedabad, 1986.

Ashis Nandy, Shikha Trivedy, Shail Mayaram and Achyut Yagnik, *Creating a Nationality: The Ram Janmabhoomi Movement and Fear of the Self*, Oxford University Press, 1995.

A.G. Noorani, *The RSS and the BJP*, Leftword, 2000.

Tapan Basu, Pradip Datta, Sumit Sarkar, Tanika Sarkar and Sambuddha Sen, *Khaki Shorts Saffron Flags*, Orient Longman, 1993.

Romila Thapar, *The Past and Prejudice*, National Book Trust, India, 2000.

Eds. A. Kundu and D. Mahadevia, *Poverty and Vulnerability in a Globalising Metropolis: Ahmedabad*, Manak Publishers, Delhi, 2002.

William L. Shirer, *The Rise and Fall of the Third Reich*, Secker and Warburg, London, 1962.

Hamish McDonald, *The Polyester Prince: The Rise of Dhirubhai Ambani*, Allen & Unwin, Australia, 1999.

Articles

Ghanshyam Shah, 'Communal Riots in Gujarat: Report of a Preliminary Investigation', *Economic and Political Weekly*, January 1970.

Romila Thapar, 'Somnath and Mahmud', *Frontline*, 10–23 April 1999, vol. 16, issue 8.

Pradip Kumar Bose, 'Social Mobility and Caste Violence, A Study of the Gujarat Riots', *Economic and Political Weekly*, 18 April 1981.

Ghanshyam Shah, 'Middle Class Politics: Case of Anti-Reservation Agitations in Gujarat', Economic and Political Weekly, vol. XXII, nos 19, 20, 21, May 1987.

Ghanshyam Shah, 'Under-privileged and Communal Carnage: A case of Gujarat', Professor Wertheim memorial lecture.

Asghar Ali Engineer, 'Communal Fire Engulfs Ahmedabad Once Again', *Economic and Political Weekly*, 6 July 1985, p. 1120.

Jan Breman, 'Communal Upheaval as Resurgence of Social Darwinism', *Economic and Political Weekly*, 20 April 2002.

Mridula Mukherjee and Aditya Mukherjee, 'Communalisation of Education: The History Textbook Controversy: An Overview', (Revised version of an article in *Mainstream,* 22 December 2001.) http://www.sacw.net/HateEducation/MridulaAditya122001.html

K.N. Panikkar, 'Outsider as Enemy: Politics of Rewriting History in India', *Akhbar*, July 2002, no. 3.

Irfan Habib, 'History and Interpretation: Communalism and Problems of Historiography in India'. www.sacw.net/India_History/IHabibCommunalHistory.html

Dominique-Sila Khan, 'Liminality and Legality: A Contemporary Debate among the Imamshahis of Gujarat', in *Lived Islam in South Asia: Adaptation, Accommodation and Conflict*, eds. Imtiaz Ahmad and Helmut Reigeld, Social Science Press, Delhi.

Ghanshyam Shah, 'BJP's Rise to Power', *Economic and Political Weekly*, 13–20 January 1996.

Radhika Desai, 'After Gujarat I and II', *The Hindu*, 19–20 December 2002.

Websites

www.indianexpress.com/full_coverage.php?coverage_id=1

www.sacw.org

www.awaazsaw.org

www.stopfundinghate.org

www.sabrang.com

www.vhp.org

http://www.hinduunity.org/bajrangdal.html

www.visionjafri.org

www.riotcell2002.gujarat.gov.in

Table 1: Casualties in the Gujarat riots, 2002

Dead			Injured		
Hindu 262	Muslim 713	Total 975	Hindu 1180	Muslim 1364	Total 2544

Source: Gujarat Police

Table 2: Progress of cases involving post-Godhra violence in 2003

	City/District	No. of cases registered	No. of charge-sheeted	Summary filed (closed cases)	Pending investiga-tion
1.	Ahmedabad city	959	517	410	32
2.	Vadodara city	617	390	203	24
3.	Rajkot city	198	8	190	-
4.	Surat city	106	75	31	-
5	Ahmedabad rural	88	71	16	1
6	Vadodara rural	242	77	155	10
7	Surat rural	3	2	1	0
8	Rajkot rural	7	2	5	0
9	Anand	199	131	67	1
10	Amreli	3	2	1	0
11	Kheda	193	113	38	42
12	Gandhinagar	66	43	23	0
13	Godhra	179	111	67	1
14	Bhavnagar	310	40	270	0
15	Sabarkantha	467	178	289	0
16	Banaskantha	61	16	44	1
17	Mehsana	172	78	94	0
18	Patan	36	15	21	0
19	Bharuch	86	58	28	0
20	Navsari	11	3	8	0
21	Narmada	46	22	24	0
22	Dahod	87	24	60	3
23	Ahwa	0	0	0	0
24	Jamnagar	3	0	3	0
25	Surendranagar	24	10	14	0

26	Kutch	12	4	7	1
27	Junagadh	50	14	36	0
28	Porbandar	4	4	0	0
29	Valsad	11	2	8	1
30	Western Railway	12	4	7	1
	Total	**4252**	**2014**	**2120**	**118**

(*Source*: Gujarat Police)

Acknowledgements

This book would not have been possible without the inputs and help of several people, some of whom remain unnamed in the list below. I am deeply grateful to them all.

I would like to thank all the people who spoke to me and shared their experiences despite their grief and trauma. Their warmth and generosity was overwhelming. There are too many of them to name and some would prefer to remain anonymous. So, first is a very general, but a very big thank you to the refugees from:

Ahmedabad: Shah Alam relief camp, Sundaram Nagar relief camp in Odhav, Peer Rasam Shah ni Roza relief camp in Odhav, Char Toda Kabrastan relief camp in Gomtipur, Dariya Khan Ghummat Relief camp in Shahibaug, Mehndi Kua relief camp, Rajpur Gomtipur relief camp, Patel ni chali in Gomtipur, Khanpur camp, Modi ni chali, Jehangir nagar relief camp in Vatva, Vadaj relief camp, Hazrat Pir Shah Hammat Roza relief camp, Madhavbhai Mill compound relief camp, Haj House relief camp, Bakar Shah Roza Relief camp, Bhil vas, Ramol, Bangali Vas.

Mehmdabad: Jhinvak, Kanij.

Vadodara city: Queresh Mohalla relief camp, Moghulwada, Pira Mitra, Dandiya Bazar, Tandalja Road relief camp, Shaheen Park.

Vadodara Rural: Kanwat, Bhaili, Tejgadh, Chota Udaipur.

Anand: Odh, Pij, Pandoli, Hameidpura, Boryavi, Vadod, Adaj, Kanjri,

Mehsana: Sardarpura, Sundarpura, Visnagar, Himmatnagar, Dasaj.

Sabarkantha: Vadnagar, Vadali camp, Modasa, Khedbrahma, Kariadra, Lakshmipura, Himmatnagar.

Godhra: Iqbal School Relief camp, residents of Signal Falia, Godhra Civil hospital.

Panchmahal: Anjanwa, Pandharwada, Halol, Kalol, Mora, Kuvajar, Derol, Dekva, Sanaiya (Halol), Baska relief camp, Nepania, Bamanwad, Sehra, Lunavada.

Dahod: Randhikpur, Fatehpura, Fatehgunj, Sanjeli, Jhalod.

Many thanks to the people whose stories are part of this book and who gave me their time and patience: To protect them I have not listed their names.

The extensive interviews I conducted would not have been possible without the assistance of relief camp organizers who were ever willing to go out of their way to help me at any time: Mohd. Umar Vora (Vijapur), Shiraz Memon (Vijapur), Iqbal Vora (Vijapur), Iqbal Baloch, Mehboob Sheikh (Halol), Mukhtar Mohammed (Kalol), Iqbal Pocha, Maulana Nisar Ahmed Patel (Jhalod), Amin Seth (Modasa), Ghulam Bhayla (Modasa), Ahmed Chadi (Modasa), Shafi Madni (Modasa), Amanullah Khan (Vadali), Haji Ataullah Khan (Dariya Khan Ghummat camp, Ahmedabad), Fr. Amalraj (Anand).

My homes away from home:
Leena Misra, Shyam Parekh, Chandrika and Khanakbhai Parekh and Ancher, dear friends, fellow journalists and host family in Ahmedabad, without whose support, help and

friendship this would not have been possible.

Rohit Prajapati, Trupti Shah and Manav, Chinu Srinivasan and Renu Khanna and in Baroda, who helped, guided and looked after me.

Navaz Kotwal, Rakesh Ganguly and Dr Sujaat Vali, my friends in Godhra, whose help and inputs to this book have been invaluable.

My heartfelt thanks to my editor, N.Ram, who suggested I write this book and is always encouraging and supportive. I couldn't have done it without him.

A big thank you to the entire Frontline family, especially —1) my deputy editors P. Jacob and Vijay Sankar who made me realize my potential, 2) Parvathi Menon and V.K. Ramchandran who had faith in me and introduced me to Frontline, 3) my colleagues Praveen Swami, Anuli Katakam, Lyla Bavadam and Venkitesh Ramakrishnan, 4) our office staff: R. Arunachalam, Usha Nair, V. Ravi Shankar, P. Shankar.

I would like to thank various people I met along the way who generously helped me with my fieldwork and research and were always encouraging:

Fr. F. Moses, Achyut Yagnik, Stalin K., M. Suhel M. Tirmizi, Cedric Prakash, Hanif Lakdawala, Bhushan Oza, Tikesh Macwana from the Dalit Youth Forum, Martin Macwan, Meera and Rafi Malik, Rajesh Mishra, Mukul Sinha, Ghazala Paul and Bhabhani Das, Govind Parmar, Wilfred D'Costa, Anand Yagnik, Nisar Chanki, Nazneen Bastawala, Urvish Kothari, Somnath, Veronica D'Souza, Sonal Pandya and Ashwin Chauhan, Adv. B.M. Gupta, Ilyas Bhagat, Vajir Khan, Anu Aga, Kishore Macwana, Samson Christian, Valjibhai Patel, Susan George, Rohini Salian.

Thanks to my fellow journalists and friends, who helped with information and interesting conversation: Bharat Lakhtariya, Rohit Bhan, Atul Dayani, Stavan Desai, Ashok Raaj, Rajiv Shah. Many thanks to Partho Ray, Neeraj

Priyadarshi, Aman Sharma, Harish Tyagi and Vivek Bendre for helping me find the photographs.

Many thanks to: Vinod Mall, R.B. Sreekumar, R.N. Bhattacharya, Rakesh Asthana, K.P.S. Gill, Ashwin Jani, Raju Bhargav, D.G. Vanjara, Haren Pandya, Vithalbhai Pandya, Girish Parmar, Shankarsinh Vaghela, Jainarayan Vyas, Yemul Vyas, Jaideep Patel, Jitu Vaghela.

Special thanks to Ami Vitale for generously helping out a stranger with her brilliant cover photograph.

Thanks to academic experts who helped me with information, insights and suggestions to the drafts of the manuscript: David Hardiman, Ghanshyam Shah, Achyut Yagnik, Ram Puniyani, Parvathi Menon, Asghar Ali Engineer, Nalini Taneja, Darshini Mahadevia, Indira Hirwe, Sudarshan Iyengar, Errol D'Souza, P.M. Patel, Prof. Varis Alvi, Girish Patel, Y.K. Alagh, Prakash Shah, Vijay Prashad, Manjiri Katju, Sujata Patel.

I am very grateful to my editors at Penguin, Kamini Mahadevan, Meru Gokhale, Ravi Singh and Sumitra Srinivasan for their faith and for all their hard work on the book.

I couldn't have written this book without the moral support and inputs from my dear friends and family who read the manuscript at various stages and offered valuable feedback. A special thank you to: P.Sainath, Rhea Bunsha, Ruchi Narain, Deepa Bhatia, Priyanka Kakodkar, Gauri Vij, Nina Martyris, Joya Rajadhyaksha, Arun Varghese, Leena Misra, Navaz Kotwal, Raam Thakrar, Victy Bunsha, Ashima Narain, Mihir Desai, Parvathi Menon, Sudhir Mishra, Jerry Pinto.

My friend Ruchi Narain, who suggested that I write the Author's Note and that I include the Gandhi quotes.

Thanks so much.

My friend Gauri, who came up with a great slug for the title.

I am very grateful to three teachers who made a big difference to my life. My swimming coach, the late Sandeep Divgikar. Monica Bose, who made me realize I could write. P.Sainath who inspired me to be a journalist and who has been a dear friend throughout. I hope I can be even a fraction as great a human being.

Most importantly, for all their love and support, I would like to thank my friends and family – Darius, Armaity, Malcolm, Yohann and Zane Pedder, Gaio, Chantal, Natalie and Shane Pedder, Nora Poncha, Kim Netto, Ratty Patel.

Akshay Kaul and Shruti Chopra, Anil Nair and Janhavi Acharekar, Aslam Shaikh, Arun Varghese, Arvind and Rewa Narain, Ashima Narain and Mathew Spacie, Ashok and Mariam Dhawale, Banu Sheikh, Bilkish Nathani and family, Chela Quinde, Deepa Bhatia, Amole and Partho Gupte, Deepak, Priyam, Saloni and Suhani Bhatija, Doris Rao, Farzana Sayyed, Gauri Vij, Hikka and Trinco, Ifty and family, Ingrid Mendonca, Joya Rajadhyaksha, Leena Misra and Shyam Parekh, Maysa Provedello, Meena Menon, Mohit Mukherjee, Namita Devidayal and Chaitanya Motwane, Nina Martyris, P.Sainath and Sonya Gill, Percy and Mahrukh Treasurywala, Priyanka Kakodkar, Raam Thakrar, Radhika Gupta, Roberta Fusaro, Ruchi Narain, Sangeeta Bordekar, Shiamak Davar, Sudhir Mishra, Teesha and Shivi Singh, the LSE gang, the KAL unit.

My dear parents Victy and Russi Bunsha, Rhea and Percy Shroff, my adorable Nana and Dinoo Aunty, without whom it would not be possible.